SECRETS OF BETTER SEX

SECRETS OF BETTER SEX

JOEL D. BLOCK, PH.D.

PARKER PUBLISHING COMPANY
West Nyack, New York 10994

Printed in the United States of America

10 9 8 7 6 5 4 3 2 1

ISBN 0-13-606666-6 (Rodale ed.)

PARKER PUBLISHING COMPANY
West Nyack, NY 10994

A Simon & Schuster Company

Introduction

Do you want a richer, fuller, more intensely pleasurable and rewarding sex life?

That's rather like asking if you would object to inheriting a few
million dollars, no strings attached and the taxes prepaid. Almost
everyone wants better sex. Even if it's good, we want it to be better.
More frequent. More varied. Longer lasting. Sexual passion has the
power to lift our spirits unlike any other feeling, just as sexual frustration can dampen our spirits unlike any other experience. We value
sex that highly.

This book is designed to help individuals and couples enhance
their sexual pleasure. Admittedly, a lot of books have that goal. The
number of books, instructional videos, and magazine articles about
sex shows how much people want and seek sexual help. How is this
one different?

In *Secrets of Better Sex*, I have gone beyond vague advice to give
concise prescriptions for solving problems and/or improving the
quality of your lovemaking in particular ways. Under each entry, you
will find a definition, an anecdote illustrating the definition or com-

mentary from people about this area of sexuality, and a prescription. In simple steps, you will learn how to delay male ejaculation, increase female arousal, talk to your partner about the touchiest issues, perform virtuoso oral sex, and much, much more.

The contents are organized alphabetically and cross-referenced to information on related topics. This is a book meant to be kept on your bedroom bookshelf and referred to again and again as your needs change and new questions arise. Today you might be concerned with dating and safe-sex issues and five years from now with overcoming the daily obstacles of children, jobs, and stress to have good sex.

The prescriptions, though quickly read and easily followed, can bring about a radical change in your sex life. Often the difference between an adequate lover and a good one is a small amount of new information, a little shift in attitude, and the learning of one or two new moves. No matter how old you may be or how inexperienced in the art of lovemaking, you can learn and change and master those techniques.

It's hoped that the entries will be shared with your partner. Sometimes they may be the catalyst for talking about a sexual issue. As important as sex is in our lives, most of us have trouble talking openly about it with mates and lovers, even with doctors and other professionals. In some cases, the information presented here will inspire you to further study of Eastern lovemaking techniques, cyber-sex, health-related issues, or other interests.

Whatever your age, health, or marital status, you can have better sex. Obstacles can be overcome. Problems have solutions. And you deserve sexual pleasure.

C ontents

Afterplay

"Afterplay" describes whatever a couple does immediately following lovemaking, most often cuddling, caressing, and sharing intimate thoughts. This experience may last no more than a few minutes before the partners go to sleep or get out of bed, but it is important to both men and women. People are more vulnerable to each other after sex than they are at other times. Tender and affectionate afterplay is one of the keys to improving a sexual relationship.

When a couple has experienced difficulty during sex, they often feel uneasy with each other afterward. Embarrassed or afraid to talk about what happened, or didn't happen, they pull away from each other, both physically and emotionally. Other couples may use the time after good sex to ask favors of each other or work out a nonsexual issue between them. Afraid of postcoital vulnerability, some men—and some women, too—turn on the television or get up and fix something to eat or roll over and go to sleep immediately after orgasm. They are wasting a good opportunity to enhance the intimate bond.

Take advantage of those minutes following sex. Stay close. Cuddle and caress and whisper secrets like naughty children—and see what a difference that time makes in your life.

EXAMPLE

"I know mine is the familiar wifely complaint," Nancy said. "After sex, my husband jumps out of bed, cleans himself, and then either comes back to bed and falls right to sleep or turns on the television and gets absorbed in Leno or Letterman. On Saturday night, he offers to fix us a snack. The sex is good, but I want a little cuddling afterward. I want him to hold me and say tender things. Why can't he do that?"

Nancy's husband, Joe, was also satisfied with their sex life. His only complaint about her was that she didn't understand his need for space afterward.

"My skin gets so sensitive after I come," he said. "I don't like to be touched. Nancy feels like I'm rejecting her in some way, but I'm not." ■

Joe's hypersensitivity following orgasm struck her as "an excuse for avoiding intimacy." He swore it wasn't. When he understood how important afterplay was to her, they reached a compromise. When he came back to bed after using the bathroom, he promised, he wouldn't turn on the television or fall asleep for at least ten minutes. During that time, he would hold Nancy; and she in turn promised she wouldn't use those intimate moments to say things he didn't want to hear, such as reminding him he wasn't doing his share of the household chores. To his surprise, he liked the cuddling. Now afterplay is important to both of them.

They've also learned more about each other's sexual desires and fantasies by exchanging confidences as they lie contented in each other's arms. He told her that he would like her to be more aggressive in bed and talk "dirty" to him occasionally. She said she wanted to play a more active and vocal sexual role but hadn't because she'd been afraid he would think badly of her. Now they are incorporating some of these desires into their lovemaking—desires that would have remained unexpressed if they hadn't grown closer to each other during afterplay.

There may be times, of course, when two people who care deeply about each other want nothing more than to roll to their opposite sides and sleep. Nearly everyone reaches a point in an intimate relationship when they just need to be alone for a while. And not every sexual encounter should play out the same way. Afterplay should not become another way to measure performance.

Five Hints for Sex-Enhancing Afterplay

1. *Don't use afterplay as a sexual postmortem.* If something was lacking in the lovemaking, that does need to be discussed, do so but in a gentle way and perhaps at a later time. Afterplay is not a platform for airing sexual grievances. Don't obsess on what went "wrong." Some people buy into the myth of the perfect sexual relationship and are disappointed if the sex isn't "best ever" quality every time. Relax. There will be a next time.

2. *Express sexual feelings and thoughts you've not shared.* What you enjoy about the sexual interaction but feel shy about pointing out during sex. Encourage your partner to share by creating an atmosphere of warm acceptance and playfulness.

3. *Don't let your problems into bed.* Conflicts that are not sexual often get played out in bed. When your partner is feeling warm and loving after sex this is not the best time to talk about the checkbook.

4. *Cuddle and caress for at least five minutes.* Fifteen is even better.

5. *Say, "I love you."* The words have a special meaning in these tender moments.

Aging

(see also Desire [loss of], Erection [disorders], Hormones, Hysterectomy, Illness and Disability, Impotence, Lubrication, Menopause, Noncoital Sex, Romance)

Sex changes as we age. There is no point in denying that. Everything changes as we age, doesn't it? Both men and women lament the loss of youth and the accompanying loss of firm skin, rock-hard erections, copious lubrication, boundless energy, and raging libidos. You would be more than human if you did not sigh for the body you once had and the heights of passion you once reached. Now, having sighed, are you ready to acknowledge that some changes are good ones?

Most healthy adults are able to lead active, satisfying sex lives into their sixties, seventies, eighties, and even beyond. Making love takes approximately as much energy as walking up two flights of stairs, a feat most of us are capable of accomplishing into very old age. Women do not lose their capacity for orgasm. If lubrication is a problem, they can use a lubricant and/or find relief through estrogen replacement. Though their response pattern slows down, men can still achieve and maintain erections that, though not as firm as the erections of their youth, are still quite sufficient for mutual pleasure.

As the male-response cycle slows down, the female response cycle speeds up, making men and women more in sync than they were in their youth. Because men typically need more stimulation to get an erection, the period of kissing, caressing, and stroking lasts longer. Also, older men tend to seek the warmth and closeness in sex that some women have waited decades for them to discover. Sex at midlife and beyond can be both tender and exciting—and filled with revelations as two people grow and change together. If they remain active and interesting people throughout their lives, they can expect to remain good lovers too.

The biggest obstacle to good sex for older people is their attitude about sex and aging.

EXAMPLE

"Ray isn't interested in sex anymore," complained Penny, his wife of thirty years. "I've tried seducing him, talking to him about it directly, giving him subtle hints—nothing works very often. He approaches me once a month, if that. I want more sex, but I am almost resigned to not having it. I feel rejected when I caress him in bed and he turns over and goes to sleep. Maybe he can't get excited by my body anymore."

In their early fifties, Ray and Penny are an attractive, slender, and active couple. They have no medical problems. Like many women, Peggy found menopause a sexually liberating experience. No more birth control or periods. She could, she realized, make love spontaneously for the first time in her life. Why, then, did Ray avoid making love to his wife?

"I know Penny wants to make love a lot of nights and I hurt her by turning my back to her," he said. "Two things happened in the last few years to make me *lose interest in sex. I had some problems with impotence and my daughter announced we are going to be grandparents. Now I look at my wife and I think 'grandmother.' I've never seen a sexy grandmother. I look at my penis and I think 'failure.'"* ■

A therapist helped Ray begin to deal with his attitudes about grandmothers by suggesting some new role models to replace the ones he had in mind: those sex symbols and grandmothers, Raquel Welch and Lonnie Anderson. Ray's fear of impotence, a common one among older males, was the real barrier for him. Talking honestly to Penny about it helped alleviate most of his concerns.

Most men have had a bout of impotence by the time they reach 40. Fatigue, tension, illness, alcohol, and heavy meals are typical causes. Older men have to realize they will be more susceptible to these factors. They need to expand their sexual repertoire so that lovemaking is not entirely dependent on an erect penis. By having confidence in their ability to satisfy their partners, erection or no, they worry less about impotence and thus make it less likely to occur.

Incidences of illness and disability do increase with age and obviously present sexual problems. But in most cases, loving couples can continue to have sexual relations, albeit modified.

WOMEN'S PRIMARY CONCERN ABOUT SEX AND AGING

He won't be aroused by my body. In our culture, which equates youth with beauty and sexual desirability, aging is particularly hard on women. Many begin worrying about losing their sex appeal with the first gray hair or wrinkle. Some women worry about being left for a younger woman.

Do men react as negatively to female aging as women fear they do?

Some do. Statistics show that men on average marry a woman three years their junior the first time and ten years their junior the second time. The more wealth and power a man has, the more likely he is to marry a woman considerably younger than he. On the other hand, many men continue to find their wives sexually attractive into their twilight years.

An astute middle-aged divorced woman once told me: "I can't possibly compete with young women my daughter's age. They will have smoother skin, higher breasts, tighter buttocks. No matter what I do,

I am not going to attract a man my age who is attracted only to such young women. But fortunately not all men are like that. Many of them value the emotional depth and sexual ability of a mature woman."

MEN'S PRIMARY CONCERN ABOUT SEX AND AGING

I won't be able to perform. In our culture, men are less penalized for having pot bellies, sagging jowls, or other signs of aging than women are. Therefore, they tend to view themselves as physically attractive even when—by objective standards—they aren't. Looks aren't the major worry for them. Performance is.

Men measure their sexual worth first by their ability to get and maintain an erection and second by their ability to "give" their partners orgasms. Women can and often do fake orgasms. An erection can't be faked.

A middle-aged man recently told me: "I went through a major crisis after my penis failed me a few times. At first I blamed it on my wife. I wondered if a younger woman could get me as hard as I used to be. Fortunately, I didn't act upon my fantasies. I'm learning to look at myself in a new way, to see that my prowess lies in being a good lover, not in having a hard penis all the time."

The natural physiological changes that occur with aging can make men better lovers. For example, you won't be able to ejaculate twice in an hour, but you will be more likely to make lovemaking last an hour without ejaculating. Your partner may now be able to have more orgasms than she did when she was young. At last you've become the man you wanted to be, bringing your partner to climax after climax before you reach your own.

⨍ive Easy Ways of Boosting Sexual Power

1. *Pretend you're dating again.* Remember when intercourse was delayed until the engagement (or marriage)? Relive those exciting days of kissing, hugging, necking, petting.

2. *Let go of old resentments.* Anger and resentment kill desire. It's time to forgive and forget whatever mistakes your partner made in the past.

3. *Laugh.* Sex is play. Have fun in bed.

4. *Exercise.* Older people who exercise have more sex and enjoy it more than their sedentary cousins do.

5. *Eat a healthy diet and take vitamins.* Foods high in saturated fat have a negative effect on your body and your libido. Eat plenty of fresh fruits and vegetables, whole grains, lean fish and poultry. Supplement your diet with a multivitamin and consult a nutritionally oriented doctor to determine if larger doses of specific vitamins would be a good idea for you.

Anal Sex

Anal intercourse takes place when the penis is inserted into the anus rather than the vagina. According to research, approximately 40 percent of heterosexual couples have tried it at least once. The anus, like the vagina, has sensitive nerve endings. Though they may fear such feelings indicate homosexual tendencies, heterosexual men as well as women often enjoy some type of anal massage. Some men and women find anal intercourse an adventurous and enjoyable act, while others regard it as dirty, perverse, and painful. There isn't much middle ground here. People like it or they don't.

This sex practice should be reserved for strictly monogamous couples and requires great amounts of mutual trust, lubrication, communication ability, and patience on the part of the male, who can't thrust as vigorously as he would during vaginal intercourse because he risks damaging delicate tissues. I can't overstress the phrase *strictly monogamous.* Anal intercourse is a high-risk activity for HIV infection.

Seven Important Guidelines for Anal Sex

If you try anal sex with your monogamous partner, follow these guidelines:

1. To protect the urethra from bacteria in the rectum, he should wear a specially designed anal condom.

2. Use copious amounts of a water-soluble lubricant such as astrolube or KY jelly, not an oil or petroleum-jelly product that could cause the condom to break. Unlike the vagina, the rectum does not produce lubrication of its own.

3. He should make sure she is very aroused before he approaches her anus.

4. She should concentrate on relaxing the anal muscles, not tensing them, and should expect some initial discomfort.

5. He should move slowly and probably not expect to insert the full length of his penis.

6. He should also be prepared to stop at any time if she experiences pain or simply wants to quit.

7. Never take a penis or finger out of the anus and insert it into the vagina without thorough cleansing.

The physical and psychological submissiveness of the act is appealing to many men and women as an occasional alternative to vaginal intercourse. In reality, the woman should control the speed and depth of penetration. No woman should feel compelled to do this for her man because he asks.

EXAMPLE

"I wanted anal sex very badly in my first marriage, but my wife resisted for a long time," Jim said. "Finally she consented. I wore a condom, used a lot of lubricant, moved very slowly, and didn't attempt to penetrate her fully. It didn't hurt nearly as much as she'd feared it would. To my surprise, it wasn't nearly as big a deal as I thought it would be either.

"My second wife is much more sexually adventurous than the first one was, more than I am, to tell you the truth. She likes to have anal sex occasionally. I enjoy it with her because she does, but it wouldn't be something I'd push for if she didn't want it."

His wife, Lucie, lets him know when she wants anal intercourse in a special way: She leaves the anal condoms and lubricant on his pillow.

"I don't want anal sex often, but when I do, I really want it," she explained. "The act has a lot of psychological connotations to me. This is something I've done with only two men in my whole life, so it is particularly intimate and meaningful for me to give myself this way. Also, I feel a little submissive and very daring, as if I'm breaking a big taboo, because I'm an independent woman and would never let Jim boss me around. It's a little painful at first, too, but painful in a good way. Very exciting! I have tremendous orgasms." ■

The rectum wasn't designed for sex and can't handle repeated bouts of intercourse without damage. Even if both partners enjoy it, anal sex is a special event. How often, if ever, that special event takes place can be a source of friction in a relationship. In the most common scenario, the man wants the woman to try it—or try it again—and she refuses. With a little creativity, both can be satisfied.

Three Alternatives to Anal Intercourse

1. *Make love "doggy style."* The rear entry position is a good substitute for anal sex. His penis is still in her vagina, but the angle of penetration and the rear view makes it seem like a different experience from intercourse in other positions. One man said: "When I am feeling aroused by her buttocks, we have sex with her on all fours and me behind her. That way I can watch her buttocks during intercourse. She likes this position too because we both use our hands to stimulate her labia and clitoris."

2. *Talk about anal sex but don't do it.* While stimulating him manually, she talks through the hottest anal scenario she can either imagine or borrow from a book or magazine. Talking "dirty" about a forbidden subject is as good—maybe better—as doing it. Tip: If you borrow from the printed page, memorize and ad lib rather than read directly from it.

3. *Practice anal massage.* For both sexes. Put on a latex glove and lubricate the area well. Tickle the rim of the anus. Circle it with your finger. When your partner is ready, insert your finger (with nail trimmed short) slowly. Have your partner contract the anal muscle around your finger, inhaling as she/he does so. Release the muscle and exhale. Repeat. As a variation, vibrate your finger gently while your partner contracts and releases the anal muscles.

Anatomy, sexual

Each person's genitals are unique. The size and shape of a woman's vaginal lips and clitoris or a man's penis and testicles do not affect sexual appetite or function. Men and women often lack information about each other's bodies and about their own as well. Most men did not even see a woman's genitals (except in the pages of sex magazines or on videos) until they became sexually active. Then they may have been too embarrassed to look closely or the light may have been inadequate for real examination. While the details of the male genitalia are more readily apparent, the male body also has its secrets. Not surprisingly, couples who have but rudimentary knowledge of the other's anatomy often find it difficult to give and receive sexual pleasure.

EXAMPLE

"My *boyfriend never gets it right when he performs oral sex," says Marcia. "I try to give him some direction but I don't want to sound like a schoolteacher at a time like that. What can I do?"*

Dave, Marcia's partner, is uncomfortably aware of his oral limitations.

"I've not been with that many women," he says. "I practice serial monogamy, and each relationship has been relatively long term. One woman didn't like oral sex. Maybe I haven't had the opportunity to learn how to do it right."

When pressed, Dave admits that he has some dissatisfactions, too. Marcia doesn't hold his penis firmly enough when she caresses him. And she doesn't pay enough attention to the head of his penis when she performs fellatio. ■

This couple needs to give each other an anatomy lesson. Couldn't you and your partner also benefit from private tutoring? You might feel more comfortable if you incorporate the exercise into foreplay. Remember to leave the light on.

HOW TO TEACH HIM ABOUT YOUR GENITALS

Sit with your legs well open. With moistened fingers, part the *labia major*, the outer lips of the vagina, to expose the *labia minor*, the smaller set of lips, ranging in shade from pink to brown, that cover the vaginal and urethral openings. Show him how to stroke the labia. Reach up inside the vagina with your fingers to bring the lubrication down. Point out the *urethra*, the opening for elimination of urine, located above the vaginal opening and below the clitoris. The area between the vagina and the anus, the *perineum*, corresponds to his perineum.

Gently spread the inner lips and direct his attention to the small pink point where they are joined together at the top, the *glans* of the *clitoris*. Sometimes the clitoris is difficult to find because it is covered by the *prepuce* or *hood*. In some women, the clitoral hood has many

folds, further shielding it from easy view. The *clitoral shaft* extends from the glans of the clitoris beneath the hood.

Invite him to touch your genitals, copying the strokes and matching the pressure demonstrated. Allow him to explore the vagina with his fingers. (see G spot, page 106). Help him find your G spot. And, finally, flex the pubococcygeal muscle (see Kegels, page140, and PC muscles, page 141) while his fingers are inside.

HOW TO TEACH HER ABOUT YOUR GENITALS

Show her how to caress your *scrotum* by covering her hand with yours and exerting the right amount of pressure. Let her feel the *testes* inside the sac. If she gently squeezes the scrotum above the testes with one finger in front and another behind the sac, she'll be able to feel the *vas deferens*—the tubes that extend from the testes to the prostate—like two pieces of wire. Have her use her fingerpads or thumb to apply pressure to the *perineum,* the highly sensitive area between the scrotum and the anus.

The *penis* actually extends into the body and consists of spongy tissue surrounded by a fibrous covering. During sexual arousal, the spongy tissues become engorged with blood and expand, producing an erection. If the anatomy lesson hasn't already led to an erection, take your partner's hand and show her the most efficacious strokes.

The most sensitive part of the penis is the *head,* especially around the *corona,* the ridge that connects the head to the shaft. Run her finger along this area and the large vein down the underside of the shaft. By now, drops of lubrication may have appeared in the slit in the head of the penis, the opening of the *urethra,* the tube through which both urine and seminal fluid travel.

Anxiety, performance

Performance anxiety (PA) is one of the most common causes of minor sexual dysfunctions, such as premature ejaculation or failure to get or sustain an erection. Though PA is more commonly associated with men, women also suffer from it. Some women, for example, avoid performing fellatio because they fear doing it wrong, not because they don't enjoy the act or want to please their partners this way. But the pressure to perform, particularly during intercourse, does lie more heavily on the man. A woman can use a lubricant if she isn't sufficiently aroused. What can a man do about a limp penis?

The fear of the limp penis becomes an obsession with some men at particular times in their life, usually after they have suffered a bout of impotence. They worry so much about whether or not they will be able to get or sustain an erection that they cause the failure they dread. Sex does happen largely in the brain. The power of anxiety is great. We know that placebos, for example, can make a patient feel better simply because he thinks they will. Why are we surprised when an erection wilts because a man thinks it will? Women who worry excessively about being passionate enough for their partners can also short-circuit the arousal process in themselves.

When a man (or a woman) is caught up in this kind of anxiety, he stops participating actively in lovemaking and starts watching himself. This process of mental withdrawal is called "spectatoring." The spectator is too busy watching and criticizing himself to enjoy sex. This detached state isn't one of arousal. Naturally his erection subsides.

EXAMPLE

"I felt as if a light was shining on me during sex," said Carl. "I'm under this light and both my wife and I are watching me carefully to see if I will be able to make it work this time."

Carl's job, stressful at best, had been a source of anxiety for him for several months. Unable to relax at home in the evenings, he paced a lot and often had clammy hands and a racing heart. His wife, Sondra, complained that he was constantly "on edge."

"I couldn't take my mind off the situation at work, even in bed," he said. "Then I began having erection problems. I couldn't get hard, couldn't stay hard. This went on for a couple of weeks. I became as anxious about my sexual performance as I was about my performance on the job."

At first Sondra didn't connect Carl's sexual problem with his work problem, partly because she didn't know how bad things were at the office for him. He told her a little, but not everything. Not surprisingly, she saw both his edginess and failure to keep an erection as indicators of trouble in the marriage. She put more pressure on him to perform by being more seductive outside the bedroom and more demanding sexually.

"I felt like a failure in bed," he said. "I couldn't have fun in bed anymore. I couldn't satisfy my wife. I felt like my last refuge was gone."

When she confronted him, he confided all his fears. Once she understood what was really wrong, Sondra was supportive rather than frustrated with him. She helped him relax by setting the mood with soft lighting, music, and massage. At her suggestion, he learned some relaxation techniques, too.

They also redefined "sex." In their new definition, sex was not primarily intercourse. Sex was any exchange of erotic pleasure. Now there was no way for Carl to "fail." No longer anxious and worried about disappointing his wife, he was able to participate fully in lovemaking again. His erection problem disappeared. ∎

Five Tips for Overcoming Performance Anxiety

1. *Confide in your partner.* She/he needs reassurance that the problem is not her or his lack of desirability.
2. *Stop thinking of sex as a personal performance.* Substitute the word "lovemaking" for sex. In lovemaking, two people give and receive pleasure in many different ways. A perfect erection is not required.
3. *Learn to relax.* Study relaxation techniques. Get more exercise. Take up a hobby. Perform volunteer work.
4. *Set the mood.* Create an ambiance for lovemaking with candles, music, flowers. Focus on the full range of sensual experience: sound, sight, smell, as well as touch.

5. *Redefine sex.* "Sex" is more than intercourse. It can be any form of stroking, kissing, touching, caressing. Sex is mutual pleasuring. Under this definition, you cannot be a failure as long as you are willing to give and receive love.

Aphrodisiacs

(see also Desire [disorders, treatments for], Hormones, Impotence)

An aphrodisiac is a substance that arouses sexual desire. For our purposes in this book, aphrodisiac is defined as a substance purchased without prescription by people who don't have a problem with desire or performance, but want to stimulate both—a human pursuit probably as old as sex. The word "aphrodisiac" is derived from Aphrodite, the Greek god of love and beauty. Throughout history, people have believed in the erotic power of certain foods, drink, or herbs and other natural substances, some of which are actually poisonous, like the root of the mandrake, a plant in the deadly nightshade family, and Spanish fly, a powder prepared from a beetle that can induce vomiting, diarrhea, severe cramping, convulsions, and even death. A product marketed as "Spanish Fly Formula" contains cayenne pepper as its primary ingredient.

Other substances believed at some time in some culture to aide arousal include oysters, ginseng, powdered rhino horn, cocaine, alcohol, asparagus, pomegranates, and figs. The French baguette got its shape from the belief that bread baked in the form of the penis would have the properties of an aphrodisiac. Have any of these and many other items ever been proven to increase potency or libido? No. And many of them, like alcohol, can have a deadening effect on the libido.

Thousands of people recently have ordered by mail a product called Natural Sex, marketed as an aphrodisiac. Both health-food shops and sex-toy stores sell a great deal of Vogorex Forte capsules, also claimed to increase sexual desire. A few years ago capsules made of yohimbe, derived from the bark of an African tree, were reputed to have erotic power. In my experience with clients who have tried these and other aphrodisiac products, the results are disappointing. Initially, they report greater desire. That can be attributed to the placebo effect. Over time, their levels of desire and potency return to normal.

When these pills do work, they work in the same way any placebo does. Keep in mind that the brain is the primary sex organ. If you believe oysters, for example, have an aphrodisiac effect on you, then they will, at least for a time. There is always risk in self-medication, even with products marketed as "natural." Before you take anything, talk to your doctor.

What can increase sexual desire and/or potency? Hormones can help. Some women report that hormone-replacement therapy to alleviate the symptoms of menopause also restores their sex drive. And small doses of testosterone, the male sex hormone present in both sexes, has a similar effect on women at that time of life as well as on men.

Research scientists are studying the areas of the brain that control pleasure, and eventually true aphrodisiacs may be developed. For example, a medical team at Tulane University in an experimental operation surgically implanted a device in an epileptic woman to deliver acetylcholine directly to the septal area of the brain to control severe seizures. The result included explosive, multiple orgasms that continued for half an hour. Perhaps someday true miracle sex drugs will be on the market.

No chemical substance yet discovered can rival *love* as an aphrodisiac. Love works at any age. Good health and regular exercise (see Health and Sexuality) also increase libido for most people.

Arousal

THE STEP BEYOND DESIRE

You can desire sex yet not become aroused during lovemaking just as you can be aroused without having a desire for sex. Some sexologists define arousal simply as the subjective experience of feeling turned on. It is actually the second stage of the four parts of the sexual cycle: desire, arousal (initial and plateau, the point of inevitability when arousal is firmly established), orgasm, and resolution. Though these stages are similar for both sexes, the timing is different. With their entire cycle typically lasting 14 minutes, four times that of a man, women require more arousal time than men do.

When a man becomes aroused, his penis becomes partially or fully erect. During the initial part of the arousal phase, his erection may subside, only to return minutes or seconds later. He has at least some power over arousal at this level and can excite himself more—or slow down the process—through controlling fantasy or physical stimulation. Once he has reached a plateau of arousal, he will usually remain erect through the point of ejaculatory inevitability when he can't control his response anymore.

As a woman becomes aroused, her clitoris grows erect and her vagina lubricates. Her nipples may also become erect and her chest become flushed. She is more likely to enjoy lovemaking and to reach orgasm if the arousal process is prolonged and intensified through kissing, caressing, and other forms of stimulation.

WHY YOU—OR YOUR PARTNER— AREN'T GETTING EXCITED ABOUT SEX

"I think about sex," Jennie said. "I want to have sex, but when we do have sex, I can't get very excited. It's not just that I don't have an orgasm. I don't even come close."

Jennie had been married five years when she talked to a therapist about her "sex problem." At first she confused her lack of arousal with lack of sexual desire, which it was not. She wanted to have sex. Once she made that distinction, she decided her problem was either sexual boredom—"probably inevitable" in marriage—or "sexual incompatibility," which had been masked in their first years together by their youthful lustiness.

A common difference in arousal timing between Jennie and her husband was causing their problems. He usually became quickly aroused and assumed she moved just as quickly to the same level of excitement in the same amount of time. They both mistook the physical signs of initial arousal, her erect nipples and clitoris and vaginal lubrication, for proof of sexual readiness. Early in their relationship, she had become aroused faster because she'd spent more time fantasizing about their encounters before they made love. And she had also occasionally faked orgasm, even arousal. Once he began spending more time pleasuring her during her arousal phase, she reported she was "getting excited about sex again."

WHEN HE LOSES HIS ERECTION DURING LOVEMAKING

"Now I think he is threatened by my sexuality," Jennie said.

She was excited about sex again, but he frequently lost his erection during loveplay. When she was ready for orgasm, he sometimes wasn't. Again, she felt frustrated. And, again, the problem was a common one with a simple solution. He had been working so hard at slowing his arousal down to keep pace with hers that he often lost his erection.

"I still want sex," he told Jennie. And she accepted that his flaccid penis wasn't a statement of sexual rejection. Now when she feels herself rapidly approaching plateau, she takes his penis in hand or performs fellatio if his erection isn't where they both want it to be.

Sometimes men do experience difficulty becoming fully aroused. They may be concentrating too hard on prolonging lovemaking and inadvertently turn themselves off. And either sex may have arousal difficulties caused by outside intrusions, such as noise, stress, physical ailments, and other distractions. A temporary lack of arousal is no reason to give up on lovemaking.

The Four Keys to Male Arousal

1. *Masturbation*. During masturbation, experiment with ways of delaying your response cycle. As you get close to the point of ejaculatory inevitability, reduce or stop sensations until arousal has subsided somewhat.

2. *Alternate sensations*. If one form of stimulation is bringing you too close to orgasm during lovemaking, stop. Use an alternate form of stimulation. Ask your partner to use light, teasing strokes during manual stimulation and fellatio.

3. *Fantasy*. When outside distractions prevent you from becoming fully aroused, fantasize. If you have lost an erection while trying to prolong lovemaking and your partner is now more aroused than you are, fantasize. Use the power of your mind to put your bodies in sync.

4. *Visual stimulation*. Most men respond to visual erotic stimulation. If your arousal level consistently falls during lovemaking, make some visual changes. Leave the lights on. Ask your partner to wear something erotic to bed and leave it on during lovemaking. Position yourself so that you can watch your own thrusting action or her face as she grows more excited.

The Four Keys to Female Arousal

1. *Masturbation*. Women often report experiencing more intense orgasms during masturbation than during partner sex. Don't be afraid to masturbate during lovemaking. When you masturbate alone, experiment with ways of intensifying your responses.

2. *Fantasy*. It is not wrong to fantasize occasionally during lovemaking and sometimes—when you're distracted by outside concerns, for example—it's necessary. Use your fantasies to take you places you wouldn't otherwise go.

3. *Extended loveplay*. Women, especially younger women, typically need more kissing, caressing, and other forms of stimulation than men do to reach their plateau of arousal. When you get there, don't feel you must hurry to the finish. Many women find the plateau as pleasurable as orgasm itself.

4. *Vibrator*. The intense stimulation of a vibrator used during loveplay can increase a woman's arousal quickly. And, no, you are not likely to become "addicted" to it as some women and their lovers fear.

THE SECRET TO INCREASING AROUSAL DURING LOVEMAKING

Slow down. Spend more time in the arousal phase than you normally do. Tease each other. Practice the stop-start lovemaking techniques found on pages 199-201. When orgasm feels almost inevitable, pull back. Do that several times. The resulting orgasm will be powerful.

Attitudes, about sex

All the tried-and-true advice about the power of positive thinking in life applies to sex, too. An attitude is a mental position one takes toward a fact or the emotional feeling one has about that fact. Attitudes can be positive or negative. In sex as in all other human endeavors, the former lifts you up, the latter pulls you down.

EXAMPLE

"John was convinced that our sex life would deteriorate after marriage," Sally said, "and so it did. We had great sex before we were married. Our sexu-

al appetites were compatible. We had no performance problems. I was equally convinced that things grew stale because he strongly believed they would. He made fun of my attempts to put the sizzle back in our relationship, calling them 'women's magazine games.'

"On our second anniversary I gave him an ultimatum. He could either accompany me to a marriage-enrichment weekend or he could sit down with me and figure out how to divide our property in divorce. I wasn't kidding. We went to the weekend seminar. It was a turning point for us. John began to shed some of his cynicism about life in general and marriage and sex in particular. We've come a long way since then." ∎

Do you doubt that a change of attitude can really change your sex life? Try an experiment. Compare your own sex attitudes to the following. If you have a negative attitude, work on changing it. Whenever you find yourself thinking, for example, "My wife doesn't have orgasms during intercourse because she's frigid"—replace the thought with, "My wife and I together can learn more about what she needs to have an orgasm during intercourse."

The right attitude is energizing, and positive actions soon follow positive thoughts.

The Thirteen Attitudes for Super Sex

1. *Knowledge.* Knowledge is sexual power. Some of our society's beliefs about sex are misinformation. (Women who aren't orgasmic during intercourse are frigid. Men who ejaculate quickly have intimacy problems. A man who loses his erection during lovemaking is angry at his partner. And so forth.) Lack of sexual information and misinformation will almost definitely lead to misunderstanding, hurt feelings, and decreased sexual pleasure.

2. *Courage.* Good sex takes a little courage. Don't allow fear and embarrassment to limit your sexual behavior. Fear of failure, of looking "silly," of not living up to one's own or a partner's expectations can stop couples from trying new techniques or experimenting with different positions or asking for the kind of loving they secretly crave.

3. *Freedom*. True sexual freedom is freedom from the tyranny of "shoulds." Lovemaking is about "wants," not "shoulds." What do you and your partner want? That is what matters, not what you think you should want.

4. *Involvement*. The most intense satisfaction comes from being involved with your partner. If you are busy monitoring your performance, you won't be sufficiently involved to have great sex.

5. *Trust*. The best sex happens when two people feel safe enough with each other to be vulnerable. To let go of inhibitions, nearly everyone needs to feel confident of being fully accepted by the partner.

6. *Generosity*. In sex as in life, those who are able to give and share enhance their own and others' experiences.

7. *Communication*. If you can say what you want accurately without causing unnecessary hurt, you are an effective communicator. That may be even more important in the bedroom than anywhere else.

8. *Loving context*. The most fulfilling sex over time occurs between partners who love each other.

9. *Willingness to seek help*. Sometimes couples have sexual difficulties they can't overcome alone. Rather than allowing those problems to tear down the relationship, the couple with a good attitude seek professional help to facilitate a resolution.

10. *Good health*. Taking care of yourself pays off in every area of life, including sex. When you feel good, you experience everything more richly than you do when you are plagued by illness or physical disabilities. Some physical ailments can't be avoided. But good personal habits increase your odds of staying healthy.

11. *Egalitarianism*. Sexism puts people in simplistic and limiting categories. (The man should initiate sex. The woman should be submissive. And so forth.) Insulting and off-putting, a narrow sexist attitude on the part of one or both partners virtually guarantees the erotic experience will be as limited as the mind set.

12. *Sensuality*. Sex is much more than orgasm. It is an erotic process that can be enjoyed immensely at each stage. When both partners are focused on sensual pleasure, they experience sex more fully.

13. *Humor*. We take sex far too seriously. Sex is supposed to be fun, and sometimes it's funny, too. Couples who can laugh at an awkward moment suffer from less performance anxiety than those who can't.

Aural arousal, the stimulation of sound

In the days when movies were silent, small orchestras or piano players or at least a gramophone provided background music. Music appeals directly to the senses by evoking feelings such as passion, tenderness, and anticipation. Lovemaking is more exciting with a sound track, too.

Many couples use music as part of the seduction process, and some keep it playing while they make love. Nearly everyone is aroused by the sounds they and their partners make during sex. Groans, sighs, moans, whispers, cries—sex has a language of its own. But words from explicit sex talk to romantic endearments can be a potent form of aural arousal too.

Sometimes people hold back expressions of pleasure during sex for various reasons. (See Fears.) They may also be afraid to ask for what they want, or they simply may not know how to ask. Their partners interpret the restraint and silence as either a lack of enthusiasm or a silent endorsement for the sexual status quo.

Use sounds to stimulate your partner and yourself, too.

EXAMPLE

"I was shy and sexually inexperienced when I married," said Christine, a 34-year-old divorced woman in a relationship with a slightly older divorced man. "My husband was also inhibited and unskilled in the ways of making love. After fumbling through sex many times, we simply backed off. For two years before we divorced, we didn't make love. Sex was a taboo subject in my home when I was growing up so my experience with my former husband nearly buried my desire.

"Then I met Jonathan, and everything changed. He's so open and natural about sex it just relaxes me. I can't believe myself now. One of the sexiest things I learned from him is to talk and make sounds during sex. The sex I had in my marriage was absolutely silent. Now we're noisy!

"I whisper in his ear that I love the way he is kissing my breasts. When we're in the middle of oral lovemaking I scream, 'Oh suck me harder!' or 'Don't stop!'

I moan, groan, scream, and just let loose. It drives him wild with desire and keeps me very excited." ■

If you're having silent or barely audible sex, try the following suggestions for turning up the sound and the excitement at the same time.

Six Hints for Erotic Expression

1. *Pant, groan, and moan.* Put your self-consciousness aside and throw yourself into the lovemaking. A sexually responsive partner increases the other person's level of arousal. The more vocal the two of you are, the more you excite each other.

2. *Learn the art of hot talk.* Men in particular get aroused by graphic sexual descriptions. Talk about what you want or what you're going to do to him in specific terms.

3. *Make eye contact.* It increases the impact of words.

4. *Use sounds to let your partner know she/he is getting it right.* Increase the volume of your moans and sighs. Call out, "Oh, yes!" or "There, yes, there!" Don't be shy.

5. *Don't come quietly.* Scream or yell when you have an orgasm. ("My lover makes a low growling sound in his throat when he comes," a woman said. "Sometimes I have another orgasm just hearing it.")

6. *Express appreciation.* During afterplay, tell your partner just how good she/he was.

Joe wanted everything to be perfect the night before Nancy left for Belgium. He had started missing her the minute she told him she'd be doing research there for three months. "I want to do something special for our last night—flowers, candles, soft music, whatever you like," he told her. But Nancy just grinned. "I can think of something we'll both remember every day until I come back," she said. "My surprise."

They met outside her office and got in a cab just after rush hour had ended. It was chilly, and they clung together in the back seat. He was astounded when he felt her slide her hand under his coat and begin to fumble with his zipper. What if the cabbie looked back? But as she worked her magic fingers around him, he realized he was getting incredibly hard. She had on a long skirt, and he watched as she manuevered her panties down one leg, then turned and sat on top of him. He wasn't inside her, but just the touch of flesh on flesh was electric.

When they stumbled out of the cab and walked in the door, she ran into the kitchen. He heard her open the refrigerator door and put something on the stove. In a minute, she joined him in the den, wearing only high heels and dangling earrings, carrying a tray. On it was a bottle of massage oil, a bucket of ice cubes, and a pot of warm, steaming honey.

"Lie down for your massage," she ordered.

He went for the blinds, since their apartment was right across from another highrise, but she stopped his hand. "I want to be seen," she insisted, pushing him down on the rug.

He couldn't wait. He tested the honey with his finger, and as he knelt before her, he applied it to the creases that ran from the tops of her thighs into the hiding place between her legs. It usually took time to arouse Nancy these days—he wondered if it was him or menopause or the fact that they'd been together twenty years—but tonight she was flowing. She dug her fingers into his hair and drew him closer. "I need you inside me," she said.

"Wait." With one hand, he poured the honey down the cleft that led to her clitoris and with the other, he took an ice cube and teased her nipples until they were rock hard. Then, before she knew what was happening, he ran the ice down her body and inserted it into her vagina, then bent and hungrily licked a circle around her clitoris, cleaning honey roughly off the shaft and sides with his tongue. She cried out and her body thrashed in his arms, but he held her tight with his mouth, not letting her escape the pleasure.

He wanted her so badly, but to prolong the ecstacy, he rolled her onto her stomach and applied the massage oil down her back and between her legs. The soft, scented essence flowed over her and made him ache. He slid across her slick buttocks and added one more small chip of ice before entering her from behind. She was wild, bucking against him, but he wouldn't let her go. He reached around in front, stimulating her as his own excitement grew intense. She began to come again and again, and her face was more beautiful than he'd ever seen it. When he came with her, he wrapped his arms around her. "I love saying goodbye to you," he whispered. ∎

Bisexuality

One meaning of "bi" in Latin is two. Bisexuality means simply having sexual responsiveness to both sexes. It is not uncommon for children and adolescents to have a fleeting sexual attraction to members of the same sex. Many experts believe that most adult bisexuals—a group of approximately 10 to 15 percent of the population—are either heterosexual or homosexual. While a small minority maintain sexual relations with men and women concurrently in an equal or nearly equal manner, most spend more time with one gender than another.

A true bisexual is more likely to be a woman than a man. Is that true for social or biological reasons? We don't know. The average man will typically report being repulsed by the idea of having a sexual experience with another male, while the average woman, even if she isn't inclined toward bisexuality, will not react with such vehemence to the idea of being sexual with another woman. If the popularity among men of erotica featuring bisexual or lesbian women is any indication, many men may be attracted to watching or fantasizing two women together. Few women report this kind of response to the idea of two men together. Also, it is probably easier for women heterosexuals to have same sex liaisons than for men because women are expected to have close and affectionate friendships with one another.

There is some reason to believe that many, if not most, people have some degree of unconscious attraction to both genders. Sigmund Freud thought we are all inherently bisexual but that most of us have repressed one side. "The Kinsey Scale" developed by sex researcher Alfred Kinsey, founder of The Kinsey Institute for Research in Sex, Gender, and Reproduction, classifies persons with only heterosexual behavior as "0" and those with only homosexual behavior as "6." Having repeated fantasies about same-sex partners would, for example, move you up a point from zero on the scale.

EXAMPLE

"*I love my husband, but I don't get the emotional satisfaction from him that I need," says Molly. "My relationship with Annie started out as a friendship. Over a two-year period we grew closer, very intimate emotionally. We were always physically affectionate with each other. Then one day it just happened. We kissed and didn't stop there.*

"Both of us felt awkward and guilty afterwards. It was a few days before we dared talk about it. That was uncharacteristic for us, because we always talked about everything right on the spot. We decided not to let the lovemaking happen again, but it did.

"This has been going on for nearly a year now. Neither of us are thinking of leaving our husband. It's just something we need, something we don't get from men." ■

Can you really have it both ways? Some people do. Bisexuality, especially among women, has become more visible in popular culture. In July 1995, *Newsweek* magazine ran a cover story on the "new sexual identity"—a sure sign that the concept, at least, of bisexuality has entered the mainstream.

Body Image and sexuality

HOW YOU FEEL ABOUT YOUR BODY AFFECTS YOUR SEXUALITY

When you feel sexy, you convey a message of desirability. In our society, few women—and an increasing number of men, too—feel sexy if they don't consider themselves physically attractive. As one woman said, "It's hard to want to take off your clothes and lose yourself in wild passion if you are ashamed of your stretch marks, cellulite, padded hips, and drooping breasts. My fat comes between me and my sexuality." We seem to believe that sex is only for the beautiful, or at least the physically fit.

The media play a major role in our culture's obsession with youth and beauty. Cosmetic surgery is a growth industry with women—and men too—opting for face lifts at an earlier age than their parents did. Magazines continually report the results of reader surveys that show women are dissatisfied with their bodies. Surely some of this dissatisfaction must stem from the constant comparison women make between their own bodies and the perfect glossy images in magazines and on the screen, big and small. While men are less likely to link body image and sexuality, they too are troubled by concerns about their physical appearances, especially the size of their penises and, as they age, hair loss.

When a Negative Body Image Douses the Fires of Passion

Jim thinks Deborah doesn't want to make love because she's too tired or "too enthralled" with their six-month-old baby to have desire for him.

"I thought our sex life would have returned to normal by now," he says, "and I'm disappointed that it hasn't. I'm crazy about my son, but I feel left out sometimes. There doesn't seem to be room for me anymore. Her job and the baby take up all her time and energy. She's oblivious to most of my sexual overtures."

Wrong, Deborah says. Far from "oblivious," she knows he wants sex, but she's avoiding him.

"Before pregnancy, I couldn't wait to go to bed, it was something I really looked forward to. From the time I started to get big right up to the present, I wait until he's asleep before I go to bed. And it's not that I'm too tired or am suffering from some kind of hormone thing. It's my body. I am twenty pounds heavier than I was before I got pregnant, and I can't seem to lose the weight. My breasts and belly have stretch marks. I have little broken veins behind my legs and across my thighs. The scar from the caesarian is ugly. I look at myself in the mirror and think, Who but a very horny man would even consider having sex with me? I just don't feel attractive. "Jim says he loves me very much, but how could he?"

Deborah's response is a common if somewhat exaggerated reaction to the physical changes wrought by pregnancy and childbirth. Many women are similarly disaffected by the sight of their own aging bodies. A woman in her fifties may use menopause as the excuse for giving up on sex because secretly she cannot imagine how her partner could desire her body in middle age. And, sadly, the group of women who report the greatest dissatisfaction with their bodies are teenagers and women in their early twenties. Their relatively firm bodies and unwrinkled skin may be envied by older women, but they rate themselves less than supermodel quality and thus not good enough.

Have you ever noticed that many women considered very sexy by men aren't classically beautiful women? They may be a little on the heavy side or may no longer be young or have uneven features, but they exude sex appeal because they are passionate human beings. While most people admire physical beauty, they really value a lover's passion more than his or her looks. Repeatedly men tell sex researchers that they want responsiveness over attractiveness. And many men continue to see their partners in their minds as the women looked when they fell in love.

The Top Five Female Body Issues

1. *Weight.* Most women think they are at least five to ten pounds overweight.

2. *Breast size.* Too large or too small. Few women believe they are just right.

3. *Signs of aging.* Sagging skin, drooping breasts, thickened middles, varicose veins. The tendency of some older men to prefer much younger women exacerbates the problem.

4. *Thighs.* They must be thin, thin, thin. As one man put it: "a woman thing." "Sure, men notice, but it's no big deal; women go over the top about this!"

5. *Scars from pregnancy and childbirth.* Stretch marks, caesarian scars, stretched vaginas (see Kegels).

The Top Five Male Body Issues

1. *Penis size.* Few men think they are big enough and many mistakenly equate penis size with sexual prowess.
2. *Balding.* Hair loss can be traumatic.
3. *Aging signs.* Though gray hair and wrinkles have traditionally been more acceptable in men than in women, standards are changing somewhat, especially in the workplace where executive men often feel pressured to retain a youthful appearance.
4. *Stomach.* Men tend to gain weight in their stomachs, while women gain in their buttocks and thighs.
5. *Height.* Studies show women still prefer a man who is slightly older, richer, and taller than they are.

How You Can Learn to Love Your Body

- *Let go of unrealistic standards.* Few of us ever look like the models, actors, and actresses to whom we relentlessly compare ourselves and our partners. In fact, models, actors, and actresses don't even look like themselves before make-up artists, hairdressers, designers, and good photographers put them together.
- *Do something positive to improve your appearance.* You *can* lose the twenty pounds you hate to see when you look in the mirror. You *can* improve overall body tone with exercise. You *can* dress to flatter your body type. You *can* even wear a little something to bed.
- *Practice creative visualization.* Examine your nude body from all angles, preferably in front of a full-length mirror. Stand, kneel. Pull up a chair and sit. Spend at least fifteen minutes looking at yourself without being critical. Then explore your entire body with your hands. Repeat the exercise a few days later and keep repeating it until you accept what you see and enjoy the feel of your own skin.
- *For men only: Know the truth about penis size.* The vast majority of penises are between three to four inches long when flaccid and five to seven inches long when fully erect. Men tend to think that other men's penises are larger than theirs are. When you look down at your own penis, it appears shorter than it is—and shorter than another man's penis glimpsed in full frontal view in the locker room.

ℋow You Can Help Your Partner Learn to Love His or Her Body

- *Praise your partner's lovemaking ability.* Let him or her know the ways in which you are pleased. "I love the way you touch me." "When you put your mouth on my penis, I go through the roof."
- *Focus on his or her best features.* Maybe she has beautiful hair. Or he has wonderful eyes and a strong jawline.
- *Encourage positive changes.* If he or she is trying to lose weight, don't sabotage the diet. Participate in the exercise program when you can. And don't fail to compliment progress.

Boredom, sexual, overcoming

(see also Marriage, Romance)

Nearly everyone feels the temptation to wander sexually in a long-term relationship. The most frequently named cause for that wanderlust is boredom, sexual, emotional, or both. Human beings are by nature attracted to variety and change. We choose to be in relationships for many good reasons, including emotional security, but in making that choice, we also limit our options. Is boredom inevitable?

Longer life spans, greater leisure, higher sexual and emotional expectations of our mates, and other factors do make it unlikely that a couple who stays together over decades will never know a moment's boredom with each other. For many, though, particularly those who believed the romanticized notions of what love or marriage would do for them, the disappointment comes quickly. Passion cools. Interest wanes. Boredom has set in.

The face that excited, the touch that electrified, the personality that stimulated eventually become merely comfortable, like the living room sofa. Sex becomes routine and mechanical. Some people mourn the loss. Others stray. And some find new ways of exciting each other.

EXAMPLE

"I love my husband very much," said Jana, a woman in her early forties who has been married for more than 20 years. "I wouldn't want to live with any-

one else. Admittedly, though, there is a high degree of monotony in marriage, especially the sexual part, that I find hard to endure at times.

"I have had a few romantic relationships in the past, not sexual affairs, but emotional ones, with colleagues at work. Those little flings made me feel more sexy and affectionate with my husband. I wouldn't recommend it as an anecdote to boredom, because it's risky. What if you do get too involved and throw away your marriage on a fling?

"I don't want to cheat on my husband, sexually or emotionally. But what can I do? I'm bored."

Her husband, Philip, responded to her complaint of boredom by saying: "You'd get tired of eating the same meal every day or watching the same movie every weekend. You're bored because we don't do enough to change the way we make love. It's me on top or you on top. Oral sex and intercourse. That's it for us." ■

Jana and Philip, like many couples, believe the antidotes to boredom are all sexual ones, an outside flirtation, different positions, new techniques, sex toys, and videos. Some people take that a step further. They believe the thrill can only be found again with a new love. Putting the excitement back into the same old relationship is possible, but it requires paying attention to the nonsexual areas of a couple's life together too.

The excitement of discovery, of having novel emotions and impressions, of conflict, of finding new ways of sharing becomes more and more infrequent as couples get to know each other more fully. If they remain the same two people they were in the beginning, the relationship becomes stale and boring. But if they continue to change, surprising each other with unexpected new emotions, ideas, and impressions, they keep rekindling that fire, sometimes just when they thought it was down to nothing but embers. The cure for sexual boredom can be found largely outside the bedroom.

Six Steps to Climbing out of the Sexual Boredom Rut

1. *Talk about it.* Say to each other, "We're in a rut," or "I'm bored with the way things are now, aren't you?" Don't make your partner feel to blame by saying, "You are boring me."

Your folks take the kids, and you take off. Just the two of you for two days in a cabin, far from everyone and everything.

You stop for dinner at an Italian restaurant right off the road. While he orders, you excuse yourself. In the ladies' room, you remove your underpants and put them in your purse.

The waiter takes your order as a pianist begins to play and a few diners take their places on the tiny dance floor. You slide your foot out of your shoe and let it rub up against your partner's leg. He is startled at first, then reaches under the table for your knee. You slide down a little in your seat and sigh, letting him know how much you enjoy this. His hand glances along the curve of your thigh, finally reaching its destination. He gasps as he feels the warm, heavy wetness between your legs.

When he has raised you to such a pitch that you're ready to scream, you push your chair back and pull him onto the dance floor. The two of you melt together—every pore, every cell is attached to him in some way. He holds you so close, you can feel his erection pressing against your leg. "I want to make you come," he whispers.

You ask for the dinners to be wrapped; something has come up and you have to go. He guns the engine and you arrive at the cabin laughing hysterically, piling out of the car and running inside. You are about to tear off your clothes when he asks, almost guiltily, "will you strip for me?"

You click on the old radio by the bed, tuning the dial until you find an "oldies" station. The wail of an alto sax is all the incentive you need. You gyrate slowly, turning so that he can see all of you. You whirl around, and your silk skirt lifts with your motion, giving a glimpse of flesh before you let it drop. You undo the tie at your neck, then loosen your sheer blouse to give a hint of cleavage. He is clearly getting impatient, and reaches into his travel bag. You can hear a faint mechanical humming as he comes toward you, holding something behind his back.

"What are you doing?" you ask, but then he slides the vibrator under your skirt, and you feel as though you're going to faint. You clutch him, and he runs the device along the front of your body to circle your nipples. It is alive, and it makes them stand at attention, straining against the light silk. You take the toy from him, easing it down the front of his pants. He holds you close so that you can both benefit from its pulsing rhythm.

Still partly clothed, you come together, unable to wait any longer. The moon is high now, and the call of an owl reminds you how late it is. But this is your time together, and you don't have to rush. Slowly, you undress and walk out along the little dock that connects your cabin with the lake. Holding hands, you jump into the warm, lapping waves, then duck between each other's legs, spouting water like fishes.

After your swim, you collapse on the soft grass. He licks the drops from your breasts; you suck the wetness from the tip of his penis. Locked in each other's embrace, you are at peace. When you finally open your eyes, you feel the weight of his head on your belly, and see his dear face turned to the rising sun.

■

2. *Don't get mad at each other for being honest.* Acknowledging the situation is the first step toward making a change. An angry or defensive response will only make honest communication more difficult.

3. *Make nonsexual changes in the pattern of your life together.* Try new restaurants, a different walking or biking path, explore museums, parks. Change routines. Take turns serving breakfast in bed on the weekends.

4. *Improve your personal appearance.* New clothes, makeup, hair style—all make us feel like a new and improved version of ourselves. Start exercising or add something new to your regular workouts.

5. *Grow as an individual.* Couples who keep the excitement in their relationship don't stop growing and changing. Take a course. Learn a new skill. Take up a hobby. Read books. Give your partner something new to discover in you.

6. *Add variety to your lovemaking.* This book is filled with suggestions on how to do that.

Breasts

(see also Body Image, Noncoital Sex)

Throughout history and in most cultures, female breasts were admired to some degree either for their nurturing capacity or their beauty or more likely for both. At least to some extent, they are subconscious symbols of comfort and security for men. But in many Western cultures, particularly that of the United States, breasts are objects of great erotic power. Why have they become much more than secondary sex characteristics, even more than an integral part of female allure?

There is no obvious explanation for a cultural preference that is the result of years of socialization. Perhaps our attitudes about nudity provide one clue. In most European countries, topless or nude sunbathing is fairly common and women breast-feed unobtrusively in public. In those countries, there is less fixation on the breast than there is here, where sunbathing topless could get a woman arrested and public breast-feeding is seldom done. Breasts have the allure of the forbidden. Fashion is probably also an influencing factor. Earlier in this century, flat chests were in vogue and women bound their breasts to achieve the "ideal figure" in their clothing. In our time, that ideal figure has become increasingly more voluptuous.

Women as well as men create the cultural dynamic of the breast as sex object. So much of a woman's sense of sexual identity and attractiveness is dependent on her breast's matching the fashion standard that many have submitted to breast-augmentation surgery and to a lesser extent breast-reduction surgery. When the Wonderbra, which promises cleavage to every woman, went on sale in the United States, stores were mobbed with female customers. The event at Macy's Herald Square in New York City was covered by CNN.

Breasts are also an erogenous zone. The breast, nipple, and areola (the darker ring around the nipple) are richly endowed with nerve endings. Nipple erection is one of the first signs of arousal. Breast sensitivity varies from one woman to another and in the same woman depending on hormonal fluctuations and other factors. Studies have shown that the majority of women enjoy having their partners fondle their breasts during lovemaking. A small percentage of women—probably 1 to 2 percent—are able to reach orgasm via breast stimulation alone.

What Men and Women Say About Breasts

A 34-year-old married man: "My wife's breasts are beautiful. The skin is soft and translucent. Her breasts grow like big pearls in soft light. I love to put my face between them."

A 40-year-old divorced man: "I never met a pair I didn't like. Women see breasts as part of their look. They worry about having the right size and the right shape. I see beauty in variations."

A single man in his twenties: "If you show me a pair of small breasts and a pair of big ones, I will pick the big ones. But there are women attached to breasts. A man might admire big breasts and fantasize having that woman, but does he make his choice of partner based on breast size? I don't think so."

A single woman: "I love the visual attention my breasts get from men. When I am shopping for clothes, I wish they were a little smaller. My friend Kate has even bigger ones, and she hates them. Her husband loves them, but her fantasy is breast-reduction surgery."

And from another woman: "Big bras aren't sexy. That's one reason I'm glad I'm a 34B. They still stand up there after two babies. That's the other reason."

The Top Six (Nonmedical) Breast Questions

1. *How can a woman increase breast size without surgery?*

Once a woman has reached maturity, her breast size isn't likely to change unless she gains weight. Breast swelling due to pregnancy, nursing, or birth control pills is most often a temporary condition. Good posture will make breasts appear larger. Exercises to strengthen the pectorals, the muscles beneath the breasts, will help lift them, also making them appear larger.

2. *How should a man handle a woman's breasts during lovemaking?*

Ask her how she likes to be touched. Some women have very sensitive nipples and some don't. They may like to have their nipples stroked or lightly squeezed or sucked—or they may not. Some women enjoy having the whole breast massaged and stroked. One approach does not fit all.

In general, however, women prefer gentle stroking of the breasts and kissing, licking, and light sucking of the nipples. Circling the nipple with the tongue can be an effective technique. Remember that breast sensitivity varies with hormonal fluctuations. Before her period, a woman may experience tenderness and swelling in her breasts and want a different kind of stimulation.

3. *Does breast size have anything to do with a woman's sexual responses?*

No. If she has negative feelings about her breasts, her attitude may influence her responsiveness. But breast size is not a measure of sexual responsiveness.

4. *Is a woman excited if her nipples don't become erect?*

While most women will have erect nipples when aroused, not all women do. Other signs of arousal include vaginal lubrication, a flush across the chest, and increased heart and breathing rates.

5. *Is there something wrong with a man who wants to have intercourse between a woman's breasts?*

Not unless he doesn't want to have intercourse any other way!

Intermammary intercourse as an occasional alternative or prelude to intercourse can be satisfying for both partners. Her breasts have to be large enough to meet when held together. She should lie on her back, half raised by pillows. The man kneels astride. Either partner can hold her breasts together, wrapped around the shaft rather than the glans of the penis. Both the physical sensations and the visual aspect of intermammary intercourse are particularly arousing to many men.

6. *Is there something wrong with a woman who doesn't respond to some form of breast stimulation?*

No. Women (and men too) vary greatly in the ways they respond sexually. Some women never have particularly sensitive breasts though they are aroused by other forms of genital and nongenital touching and stroking. Other women report that breast sensitivity decreases after breast-enlargement or -reduction surgery or treatment for breast cancer or after pregnancy and childbirth or with age, leaving them more or less indifferent to touch. And some women will not be aroused by breast stimulation for psychological reasons. They may, for example, be embarrassed by the size of their breasts, considering them too small or too large to be erotic.

Note: Women should talk to their doctors about breast health concerns and learn how to perform a monthly breast self-exam.

Calendar, creating a romantic

Therapists sometimes help couples completing treatment to develop a calendar so they can maintain their romantic momentum throughout the year. This simple concept for keeping romance alive can be used by any couple. Planning the year together is part of the fun.

The following are suggestions. Your anniversary and other special dates will probably help determine your own romantic calendar.

January. Reaffirm your commitment to each other. How would you like to improve your sexual relationship this year? What steps can you take to do that?

February. Valentine's Day may have been turned into another children's holiday in your household. Take it back as a day for lovers.

March. Fill the bedroom with tulips and other spring flowers. Use some of the petals beneath your fingerpads while massaging your lover's nipples.

April. Take a walk in the rain. Don't wear anything under your raincoats.

May. Plant flowers together in the moonlight.

June. Dance together sensuously at someone else's wedding reception. Kiss on the dance floor.

July. Have a midnight picnic outdoors. Don't wear any underwear—or any clothing at all if you have enough privacy.

August. Be teenagers for a day. Go somewhere, like an amusement park, you wouldn't typically go without the children. Make out.

September. Learn something you didn't know about sex together. Buy a book on sex techniques or an educational video or sign up for a class on Tantra.

October. Have a private Halloween party for two. Dress in sex-fantasy costumes.

November. Eat the leftover mashed potatoes and gravy off each other's bodies.

December. Give each other a sexual or sensual present, preferably something requiring action on your part, such as a bottle of scented massage oil.

Celibacy, creative

WHY DO SOME PEOPLE CHOOSE TO BE CELIBATE?

Sexual abstinence (celibacy) is popularly considered to mean not having partner sex, often by choice. The celibate typically do masturbate. Masturbation is, of course, a sexual activity, which in previous historical periods was also forbidden to the celibate and is still off limits to some under particular religious doctrines. Monks, nuns, and priests, for example, are not supposed to masturbate. Interestingly, the sexual prohibitions of the Victorian era against masturbation and any form of sex other than vaginal intercourse have their roots not in religion but medicine. Physicians mistakenly believed that loss of semen caused a corresponding loss of health and vitality and advised men against sex when not intended for procreation.

Celibacy has been designated by the media as a minor social trend. Books and articles claim that men and especially women choose celibacy as a way of promoting or improving their own psychological and spiritual growth and as a means of avoiding the emotional complications and physical risks of sex. Some educators, politicians, and other leaders claim that celibacy is the only safe choice, a protection against HIV infection and other sexually transmitted diseases. As in previous times, celibacy in these contexts is held up as a superior way of life or as a means of building character. A close reading of history shows, however, that some members of the celibate clergy throughout the ages have been guilty of horrendous acts of cruelty. Forsaking sex alone won't make you a better person.

Some people abstain from partner sex not by choice. They may be committed to people who are physically not available due to illness, geographical distance, or some other factor; or they may be unavailable themselves due to illness or accident. Others may be "between partners," out of one sexual relationship and not yet into another during a period of emotional healing. And some are ready for and desirous of sex but unable to find an interesting and interested partner.

The physical and psychological impact of sexual abstinence varies from one person to another and also depends on other factors including the length of the period of celibacy, the age of the person, the reasons for abstaining, and whether or not the person gratifies his or her sensuality and achieves sexual release through masturbation.

EXAMPLES

Allison's husband, Rick, works for a multinational corporation and periodically has overseas assignments lasting anywhere from two to six months. She isn't free to join him when he travels because of her own professional responsibilities. A healthy couple in their early thirties, they find the extended separations a sexual hardship.

Jill is a 22-year-old virgin who has chosen to remain celibate until marriage. More than one relationship has ended because of the sexual barricade she puts up between herself and the man. She is frustrated by her inability to sustain a close emotional connection but wants to hold on to her "principles."

And, finally, Maureen has "sworn off sex" following a brief affair with a man who, she presumes, transmitted chlamydia, the most common STD, to her. Though chlamydia is easily treated and cured, she felt hurt, betrayed, and "cheapened" by the experience. For this and other reasons, she says, she can't trust men and won't risk sex again. ∎

SHOULD PEOPLE CHOOSE TO ABSTAIN FROM SEX?

That's a personal decision and in some cases a good one. For example, brief periods of abstinence may increase the volume and potency of semen—giving a man with a low sperm count a better chance of impregnating his wife. (No research, however, substantiates the myth that abstaining from sex before an athletic contest gives men greater power.) For couples who are experiencing sexual boredom, abstinence for a week or more can make the sex more exciting by increasing their hunger for each other.

Choosing to be celibate while your partner is away or ill, as Allison and Rick have done, is not the same as choosing to be celibate within a relationship where the couple has access to each other. (See Sexless Marriage.) Under those circumstances, it is an act of love and a display of commitment. A benefit of their enforced sexual breaks is their ongoing passion, not dulled by daily routine and complacency.

Abstinence can be a useful break for someone who is recovering from a traumatic relationship or has a history of unhappy or unsatisfying sexual relationships, either one after another or in multiple fashion. By not rushing immediately into sex, men and women can learn to see each other as individuals and perhaps spare themselves making a wrong partner choice simply because they let the sex take them further together than they really wanted to go. Some people, including Jill, sincerely believe in religious or moral proscriptions against sexual activity outside marriage. But abstinence as a way of hiding out is no more admirable than any other ways people have devised of avoiding intimacy. And there is no proof that sublimating your sexuality will turn you into a genius or an artist.

Orgasm, via masturbation or other means, and sexual activity that includes touching, stroking, and caressing are beneficial to one's physical, psychological, and emotional health. But there is no reason to believe that periods of abstinence are harmful, particularly if the person does masturbate and satisfies the need for contact by hugging friends, cuddling children, stroking pets. Even the act of applying hand and body lotion can gratify the senses if you allow yourself to enjoy the sensations of your own hands stroking your flesh.

HOW CAN PEOPLE HANDLE ABSTINENCE?

There are ways of being sexual with a partner without risking STD infection through unprotected intercourse. (See also Condoms,

Foreplay, Noncoital Sex, Phone Sex, Safe Sex, Sexually Transmitted Disease.) Maureen, for example, has taken the all-or-nothing sexual position. In blaming her partner for passing on an infection he probably did not know he had—chlamydia is largely asymptomatic in men—she fails to take responsibility for her own sexuality. Any sexually active person not in a monogamous relationship should practice safe sex and be periodically tested for STDs. In not accepting that responsibility, it is likely that Maureen, finding herself overcome by love or desire, will put aside her vow of celibacy in the near future and take the same sexual risks again.

If no partner is available, fantasy and masturbation are satisfying alternatives. Women especially need to continue some form of sexual activity as they age if they want to prevent vaginal atrophy, a condition in which the vagina grows progressively drier and less elastic until intercourse would be painful or even in some cases virtually impossible. Studies have shown that women in their sixties and seventies who masturbate suffer significantly less vaginal atrophy than those who don't.

The Five Keys to Surviving a Sexual Drought

Prolonged and involuntary celibacy is perhaps the most difficult sexual condition. Nothing takes the place of sex, but if you break it down into its components, you can make sure each of those needs is being met in your life. In simplest terms, sex is warmth, closeness, physical touching, and orgasm. The keys to surviving a drought in comfort are satisfying each element in the following ways:

1. *Create and strengthen intimate bonds.* Find warmth and closeness with friends and family.

2. *Indulge your sensual side.* Too many people think that candlelight is for shared meals, bubble baths are a part of the preparation for partner sex, and that the best fabrics and perfumes should be worn for lovers only. Be romantic with yourself.

3. *Fantasize.* Don't censor your sexual thoughts. Choose books and films that encourage erotic fantasy.

4. *Touch.* Yourself and others, too. Take your hugs where you can get them. And consider adopting a pet.

5. *Masturbate!*

Checklist, the sexual relationship

These twenty questions will help you evaluate your sexual relationship. There is no right or wrong answer to any question. You and your partner can review the list together or separately and then compare results. Your answers should tell you what each finds satisfying or dissatisfying in your sexual relationship and point you in the direction of positive change.

The first step is to put aside an afternoon or evening when you and your partner can share several hours of uninterrupted time. Make sure both of you have the opportunity to read through the questions before proceeding together. That way you will be equally informed.

Twenty Questions About Sex

1. How often do you make love? If frequency is an issue, what suggestions do you have for improving or resolving this?
2. How do you feel about the form of birth control/safe sex protection you're using?
3. How do you feel about your partner's sexual responsiveness, including orgasmic reaction? About your own?
4. Who usually initiates sexual activity? Is this satisfactory? Is there satisfaction with the time of day sex occurs, the place, the privacy?
5. Do you and your partner tell and/or show each other how you want to be touched, stroked, kissed, and caressed?
6. Are you satisfied with the degree of foreplay in your lovemaking? What are your suggestions for making it even better?
7. Do you have sexual thoughts and fantasies—and do you enjoy them? How do you feel about sexual thoughts and fantasies being shared between you and your partner?
8. What part does masturbation play in your sexuality?
9. What three elements of your sexual experience do you enjoy most?
10. What are your top three suggestions for heating the fire between you and your partner?
11. What suggestions would you offer yourself to romanticize your relationship? What would you like from your partner?
12. What is your prescription for strengthening the sexual communication between you and your partner?

13. What could you do for your partner outside the bedroom that would have a favorable effect on your sex life?

14. Name your partner's secret places, the spots where he or she is most sensitive to touch.

15. How do you feel about your body? Your partner's body?

16. What are you willing to do to improve your current state of health and fitness?

17. What does your partner do to arouse you?

18. When you're not quite in the mood, what can your partner do to kindle your embers?

19. Describe your partner's most effective lovemaking technique.

20. How does your partner's most effective lovemaking technique make you feel? Describe it to your partner down to the smallest erotic detail.

Clitoral Stimulation

(see also Cunnilingus, Orgasm)

In the majority of women the clitoris is the most sensitive area of their genitals. A button-sized organ located just below the place where the top of the inner labia meet, the head of the clitoris is often partially or totally hidden by the clitoral hood, a fold of skin. The shaft is largely covered by the labia and extends inside the body into the pubic region.

The clitoris is highly sensitive to stimulation. As a woman becomes aroused by clitoral stimulation or other means, the organ pulls back against the pubic bone and the labia swell, combining to make it appear erect. This is why it is sometimes compared to the penis.

Because of its small size and hidden location, the clitoris has been—and to some extent remains—shrouded in mystery. Men often report trouble in locating it or confusion about how and when to stimulate it. Though less than a third of women can reach intercourse without clitoral stimulation, many women are shy about asking for it and afraid of intimidating their partner if they touch themselves during lovemaking. Compounding the problem, theories about how women "should" be orgasmic have come in and out of fashion over the years, with some schools of thought, most notably Freud's, maintaining the superiority of vaginal or nonclitoral orgasms. This kind of thinking has done a great deal of harm to women and to their relationships with men.

While the clitoris is not a "magic button," it is in most women the key to orgasm and in nearly all women a source of pleasure that should not be overlooked.

What Women Say About the Clitoris

From a 41-year-old woman married 13 years: "I've never had an orgasm through intercourse. I met Frank when I was 28 and had been sexually active for nearly 10 years. There were lots of lovers before him, with different techniques and different staying power, but I didn't have an orgasm with any of them. After Frank and I were married a while, we had established the trust and comfort with each other that we needed to work out the right kind of clitoral stimulation to make me orgasmic."

A 27-year-old woman who does not have a steady partner says: "I've never had a vaginal orgasm, an orgasm that didn't include direct clitoral stimulation. I feel most confident that I will be orgasmic if I stimulate myself, because I need specific rhythm and pressure. Sometimes a lover can do it, especially with his tongue, which I find very hot! When I have intercourse I prefer positions that allow me to touch my clitoris. That way I can have an orgasm during intercourse and *really* enjoy it!"

From a 33-year-old divorced woman: "I am easily orgasmic, which I am sure has more to do with luck than anything else. I can have orgasms during intercourse without direct clitoral stimulation. But sometimes I prefer to touch myself during intercourse and come that way. The orgasm feels stronger, as if it were coming from several places at once."

How to Make Love to a Clitoris

1. *Overcome a woman's shyness about touching herself.* A man can best learn how she likes to be stimulated by watching her stroke herself. Yet many women consider touching themselves a private, even shameful, thing to do. Or they may believe that lovemaking means one only touches the other, not the self. A man can help his partner overcome these inhibitions by asking her to stroke herself for him and telling her how aroused he is when she does.

2. *Alleviate a man's anxiety about the need for clitoral stroking.* Conversely, many men still believe that they should be capable of sat-

A Sumptuous Sunday Morning

Y ou stretch and yawn. The rain is drizzling softly on the windows, drumming a gentle tattoo that lulls you back to sleep. You can be lazy all day—it's Sunday.

You feel a hand snaking across your warm limbs, and it's impossible to ignore. Are you dreaming or waking? Your limbs start to shake in sensuous delight. You can feel a roving mouth and tongue between your legs, and an explosion begins somewhere inside you that you cannot control.

You open your eyes and glance at your lover, whose face bears a silly grin. "Isn't that better than the newspaper and coffee?"

You take your time getting up and dressing, then decide to go out for a drive. The rain has nearly stopped, but everything has a dewy wetness about it. You come to a completely deserted road just off an abandoned highway. It is straight as a pin. "Keep driving," you say, putting one hand on your lover's leg. You begin to stroke it lightly, making circles on the thigh, moving upward an inch at a time. You undo one button, then a zipper, and slip your hand inside. You can feel a quickened pulse under your fingers. There is no one else around—no one else in the world—as you work faster and harder, aiming for delirium. Suddenly, the car jerks to a halt and you are thrown back in your seat. Both of you sit, panting, and then your lover pulls the car over to the side of the road.

You climb into the back seat and loosen each other's clothing. One leg is on the headrest of the front seat, the other presses against the door latch. Each kiss, each caress, feels like the breeze through the open window. You welcome your lover into your arms, pulling pants in one direction and shirts in another. You lie head to head, trying to accommodate in such close quarters. You feel the pressure of limb on limb as you welcome this wonderful body inside yours.

Monday morning seems as far away as the moon. ■

isfying their partners without any help and by their penises alone. Tell him that you want to share something special with him. Tell him you have trouble asking for the kind of clitoral stimulation you need and feel more comfortable showing him. Most men will be turned on by the demonstration. Later, they will feel less threatened if you stroke yourself during intercourse.

3. *Assume a comfortable position.* That may be the one you use during masturbation or your favorite lovemaking position.

4. *Techniques for men.* Whether using you fingers or lips and tongue, use a very light touch. Wet your fingers with saliva or a lubricant. Let your partner's response guide you if a firmer touch is desired. Use different movements, for example, switching from circling the clitoris to moving up and down along the shaft. Try holding two fingers in a V position with the point above against her body above the clitoris and the fingers extending along each side. Gently press with your fingers.

5. *Don't try to have—or give her—an orgasm.* Using a familiar pattern of stimulation, a woman will find it still takes longer to reach orgasm when she's not alone. The times she stimulates her clitoris while he is watching or during lovemaking—or asks him to do it for her—should be free of the pressure to reach orgasm.

Communication

HOW IMPORTANT IS COMMUNICATION?

Admittedly "communication" is an overworked word. When talk-show audiences began routinely advising guests with relationship problems to "communicate," the social saturation point had clearly been reached. Research literature does show rather conclusively that skillful communication is an essential element of an intimate relationship. Not surprisingly, couples who have a solid, communicative relationship report greater happiness, including more satisfying sex lives.

While it has become fashionable to talk about "communication problems," many couples influenced by the folklore of romantic love believe that an innate sensitivity should link them with their partner. Others assume that being in a relationship affords them the privilege of being less diligent in their efforts to communicate than they would be in casual contacts. And most middle-aged adults grew up in households in which marital intimacy between their parents was not even a goal. Deceptions and lies are almost institutionalized, standard operating procedures between the sexes. As a result of these and other factors, many husbands and wives, rather than sharing the closeness of an intimate relationship, live in very separate emotional worlds. That kind of separation has a negative sexual impact.

Couples who "never talk anymore" typically "never have sex anymore" either. Their conversation is limited to necessary exchanges about the running of a household, a joint social life, and family obligations. Why should their sex life be richer? Good sexual communication is rooted in good intimate communication. Establish verbal intimacy by talking to each other about your emotions, opinions, ideas, hopes, and fears. Then it will be easier to talk about sex.

EXAMPLE

Married 15 years, Jeff and Sally have been "drifting apart" over the past several years. Their sex life is not fulfilling for either one of them. She frequently fakes orgasms and complains to her friends that he doesn't satisfy her in bed. He would like to make love more often in more varied positions and have more oral sex but he doesn't tell her specifically what he wants. Each feels their needs are not met and silently resents the other for not meeting them.

"He's always saying he doesn't 'get enough,'" Sally complains, "whatever that means. I don't get enough of anything. He isn't affectionate and he never has time for me unless he wants sex. Most nights he falls asleep on the sofa watching television. But when he's ready for sex, he expects me to be ready too; and I'm not."

"She's always tired or busy," Jeff complains.

"We never talk," Sally says.

"No, we don't," Jeff admits. "In the beginning of our relationship we talked to each other about everything. I called her from work to talk over things with her. We were very close. We told each other things we'd never confided in anyone else. Now I feel like she's closer to her friends than she is to me. I'd like to talk to her about our sex problems, but I'm afraid she'll tell them whatever I say."

"How am I supposed to tell him I want the sex to be different when he doesn't know I've been faking?" Sally asks. "After all these years, shouldn't he know how to please me? I don't understand why it's up to me to provide instructions." ■

To improve their relationship, Sally and Jeff must first reestablish the intimate connection they once had. Then they have to discuss some touchy issues. None of their problems are insurmountable. As they talk more openly to each other, they should observe the five principles of communication.

The Five Principles of Communication

1. *The empathetic listening principle.* In effective listening, we fully hear the speaker's message, particularly the emotional component, and relay our understanding of the message to the speaker in such a

way that he or she feels accepted and understood. It is easy to misread or overlook feelings. Many of us learned to hide our feelings in childhood. By the time we are adults, most of us have mastered the rituals of the superficial exchange of feelings, the harmless small talk that is expected in polite society. Empathetic listening requires us to listen on a deeper level, connect to the feelings of the speaker, and communicate the connection.

2. *The "I-message" principle.* Whether you're asking a question or making a statement, take clear responsibility for every message you send. Often "you" statements are "I" statements in disguise. For example, when people say, "You make me mad," they are really saying, "I am angry." And sometimes questions are really disguised accusations or traps. Ask legitimate rather than rhetorical and manipulative questions.

3. *The direct communication principle.* When you want change, clarification, reassurance, companionship, support, or something else—be direct. Don't speak in generalities. And don't expect the listener to read your mind by correctly filling in the blanks. Misunderstandings inevitably grow from unclear communication.

4. *The principle of weak words and strong gestures.* When our words convey one message, but our tone of voice or body language says something else, we are likely to arouse suspicion and confusion in the listener. The nonverbal dimension is critically important in human communication. In fact, research indicates that about 70 percent of our communication with others is carried out on a nonverbal level. Develop consistency between what you say and how you say it.

5. *The principle of descriptive language.* When behavior is described rather than labeled, the outcome is likely to be more positive. Too often in an effort to make sense of the world around us, we categorize and label complex behaviors. Also we fail to take into consideration the fluctuation in human behavior. Rather than saying, "You are selfish in bed," for example, say, "I would like you to spend more time arousing me orally and manually before we have intercourse."

HOW TO DISCUSS THE TOUCHIEST SEXUAL ISSUES

"Won't you ruin sex if you talk about it?" Jeff asks.

Jeff, like many other people, ascribes to the swept-away school of romance. The silence surrounding sex is mystical. Love has a language of its own. You know what the other wants. Together you are swept away to ecstasy.

In actuality, no matter how much you love someone, you don't automatically know how to please him or her. That means Jeff and Sally, who are learning how to talk to each other again, must also learn how to talk about the most delicate of subjects, their sexual pleasures. Talking about sexual issues requires that you be able to ask without demanding, tell without criticizing, and to do all of this without displaying embarrassment.

- *Share.* First, exchange information. Tell your lover about your own needs, desires, wishes, secrets, fears and fantasies. Make it clear that sharing—a fantasy, for example—is not the same as asking for action.

- *Ask for information.* Maybe you want to know how many partners a new lover has had or whether he or she intends to make a commitment to you. Or maybe you want to know if your spouse of 20 years has ever wanted to make love in the backyard. Don't assume you know the answers to your questions. Don't be afraid of hearing answers that may not match your hopes. Ask—and be prepared to hear.

- *Ask for what you want.* If you want to make love standing up in the bathroom, say so. Don't expect your partner to guess what's on your mind. But remember, a request is not a demand. Make sure your tone of voice and body language convey the same message as your words. Keep the request simple and to the point. Don't precede it with a litany of sexual grievances. And ask your partner to clarify what he or she wants if you don't understand.

- *Use positive rather than negative statements.* "I want to make love to you more often" is a positive statement. "You don't give me enough sex" is a negative statement. Stay in the positive.

The Secret to Creating Positive Sexual Change

- *Saying "no" without being rejecting.* One partner may not want to participate in a sexual activity that the other avidly desires. Treat the difference as you would any other. He likes steak and she likes lobster. Does that make either one of them a pervert, a sex maniac, a frigid person? No. You have the right to reject any sexual practice, but do so without rejecting your lover.

- *Asking without being critical.* He or she doesn't perform oral sex the way you want it performed. The temptation to say, "Don't do it that way" is great. Don't say it. Build on the positive aspects of your lover's performance and augment those with shared learning. Buy a book, rent a video. Focus on ways you can both improve your oral performances.

even Nonverbal Ways to Let Your Partner Know What You Want

1. Sigh softly when it feels good.

2. Moan when it feels even better.

3. Suddenly shift positions if the stimulation is becoming painful.

4. Gently move your partner's hands to where you want them to be.

5. Show him or her how to stroke your genitals by stroking them yourself.

6. Write a graphic love note.

7. Move with greater urgency when the stimulation is right.

Compulsive Sexual Behavior

(see also Paraphilias)

Compulsive sexual behavior is the joyless repetition of particular erotic acts. Whether the sexual compulsion is endlessly phoning sex lines, having one-night stands, or masturbating several times a day, he or she reports feeling "out of control" before the activity and guilty and ashamed afterward. What gratification the person does experience from his or her sexual activity is dulled and fleeting.

In recent years, the concept of "sex addiction" has been one of the most hotly debated issues in sex therapy. Proponents of the theory contend that some people—who might have been labeled "womanizers," "rakes," or "sluts" in the past—are not only behaving in a compulsive way but are also addicted to sex because they are powerless to control their sexual urges and will indulge them at any risk or consequence. Treatment centers and 12-step self-help groups based on the precepts of Alcoholics Anonymous have sprung up all over the country to deal with Western society's newest dysfunction. The sex-addiction theory, however, has more detractors within the professional community than it does supporters.

Those who do not believe sex can be an addiction argue that no substance is involved, as in alcohol or drug addiction. Assessment of sex addiction tends to be subjective with the moral and religious values of the treatment specialist or recovery group shaping the diagnosis. Such biases have led dissenting authorities to call sex addiction a punitive myth growing out of our culture's newly conservative, if not repressive, attitudes on sex and pleasure. Unfortunately, this negative climate on sex causes many people to feel guilty about their behavior, urges, and fantasies, especially women who are inundated with more antisex messages than men are throughout their lives.

Promiscuous behavior is not indicative of addiction. Nor is the use of prostitutes, phone sex lines, or the practice of other sexual behaviors not sanctioned by the majority of mainstream Americans. Anyone who leads a freer sexual life than the current norm is liable to censure from the therapeutic community, not just the religious one.

While I recognize that a small percentage of people do suffer from sexually compulsive behavior, I don't think the label "addict" applies to them. If you are troubled by your sexual behavior for any reason, however, you should talk to a therapist.

EXAMPLE

"I feel out of control," said Abe, a man in his late twenties. "Since I was a teenager, I've been chasing sexual gratification. I never seem to get enough, but what I get doesn't satisfy me. I need some kind of sex several times a day."

Abe began in adolescence by masturbating several times a day. Gradually, he added other activities such as "picking up" women in bars for "nameless" encounters, often in the bathroom of the bar, and sometimes several times a night, always with different partners. He also calls phone sex lines and procures prostitutes. None of his encounters are in any way psychologically intimate.

"When I am looking for sex, I feel almost as if I'm in a trance," he said. "While searching for a partner, I get more and more aroused until I finally score. Afterward, I feel despair. I hate myself. I'm ashamed of the way I live. I feel bad about myself until I go into the next trance and do it all over again." ∎

The cycle Abe described is familiar to victims of compulsive behavior. Their search for gratification is obsessive, sometimes ritualistic. They feel unable to control themselves during the search, and afterward they experience despair, shame, and self-hatred. The only way they can escape the negative feelings is through the repetition of the search for gratification, which numbs and obliterates the feelings of shame and self-hate—temporarily.

Abe is in therapy now for his problem, and the prognosis is excellent. The goal of his therapy is to help him understand why he behaves as he does and stop acting out as he learns how to create a more positive sexual dynamic in his life. In his case and many others the use of medication, such as the antidepressant Prozac, is sometimes part of treatment. If you do exhibit compulsive sexual behavior that leaves you with feelings of shame and despair, seek help.

If you're just having more sex, or more varied sex, than your friends think is appropriate, openly consider what they have to say. After due reflection if you're feeling comfortable with your sexual behavior, perhaps it is time to stop confiding in your friends rather than changing your lovemaking patterns.

Condoms

(see also Female Condom, Sexually Transmitted Diseases)

Incredibly, only 14 percent of sexually active unmarried heterosexuals not in monogamous relationships report using condoms every time they make love. Why don't more people consistently use condoms? Denial and ignorance about the prevalence of STDs and how they are transmitted. Embarrassment. Fear of "spoiling the mood" if they ask a partner to use one. The mistaken belief that someone who seems "nice" and looks "clean" won't have a disease. The sense, especially among the young, of "invincibility." Unfortunately, many women and some men, too, believe that being prepared for sex makes one appear to be promiscuous.

Sex in a nonmonogamous relationship without a condom is truly a dangerous liaison.

THE SHOPPERS' GUIDE

Every sexually active and nonmonogamous man and woman should know how to choose and use a condom. Effective both as a contraceptive and a barrier preventing the spread of STDs, the simple classic sheath comes in a considerable array of styles. Made of either lambskin or latex, condoms are available in lubricated and nonlubricated versions. Some are treated with nonoxynol-9, a spermicide considered beneficial in the prevention of HIV transmission. Others are neon-colored or flavored in selections ranging from mint to passion fruit. You can buy specially designed anal condoms and French ticklers, ribbed for satisfaction. Sizes include average, which fits most men, as well as larger sizes.

THE TEN MOST OFTEN ASKED CONDOM QUESTIONS

1. *Which one should I buy?*

First, buy them in this country where testing criteria are more rigorous than they are in other parts of the world. Condoms manufactured in or imported into the United States must meet FDA standards: 99.6 percent of a randomly selected batch must pass leak tests. That means four condoms out of a thousand *could* leak, making the use of spermicidal lubricant important. The latex condom and nonoxynol-9 lubricant used together offer the best protection available against STD and HIV transmission.

Nonlubricated or flavored brands are preferred by many women for performing fellatio. After oral sex, switch to a nonoxynol-9 lubricated condom or add the treated lubricant to the condom he's wearing. Never use an oil-based lubricant on latex because oil can dissolve the latex in places, leaving tiny holes you may not even see.

Lambskin condoms provide more sensation according to many men *but* they do not provide protection against infection. The walls are more porous than latex and can leak. A latex condom is the best choice for intercourse and oral sex. If you want to experiment with a ribbed or ridged condom or a French tickler dotted with protrusions for different sensations, just be sure they're made of latex.

Never use a condom that is broken, sticky, or discolored. (Store in a cool, dry place.)

And *always* choose an anal condom for anal intercourse.

Consumer Reports tested 37 styles of condoms. Thirty passed their tests. (See back issues of CR, available in most public libraries.) Their top seven condoms are: Excita Extra Ultra-Ribbed with spermicide; Ramses, Extra Ribbed, with spermicide; Sheik Elite 1; LifeStyles Vibraribbed; Ramses Extra, with spermicide; Ramses Sensitol; Sheik Elite, Ribbed, with spermicide.

2. *When should I use a condom?*

Every time you have intercourse or fellatio with any partner not involved in a long-term monogamous relationship with you. You can safely stop using condoms after you have made a monogamous commitment to each other and tested negatively for STDs. Studies have shown that couples typically use condoms three to six times, then discard them because they "know each other well" or "are in love." Science has yet to prove love a deterrent to the spread of disease. And nice people get STDs, too.

3. *How can I ask my partner to wear a condom if he says they interfere with his pleasure?*

Don't ask. Asking implies the subject is open to negotiation. Just say, "Yes, you are going to wear a condom—unless you would rather completely interfere with your pleasure."

4. *Can you put a condom on a flaccid penis?*

No, but you can put a condom on a semi-erect penis.

5. *How different is the experience of sex for a man when he's wearing a condom?*

Men generally agree there is less sensation while wearing a condom. Some men report considerably less sensation, while others say the difference is not too significant. On the plus side, some men say that using a condom helps them control the tendency toward premature ejaculation.

6. *Can we use the same condom if we make love again that night?*

No. Never reuse a condom.

7. *What is the correct way to put on a condom?*

Put the condom on the penis before it touches any part of a woman's vagina. Leave room at the top for trapped air and ejaculate. Some condoms are made with a reservoir and some aren't. Pinch a half inch at the top of a condom before you begin to roll it down the penis all the way to the base.

8. *What is the correct way to remove a condom?*

After ejaculation, the man should hold the condom in place at the base of his penis while withdrawing. Don't wait until the penis has lost its erection because the condom will be more likely to slip off. Carefully remove, discard, and wash both hands and penis.

9. *How long do condoms keep?*

They begin to deteriorate after two years. Check the expiration date on lubricated condoms, required by law to carry one. If it's been a long time between relationships—expiration date or not—buy a fresh supply. And never pull a condom from an opened box with a new lover. It's tacky.

10. *Are colored condoms safe?*

According to the FDA, the dye in black condoms *may* be a carcinogen. Dyes in other colors may cause irritation or an allergic reaction in some people. Usually, colored condoms do not contain nonoxynol-9. Check the label before buying. They are probably not as safe as regular condoms, but they are fun and not nearly as risky as unprotected sex.

CONDOM PLAY: HOW TO INCORPORATE CONDOM USE INTO LOVEPLAY

He says, "I go soft whenever I put that damn thing on!"

She says, "Here, honey, let me do it for you."

Some men find it arousing when a woman puts the condom on. She can use her hands. (Grasp the base of the penis firmly and then follow the directions given in step 7. Roll the condom down as you would roll a ski cap down over your head.) Or, she can put it on with her mouth, which is a little trickier but a skill worth developing. Use your hands to stroke and fondle his penis and testicles while you're perfecting the technique.

Choose a condom you don't mind tasting. Take a drink of water so your mouth will be wet. Suck the tip of the condom into your mouth. Anchor it against the roof of your mouth with your tongue.

Keeping the tip firmly in place, put the entire condom inside your lips and in front of your teeth. Flatten the tip with your tongue. Otherwise air may enter the condom and cause it to break.

Gently circle the shaft of his penis with one hand and the thumb and forefinger of the other hand leaving only the head and approximately an inch of the shaft uncovered. Place your mouth with the entire condom on the head of the penis. Immediately slide your lips behind the ring of the condom and press it against the head of the penis with your mouth.

At this point, the tip is still inside your mouth and the ring outside and flat against your lips. Now use your lips to slip the condom down over the head of the penis. Take it down as far as your mouth can go. Use your hands to slide the rest of the condom to the base of the penis.

FEMALE CONDOM

A relatively new product, the femal condom consists of a lubricated polyurethane sheath roomy enough to cover the vaginal area with a flexible polyurethane ring on each end. One ring is inserted into the vagina almost as if it were a diaphragm. The other ring remains outside.

The female condom has a higher failure rate both for preventing pregnancy and STDs than does the male condom. If you do use it, be sure you also use a spermicidal lubricant.

Conflict Resolution

People in relationships may argue about how often to have sex or about what kind of sex to have. Sometimes these conflicts are rooted in sexual differences and sometimes they have nothing to do with sex. A couple who has serious problems about how to spend money or raise children may put their issues in sexual terms. She may withhold sex because he spends too much money on frivolities or he may withhold sex because she undercuts his authority with the children.

Some couples handle their unresolved conflicts by leading double lives. They emotionally divorce themselves from each other. One or both may have an affair. Or they may drift into a sexless marriage with neither one of them seeking outside lovers.

Resolving conflicts, whether they are sexual or nonsexual, is essential in a healthy erotic relationship.

EXAMPLE

"I don't get sex unless I'm good," complained Keith. "I feel like a little boy in this marriage; and I resent it. Catherine punishes me when I stay out late with friends by withholding sex. She punishes me if I put too much on the credit cards by withholding sex.

"I feel powerless with her. Nothing I can do will arouse her if she doesn't want to be aroused."

For her part, Catherine said that Keith made lovemaking "impossible" because of his blatant disregard for their budget.

"I don't feel sexy with him when he repeatedly violates our agreements about money and time," she said. ∎

Unlike many couples in the withholding position, Catherine and Keith recognized and admitted to the connection in their relationship between nonsexual behavior and sex. They argued about sex, however, more often than they argued about money or time. When they were able to separate sex from their issues, they began to resolve the conflicts and enjoy making love again.

The Six Steps for Conflict Resolution

1. *Do not link sex with nonsexual issues.* Using sex as a reward or a bribe devalues the erotic experience and drives a wedge between partners.

2. *Tackle one problem at a time.* In a problem-solving discussion, only one problem should be discussed. Additional problems or discussions are to be avoided or redirected.

3. *Define the problem clearly.* A well-defined problem statement involves a description of the undesirable behavior, specifying the situations in which it occurs, and the nature of the distress accompanying it. A problem statement should be specific, feeling-oriented, responsible, and brief.

4. *Practice creative brainstorming.* Generate a list of solution possibilities without evaluating their merits.

5. *Be willing to compromise.* Both partners are affected by and involved in a problem. Solutions should involve change on the part of each partner.

6. *Clarify and summarize the final agreement.* Once agreement has been reached, each party should clearly state what he or she is going to do differently. Putting it in writing may help.

Cunnilingus

(see Oral Sex)

Cybersex

You can become part of the cyberworld that links people across the nation and throughout the world by joining one of the information services such as CompuServe or America Online. All you need is a computer, modem and a credit card. These services connect computer users via E-mail, a system of sending messages that some people use as a dating service, a source for erotica, and even a way of having "sex" on line. Cybersex involves no physical contact. Heated written exchanges describe simulated sexual maneuvers between two people either in confidential messages or within a group or "chat room."

Why would anyone want to do this? Cybersex is a sexual stimulant for some people, a way of becoming safely aroused without cheating on a partner or taking emotional and physical risks in an encounter with a stranger. They enjoy the fantasy element of their encounters on line and are excited by the large number of available partners. One can have as many cyberlovers as one likes with no guilt. Others may find cybersex inspires them to try new ways of making love with their partners or frees them to discover something new about their own erotic natures. And some people do move from connecting via the cyberworld to meeting each other in the real world.

The downside? Some people spend far too much time in cyberworld, cutting themselves off from the physical and emotional comforts of real relationships. Also, a lot of cyberlovers aren't who they say they are. They exaggerate their physical attributes, lie about their ages, occupations, and marital status, and sometimes their genders. Someone who makes an emotional commitment to a cyberlover may be committing to a fantasy, nothing more.

Cybersex can be liberating, a sexual fantasy with an edge of realism, or it can be a way of avoiding human contact, an outlet for workaholics. How much time are you spending in cyberworld?

EXAMPLE

"I liked cybersex because of the freedom to be whoever I wanted to be," said Jane. "I could say whatever I wanted to say about myself. Also I liked the element of danger. I never knew who I was talking to. Maybe he was a potential hacker/stalker.

"My best cyberlover approached me with the line, 'Can I hold your hand?' I thought that was romantic. He said he was an Olympic skating hopeful. Maybe he was. I said I was an actress/model. I wasn't.

"We made a weekly date for sex on line. In addition to him, I had three or four other encounters each week with strangers I picked up in chat rooms. That worked for me because my boyfriend traveled a lot. I was very attracted to my skater. We talked about meeting each other, but never did. My friends who have *met face to face with men they've met on line were all disappointed. Reality makes things worse.*

"After a while, I got tired of simulated sex on line. I realized I didn't have a life, so I quit playing around in cyberworld and got more involved with my boyfriend." ∎

Jane never considered her cybersex dates a form of "cheating" on her relationship, but some people do. Is it cheating? That's not an easy question to answer. If you are withholding a great deal of yourself in a committed relationship, you are cheating in a sense, whether the withholding takes the form of cybersex, a real lover, or simply keeping important secrets.

Desire

Desire is the erotic urge that precedes arousal. It is possible to become aroused without having first experienced desire just as it is possible to have desire without acting upon the feeling. The two are separate and different processes. Problems with sexual desire are the most common complaints treated by sex therapists today.

While the process of sexual arousal has been studied in detail, research on sexual desire has been done only in the last decade. Some of those studies indicate that the sex hormone testosterone, present in both sexes, is responsible for sexual desire, or libido, in both men and women. But there is more to desire than hormones. Desire is sometimes elusive, often compelling, and frequently complicated, affected in varying degrees by marital conflict, repressed anger, broken trust, stress, anxiety, and many other factors within and outside the relationship.

In addition, each of us goes through cycles of desire having to do with fluctuating hormonal cycles, our health and physical condition and how we feel about our bodies, our workloads, how well we're getting along with our partners. Many women, for example, desire sex more at certain points of their menstrual cycle than others. Two people will periodically go in and out of sexual sync in a long-term relationship. Couples who have never been sexually out of sync with each other probably haven't been together long. It's that common. Like the common cold, this condition may make you miserable, but it isn't going to kill you or the relationship.

More serious problems include lack of desire and incompatible desires, when one partner always wants more sex than the other.

EXAMPLE

The sex virtually ended when Laurie and Jim moved in together. She tried the conventional home remedies for arousing his flagging libido. When she met him at the door in a red silk negligee and high heels, he said, "Jesus, Laurie, don't you ever think about anything but sex?" She cried while he stomped around the room blowing out candles—not the sensual scene she'd pictured standing in line at Victoria's Secret, red silk and credit card in hand.

She says he never wants sex. He says she always wants sex. That's an amusing set-up in a Woody Allen movie, but not funny in real life.

"My boyfriends before Jim couldn't get enough of me in bed," she said. In the beginning of their relationship two years ago, neither could he. "What's wrong with me now?" she asks. Have I lost my appeal? I'm going to be 30 in a year and a half. Does he want someone younger?"

Jim said, "No, I'm not tired of her, she hasn't lost her appeal, I don't want someone younger. I want sex once, maybe twice, a week, not the five or six nights a week Laurie wants to make love. She has sex on the brain."

She questioned her desirability, but Jim said his manhood was in question, not her womanhood. He felt pressured to perform by Laurie. What was happening to Jim and Laurie eventually turned out to be nothing more serious than their first out-of-sync cycle. He was putting in long hours at the office and was worried about his future with the company and perhaps his future ability to support a family. Dissatisfied with her own job, she was expecting the relationship to meet more of her emotional needs just as he was willing to put less of his emotional energy into it. The more he withdrew, the harder she tried to get his attention by wearing higher heels, shorter skirts, and showing more cleavage. When she backed off, he came out of his sexual slump.

For other couples, a disparity of desire may be an ongoing fact of life. Some people have higher sex drives than others. That does not make one person "normal" and the other "abnormal." They simply have different appetites for sex as they might for food, sleep, exercise. And sometimes the people with high sex drives fall in love with and marry the people with low sex drives. How does that happen? During the courtship phase, the partner with lower drive will probably want a lot more sex than he or she normally does. The natural differences in libidos are masked by the excitement of the new relationship. ∎

$\mathcal{S}$ix Tips for Handling Disparate Levels of Desire

1. *Accept that being out of sync happens to every couple now and then and doesn't signal disaster*. Don't take it personally. If you take the issue out of "me" and "I" terms, you'll be more tolerant of your partner's different needs. Instead of saying "What's wrong with *me*? Why doesn't he want *me*?" or "*I* am unhappy because I'm not getting what *I* want from him" — say, "He's tired and stressed. This has nothing to do with me. And I can't expect him to want sex every time I do."

2. *Be more attentive to your partner's needs when you do make love.* When the reluctant partner is in the mood, make the sex sizzling. Great sex once a week is better than lackluster lovemaking two or three times a week.

3. *Don't be overtly seductive or demanding if frequency has become an issue.* The woman in front of the TV in her garter belt and stockings can be viewed as an invitation or an ultimatum. Be more subtle. Remember how you feel when your partner is in the mood and you aren't.

4. *If the same person always wants more and the same person always wants less, accept the difference in levels of desire as a fact of life in the relationship.* Don't call names, like "sex maniac" and "frigid" or suggest that he must be secretly gay or she must be seeing another man because he/she doesn't want to make love as much as you do.

5. *If you're the less interested partner, don't automatically say no.*

- Say, maybe—as in, maybe you will change your mind in a few hours. Encourage nonsexual touching. Maybe later in the evening, you will be in the mood.

- Spell out your conditions for ideal sex. If you want more or less oral sex, loveplay, romantic ambiance, prolonged kissing, tell your partner in specific details. She/he meets your conditions for ideal lovemaking more often and he gets more of what she/he wants, too.

- If you're masturbating regularly, don't. Work on sharing your sexuality with your partner. If you're not masturbating at all, start. Masturbation may prime the pump, perhaps stimulating a dormant sexual/sensual interest.

- Use sex fantasies to help turn yourself on if you would like to desire sex more often. Take some responsibility for arousing yourself.

6. *If you're the more interested partner, don't expect your mate to gratify all your sexual desires.*

- Masturbate. Being in a relationship doesn't entitle you to use another body to relieve your sexual tension.

- Realize that your partner may need extra stimulation to become aroused. Become more adept at arousal.

- Find other ways of being close, from cuddling with your lover to stroking a pet or hugging your children. Sex is not the only expression of love and intimacy. Redirect some of your sexual energy.

- Fantasize. A fantasy can sometimes be almost as good as the real thing.

WHAT CAUSES LOSS OF DESIRE?

One or both partner's chronic lack of desire has a serious impact on the relationship. This extreme absence of desire—hypoactive sexual desire disorder—is usually caused by illness, medication, depression or other psychological problems, or, less frequently, by total discord between partners. (A person who actively avoids nearly all genital contact suffers from sexual aversion disorder.) Some people who have been victims of sexual, psychological, or physical abuse as children or adults may also manifest a total lack of desire. Extremely harsh and rigid parental or religious training about sex can inhibit desire in adults too. And loss of desire can also be caused by hormonal changes that occur during menopause, following hysterecto-my, or in both sexes with age.

Occasionally, one partner loses interest in sex because lovemaking has been consistently frustrating and unrewarding. A woman who cannot reach orgasm or a man who suffers from an erection problem, for example, may turn off to sexual feelings rather than risk disap-pointment again. When the technical difficulties are corrected, desire returns.

If you or your partner are experiencing chronic and pervasive lack of desire, see a physician first. When all medical causes have been ruled out, make an appointment with a therapist.

Divorce, impact on sexuality

Some divorced people rush into a new relationship or have a series of brief sexual affairs. Others go through a period of emotional detachment, maintaining a distance even after they begin seeing someone. Whether seeking emotional intimacy or avoiding it, divorced men and women—including those who embrace their new freedom as well as those who have been forced into it—may suffer sexual difficulties with a new partner.

For men, those problems may include premature ejaculation or dif-ficulty in achieving or maintaining an erection. Women may suffer from insufficient lubrication or be unable to reach orgasm. Both men and women may feel uncomfortable or embarrassed about aspects of lovemaking they once regarded as natural, like undressing in front of a partner, performing or receiving oral sex, or assuming certain inter-course positions. This state of reserve is typically short-lived.

Sometimes fear is causing the sexual problems. A man or woman may be afraid of another involvement, a reasonable fear in some cases, particularly if the partner has been hastily or unwisely chosen. They may fear sexual rejection or performance failure or another failed relationship. Most of these fears subside in a reasonable amount of time; and the sexual difficulties work themselves out, too.

Occasionally a sexual problem such as premature ejaculation will take on a life of its own and become self-perpetuating. The sufferer worries so much about the problem that he causes it to happen again and again. Or there may be a deeper problem relating to the timing of the new relationship or to the choice of partner.

EXAMPLE

Michael and Linda divorced shortly after their twentieth wedding anniversary. Both attractive people in their mid-forties, they were each determined to get on with life and find a new partner as quickly as possible. They had been, they agreed, "disconnected" for many years. Why not move forward quickly then?

"Before our marriage fell apart, I was crazy about Linda; she was the girl of my dreams," Michael said. "When I started dating again, I was looking for the new Linda, the new girl of my dreams. The women I met looked good, but fell short when I got to know them."

Michael at first blamed their "shortcomings" for his lackluster sexual performances.

"I had trouble keeping an erection," he said. "Sometimes I felt as if I was losing interest in the middle of sex, which had never happened to me before. One night I had a really hard time getting an erection. This beautiful young woman was performing fellatio and I couldn't get hard. It was demoralizing." As his performance problems increased, Michael began to romanticize his marriage. "I thought maybe my penis was trying to tell me something," he said.

He called Linda, who was having some sexual problems of her own.

"I wanted to have sex, but I couldn't get aroused," she said. "Michael called me the morning after I'd faked not just an orgasm but an entire sexual performance."

Michael and Linda met for dinner. And that led to sex. Briefly, they tried to rekindle their relationship because they were able to make love to each other without experiencing the difficulties they'd encountered with other partners.

"We soon realized we had the same problems we'd had before," Linda said. "We stopped seeing each other and went back into the dating pool again. But that little fling with my ex was great for my ego. I got my sexual confidence back."

"I don't know if it was good for me, but it did me no harm," Michael says. "I decided to spend some time alone after Linda and I stopped seeing each other. Maybe that's what I needed to do. When I finally felt as if I had reached closure on the marriage and was really ready to look for someone else, I put myself out

there in the marketplace again. Luckily, I met a good woman and didn't have any sexual problems with her." ■

This couple's brief sexual reunion is not all that unusual. Relationships do not abruptly collapse. Sometimes divorced partners do turn to each other for solace, sexual and otherwise, after they have been disappointed, scared, or hurt by experiences with new people.

The first year—and sometimes longer—after divorce is a period of adjustment that may include sexual difficulties. Reminding yourself that this is generally true for most people should help you cope.

The Ten Steps to Becoming Sexually Active After Divorce

1. *Avoid emotional and sexual intimacy for a time.* Avoidance is not necessarily an unhealthy response. For most people, time is an integral part of the healing process. For some, it is essential.

2. *Seek emotional and sexual intimacy in limited doses.* Limiting the amount of time you will spend with a new person can help you move the relationship along at a comfortable pace.

3. *Make careful partner choices.* Some people choose an affair with a married person as a means of limiting involvement, but that complicates the healing process. Others choose someone who will reject them or live up to their worst expectations in some way.

4. *Be honest with a new partner.* Say you're not ready for commitment. If you're having problems with intimate disclosures, acknowledge that. And be your authentic self. Some people wear "disguises" in an effort to protect themselves from intimacy and potential hurt.

5. *Accept some sexual awkwardness or difficulty as inevitable.* After you've been with the same person for years, taking your clothes off in front of a stranger can seem daunting. Don't be hard on yourself if you aren't the lover you know you can be.

6. *Pay attention to your new partner's sexual needs.* For example, a woman may hardly notice your erection difficulties if you please her orally or manually. Pleasing someone else makes us feel good about ourselves.

7. *Don't have unrealistic expectations of a new partner.* It is not your new lover's responsibility to heal your past wounds.

8. *Avoid the tendency to idealize a new partner.* Women may be more prone to this myopia than men, but both sexes tend to be vulnerable in the so-called "honeymoon phase" of a relationship.

9. *For help in dealing with sexual difficulties, see the specific entries in this book.* Most sexual problems can be resolved. And don't overlook the entries designed to enhance sexuality.

10. *If sexual difficulties persist after you feel comfortable with a new person, examine the relationship.* Maybe this isn't the right person for you or the right time for a serious involvement.

Dysfunction, sexual

(see Desire, Ejaculation, Paraphilias, Sex Therapy)

Ejaculation

PREMATURE EJACULATION

Premature ejaculation (PE) occurs when a man ejaculates before or immediately after penetration, that is, with minimal stimulation. In some men, simply touching their partner can cause them to ejaculate. Just as this can be very upsetting for his partner, in practically all instances of premature ejaculation the man is also experiencing frustration and anxiety about his poor control, feeling each time that he "slipped," or "failed."

A common problem, particularly among young men, PE is caused by psychosocial factors. Rarely is there a physical basis. Most men have experienced an episode of premature ejaculation at least once in their lives. For some men, however, poor ejaculatory control is chronic and lifelong.

My view is that men (and women) have a "preset" orgasmic threshold, with the majority being set at "average." This means that a rapid ejaculator doesn't necessarily have some deep pathology. In the past, sex therapists suggested that a man who ejaculated quickly had an intimacy problem and was trying to make a fast getaway. Rather, some men reach orgasm quickly, as do some women, but in women this is not considered a liability.

PE is not necessarily an indication of an underlying intimacy problem. Some men have exacerbated their control problems by taking stress to bed with them, by being anxious about ejaculating rapidly, which becomes self-fulfilling, and by having developed the habit of rushing through everything in their lives, including sex.

Fortunately, PE is not a difficult condition to improve, but untreated, it can lead to problems of anger and resentment in the relationship. In fact, some men with erection problems developed them as a result of the tension in the bedroom about their PE. In time, tension and worry becomes increasingly distracting, leading eventually to loss of erection.

For many men, the problem can be resolved without therapy through good communication and cooperation between him and his partner in employing some techniques to delay ejaculation.

EXAMPLE

"In my previous relationships, I was able to reach orgasm at least sometimes during intercourse," said Marilyn. "I've never had an orgasm this way with James because of his inability to control himself. And that really bothers me."

Marilyn and James, both in their early thirties, sought help for their sexual problem after four years of marriage. Both considered the marriage a good one in all respects but this one: James ejaculated upon entering her, or at most, after a few quick thrusts.

"This has been my pattern with other women, too," admitted James. "I try to control myself, but I can't. Sometimes I try so hard that I lose my erection. I don't blame Marilyn for being dissatisfied with me. I bring her to orgasm orally and manually, but she has a right to expect more." ■

Both were tense about their sexual encounters when they consulted a therapist. In fact, they were beginning to avoid sexual contact altogether. Fortunately, James' premature ejaculation problem was easily treated through using a series of physical techniques detailed as follows. An important aspect of therapy for them also included reassurance that his physical problem was not an indicator of fear of intimacy on his part or lack of desirability on hers.

Three Techniques for Curing Premature Ejaculation

Practice these exercises while masturbating and, of course, during lovemaking. During masturbation, most men fail to learn much about their arousal process in their rush for quick release. Slow down, enjoy the process, and learn something about yourself. Focus on sensual and sexual feelings so that you will recognize the early sensations preceding climax. Most men pick up the cue, "I'm going to come," simultaneous with coming. Through regular masturbation, you can learn how to pick up that cue sooner and also gain control of your sexual response cycle.

1. *The Squeeze.* (Also sometimes called the pinch.) Developed by Masters and Johnson, the squeeze is exactly as it sounds. When a man feels he is about to ejaculate, he or his partner gently squeezes or pinches the end of his penis where the glans joins the shaft and holds the squeeze for several seconds. After squeezing, stop the stimulation for 30 seconds or so. He may lose some of his erection but will regain it when lovemaking resumes again. This technique can be repeated as many times as necessary or desirable during intercourse.

2. *Tensing.* When ejaculation is imminent, tense the muscles at the base of the penis. (See Kegels for strengthening exercises.) After several seconds, relax. Alternately tensing and relaxing those muscles can help prolong intercourse.

3. *Teasing.* Either you or your partner stimulates your penis manually. Stop the stimulation when ejaculation is imminent. After several seconds, resume again. With practice, you can learn to keep yourself at a high level of arousal. When orgasm does occur it will be more intense.

DELAYED EJACULATION OR MALE ORGASMIC DISORDER

Delayed (or Retarded) ejaculation, now called male orgasmic disorder, occurs when a man has chronic difficulty in reaching orgasm even during prolonged periods of intercourse. I emphasize the word *chronic*. Most men will occasionally not be able to reach orgasm when they are tired, depressed, under the influence of too much alcohol, taking drugs or prescription medication, or for other reasons.

Some men cannot ejaculate during intercourse when they aren't getting along with their partners.

The disorder may be manifested in several ways: A man may be able to ejaculate only during masturbation; or only during oral or manual pleasuring by his partner and not in her vagina; or only after bouts of prolonged and vigorous intercourse that leave his partner sore and tired. In extremely rare cases, he may have never experienced ejaculation, not even in a wet dream.

Sometimes physical conditions such as diabetes or certain medications such as Prozac and other antidepressants can caused delayed ejaculation. Severe depression and other emotional or psychological factors can also be at the root of the problem. A man may, for example, have unresolved feelings of ambivalence toward his partner or guilt about sex.

Before seeking therapy, he should consult his physician to rule out all possible physical causes. In treatment, he will have to examine his attitudes and feelings about sex and his partner. Fortunately, retarded ejaculation can be overcome with the help of a competent therapist.

EXAMPLE

"I'm very attracted to my wife," said Ted, 27, who had been married 18 months at the time. "She arouses me easily. I have no trouble getting and sustaining an erection, but I have a great deal of trouble ejaculating."

Ted's wife, Monica, didn't know how much trouble he'd been having with ejaculation until he told her in a therapy session. He was unable to ejaculate inside her vagina. In fact, he could ejaculate only after intense manual stimulation. Because he feared her reaction to this, he'd been faking an orgasm during intercourse, waiting until she fell asleep, then sneaking into the bathroom to masturbate, applying vigorous pressure, sometimes using a towel for greater friction.

Frantic in his attempts to overcome his difficulty, Ted approached Monica daily for intercourse. This constant pressuring for sex, the prolonged periods of intercourse, and the desperation she sensed in him were all taking their toll on their relationship. Then he confessed to never having ejaculated inside her.

"I was hurt and confused," she said. *"I felt betrayed because he had been lying to me about something so important. Wasn't I attractive enough? Sexy enough? Was it my fault?"*

After sending him to a physician to rule out medical reasons for Ted's difficulty, the therapist reassured the couple that their relationship was basically sound and his orgasmic disorder had a positive prognosis. Within four months, Jeff's physical difficulty was successfully resolved and the damage to trust done by his deceit had also been repaired.   ■

How to Handle Male Orgasmic Disorder

1. *Get a complete physical.* Be honest with your doctor about your difficulty. She/he needs to know your symptoms or she/he might overlook a possible cause.

2. *Share your concerns with your partner.* You will need her help and reassurance; and she probably needs your reassurance, too.

3. *See a therapist.* Usually this disorder does not require lengthy therapy. Ten or twelve sessions will probably be enough. In treatment, you will work through the psychological issues and learn how to adapt your lovemaking to make ejaculation inside your partner possible.

    For example, a man who can ejaculate only during masturbation may first learn to ejaculate when his wife is masturbating him in the way he usually does it and while employing his favorite fantasy. Later on, he may penetrate her with a combination of hand and vaginal stimulation. They move progressively nearer the point where he can ejaculate inside her during intercourse.

FEMALE EJACULATION

Some women expel fluid at orgasm. Opinion is divided on the source of the fluid, which may contain some urine in a mixture of secretions from vaginal glands. This expulsion of fluid, while loosely termed "female ejaculation," is not analogous to male ejaculation. Whatever the fluid may be, it is definitely not a female version of sperm.

Women who experience this "ejaculation" often report they do so only when the G spot has been stimulated. Some are embarrassed by the secretions, which lovers may assume results from a loss of bladder control. If you do expel fluid at orgasm, don't feel uncomfortable about it. Bring a towel to bed and enjoy.

Female ejaculation has been a frequent theme in erotica throughout the ages. Should your lover think you have a bladder-control problem, find an erotic story featuring the practice and share it with him.

Erection

(see also Desire, Ejaculation, Impotence)

ANATOMY OF AN ERECTION

Erection seems to be a simple process: When sexually stimulated, a man's penis becomes engorged with blood and gets hard. An erection is, in physical fact, nothing more than the firmness caused by the pressure of extra blood inside the walls of the penis. But the male sexual organ, a complex system of nerves, blood vessels, and specialized tissues, is affected by many factors. There is both a physical and a psychological component to erection.

Many men who experience erection difficulties report strong sexual desire but experience frustration translating that into an erection. They feel as if their interest doesn't quite reach their genitals. Then again, some men with lack of desire may have the ability to achieve an erection but have no interest in sex. In other instances, lack of desire may be a significant contributor to erection disorders. To make things even more complicated, lack of desire may also be a consequence of erection disorder. Continued failure has a discouraging effect.

In the arousal phase, the penis becomes erect and the skin of the scrotum sac thickens as it contracts. Young men generally achieve erection with very little stimulation. As a man ages, he needs more stimulation and typically finds his erection is not as hard as it was when he was young. The arousal stage can progress right into orgasm or be delayed. Since orgasm and the arousal stage are not dependent on each other, a man may find that he can be orgasmic without having an erection or, conversely, he may have an erection and experience difficulty being orgasmic. In the final stage of sexual response, resolution, the penis slowly returns to its flaccid state.

Sometimes a man has trouble achieving an erection—or a "good enough" one—or loses his erection during lovemaking. That will happen to every man occasionally. Illness and medication, heavy indulgence in food and alcohol, stress, and exhaustion are the usual culprits. Chronic erection problems (see Impotence) are often caused by anxiety, anger, and sexual inhibition.

WHAT MEN SAY ABOUT ERECTIONS

From a 45-year-old married man: "I used to think my virility depended on being able to get one of those 'look, Ma, no hands!' erections. Now I have accepted the fact that it takes more for me to get hard. My wife helped me to see that as good news. I last longer. Sex isn't so frantic anymore, which means I'm a better lover. I get a lot of satisfaction out of that. Do I miss the instant hard-ons? Sometimes! But life's a trade-off."

From a 22-year-old single man: "Sometimes I get erections when I don't want to have them, like in public places. That can be embarrassing. I wish I had a little more control over my penis than I do at those times. But, hey, I love the feeling of that power surge!"

And from a 35-year-old recently divorced man: "My erections aren't as dependable as they once were, which causes me some concern. The last time I was single, in my early twenties, my penis was like a rock. Now it lets me down sometimes."

*T*he Four Steps for Handling Your Erection Difficulties

1. *If you lose your erection during intercourse, let it go.* You're not a failure. Sex isn't over. Don't frantically try to get the erection back. Continue making love to your partner in other ways and ignore your penis. It will probably revive.

2. *You can maintain an erection for a longer period of time by alternating the stimuli.* Sex is more than intercourse. Vary your lovemaking and also vary your pattern of thrusting during intercourse.

3. *Use a partial erection.* Having difficulty achieving or sustaining a full erection? Take your penis in hand and rub it across your partner's clitoris. Or, while holding your penis firmly, insert it inside her vagina and ask her to flex her PC muscles.

4. *Don't blame your partner.* Sometimes men turn on their partners and blame them for not being attractive enough or being too assertive or not assertive enough in bed. No one is to blame for something that naturally occurs now and then in all men.

$\mathcal{T}$he Four Steps for Helping Him Handle His Erection Difficulties

1. *If he loses his erection during intercourse, let it go.* Don't immediately try to make him hard again unless he asks you for manual or oral stimulation. Try pressing your pelvis tightly against him if he hasn't fallen out, but don't work to keep him inside.

2. *Suggest something specific he can do for you that doesn't involve his penis.* Ask him to stroke your clitoris, fondle your breasts, perform cunnilingus. Your arousal will do more to restore his erection than "working" on his penis will do now.

3. *Don't stop and ask "What's wrong?"* He already feels as if he's letting you down. This isn't the time to be solicitous. And a discussion about his penis and why it isn't working will only keep the focus on the problem.

4. *Don't blame yourself.* Many women ask, "What's wrong with me? Why am I not turning him on?" They feel self-conscious and sexually inhibited, reinforcing his discomfort by their own.

Erotica

What distinguishes erotica from pornography? Some people think that whatever turns them on is erotica while whatever turns on the next person may very well be pornography. Coming up with the definitive definition for either word is impossible. For our purposes, erotica is sexually explicit and arousing material that does not feature children or violent acts.

In the past, erotic material was designed primarily to arouse men. Primitive works of art include clay figures of women with exaggerated breasts and buttocks. In modern times, videos were first known as "stag films," because they were made for men and typically shown at all-male gatherings. Until recently people assumed that women are not aroused by sexually explicit material. Men are more aroused by visual stimuli than women are, but women are aroused, though not always by the same kinds of material men find exciting.

Bookstores and video stores now have an unprecedented selection of erotica written by and for women and videos marketed to women and couples in both the entertainment and sex instruction categories. Many therapists consider these to be legitimate sex aides. And many women say such books and videos have helped them define and expand their erotic tastes. Generally, the more secure a woman is about her sexuality and within the relationship, the more likely she will be unthreatened by erotica.

EXAMPLE

"*My wife, Carol, was really offended because I didn't drop my subscription to* Playboy *when we got married," said Mike. "She thought I should never want to look at another pair of breasts except hers again. Her teasing about it was good-natured with an edge.*

"*Then I started suggesting to her when we were in the video store that we rent an X-rated video. She was adamant about how sleazy and dirty they were until she read an article in one of her women's magazines that said some videos were okay. Finally, she relented. We picked one from the list in the magazine article.*"

Carol found she wasn't as offended by the videos as she'd thought she would be. Nor was she as aroused as Mike was by them, but she did find them exciting and certainly did enjoy the extra enthusiasm he brought to their lovemaking after they had watched one together. For Christmas he gave her a book of erotica.

"*I find the writing much more arousing than the films," she says. "I like making my own pictures in my mind. And I've always been a reader. Words are exciting to me anyway. Sometimes I read out loud to Mike, an experience we both enjoy.*" ▪

If your partner is reluctant to try erotica:

- Don't pressure her into watching videos.
- Don't make a point of admiring the actress' bodies. Many women compare their own bodies to those on screen and feel inferior.
- If she consents to try, choose something more to her tastes than yours. In general, women like erotica with a storyline and romance. Most women are turned off by images that are violent or degrading to women. Consider prescreening a video before you see it together.
- Give her veto power. Tell her you'll stop watching if she feels uncomfortable.

- As a variation on the erotic theme, read out loud to each other from sexy books.

Ten of the Best Books and Videos Aimed at Women and Couples

1. *The Erotic Edge: Erotica for Couples,* edited by Lonnie Barbach, Ph.D.
2. *Herotica 2: A Collection of Women's Erotic Fiction*, edited by Susie Bright and Joani Blank (Plume, paper)
3. *Tart Tales: Elegant Erotic Stories* by Carolyn Banks (Carroll & Graf)
4. *The Erotic Impulse: Honoring the Sensual Self,* edited by David Steinberg (Jeremy Tarcher, paper)
5. *Little Birds* by Anais Nin (Bantam, paper)
6. "A Taste of Ambrosia," video directed by Candida Royalle and Veronica Hart
7. "Rites of Passion," video directed by Annie Sprinkle and Veronica Vera
8. "Sensual Escape," video directed by Candida Royalle and Gloria Leonard
9. "Cabin Fever," video directed by Deborah Shames
10. "The Masseuse," video starring Hyapatia Lee

Exercise

(see Health and Sexuality)

Extramarital Affairs

(see also Trust)

An affair is a sexual relationship or liaison outside marriage. It may be brief or of lasting duration, of low or high emotional involvement. In most cases, the partner does not know about the affair and would not give consent to it.

The Top Eight Reasons People Have Affairs

1. Emotional alienation from mate.
2. Curiosity about what sex would be like with someone other than partner.

3. Unexpressed anger or hostility toward partner.

4. The desire for more sex or a different kind of sex from what partner wants.

5. The need for an ego boost.

6. The inability to form deep commitments.

7. Avoidance—of marital or personal problems.

8. To dull the pain of a loss, for example death of a loved one or a child going off to college.

Types of affairs

How common are affairs? Survey findings range from a low of approximately 25 percent of all married couples having affairs to a high of 50 percent and more. Affairs are probably more common now than they were in generations past. Certainly they are more public and have less disastrous consequences for the participants.

Infidelities, either in marriages or in committed relationships, range from the occasional one-night stand to the once-in-a-lifetime grand amour. Admittedly, there is great diversity between those two extremes, but affairs can generally be divided into two broad categories: low emotional-involvement affairs and those of higher emotional involvement. The types of affairs men and women choose vary in their implications and consequences both for the person and the marriage or the relationship.

Low-involvement affairs

Occasional low-involvement affairs are the most common form of infidelity. Meetings are probably sporadic, though the partners may see each other frequently, even on a regular basis. More regular meetings may take the form the French label *la matinee,* a light-hearted affair between working men and women who use the lunch hour for their rendezvous. The relationship, however, does not deepen significantly no matter how often they meet. The feelings exchanged, not time spent together, determine the true nature of an affair.

The one-night stand is a particular form of low-involvement affair. One or both of the participants treat sex as a form of energetic play. He or she may have frequent one-night stands, utilizing the opportunities afforded by business travel, for example. Or he or she may indulge only rarely, regarding extramarital sex as a sometime thing, the moral equivalent of indulging in too much wine or food. One-night stands usually leave little emotional impact, except perhaps for guilt.

The basic rule for low-involvement affairs is: Never become "serious."

The risks include being caught by a spouse or employer, inadvertently getting involved with someone who is prone to obsessive love relationships, and contracting a sexually transmitted disease (STD)—which are also risks for the high-involvement affair. An additional risk is that one partner may fall in love with another and want to escalate the relationship to the "serious" level, a real danger when one or both is unhappily married and perhaps looking for a way out of the marriage.

EXAMPLE

"When I go out of town on business, I find a woman to share my bed, unless I'm just too busy," says Roger. "It's novel and exciting to be with a woman for an hour, a day, a week—and then to say good-bye. Of course, I am careful to use condoms. I wouldn't want to bring anything home to my wife. And I am also careful about the kind of women I choose, women who know the score and have no illusions about their place in my life. It's better if a woman is married and has as much to lose as I do.

"Sometimes I think of a lover for a week or two after the encounter. We may even work out our schedules so that we can meet again from time to time, but I never let myself fall in love with any of them. Nor do I think any of them have fallen in love with me. My primary commitment is to my wife. Besides, I am very busy. I couldn't handle more than an occasional fling.

"There are even times when I'm away from home and too busy to devote the time to wining and dining a woman. Of course, if I could have a woman delivered to my room, I wouldn't turn it down."   ■

High-involvement affairs

When the lovers describe themselves as sexually, emotionally, and intellectually attuned, they are partners in high emotional-involvement affairs. The conventional notion of highly emotional affairs is that such relationships follow a cycle: intense infatuation with a new person, a relatively quick decline in passion, disillusionment, dissolution. Certainly some affairs fit this model, particularly since enormous emotional resources are required to lead two lives. Others may develop slowly over time. They may have begun as low-involvement affairs and escalated when the partners developed strong feelings for each other. Some parallel a good marriage in the way they have moved from a strong erotic attachment to a more comfortable and enduring closeness.

High-involvement affairs are less common than low involvement relationships for the obvious reason: It is simply too difficult for most married people to steal away for more than a few hours a week. Although many people may dream of a grand amour, they can't find the time to have one.

EXAMPLE

"*Sex to me is more than just a roll in the hay,*" says Monica. "*It's very important. When I first met Barry seven years ago and he came on to me, I quickly straightened him out. I told him I was married, and I didn't believe in casual sex. He was insulted, but I thought he got what he deserved.*

"*Over the next year or so we continued to run into each other with our respective spouses at social gatherings. I was attracted to him and I knew he was attracted to me. But I had never had an affair and couldn't imagine having one.*

"*Then my husband suggested we invite Barry and his wife over for dinner. I went along with this and soon we were seeing a lot more of each other as couples. I had this vague feeling of discomfort, but I enjoyed seeing him too much to put a stop to our couples' friendship.*

"*I realized one night that I was falling in love with him, which spelled trouble for me. Once I knew I loved him, I was vulnerable to his advances. We began having an affair.*

"*We've been seeing each other five years now, three or four times a week. We still get together socially with our mates, but not often. Neither Barry nor I encourage it. It's not a comfortable situation for either of us. My hope is that one day we will be able to untie our present marital knots and live together openly as husband and wife.*"   ■

The Five Most Commonly Asked Questions About Affairs

1. *Should I have a casual affair?*

No one can make that choice for you. There are typically several motives for extramarital involvements beyond the obvious one. You need to ask yourself some questions to determine your motives. For example: What do you want from an affair? Do you find your marriage boring because you need that excuse to have an affair? Are you considering an affair as a means of avoiding working on the marriage? Is your dissatisfaction with the marriage genuine, or is it a part of your dissatisfaction with yourself?

If you do have an affair, you must use condoms, preferably those treated with nonoxodyl, for the prevention of STDs. And you need to screen a prospective partner carefully. Is this person emotionally stable? Are his or her expectations for the affair the same as yours? The movie, *Fatal Attraction* popularized the obsessive lover. You probably won't meet a knife-wielding woman (or man) who kills your daughter's bunny, but if you don't choose carefully, you may find yourself involved with someone who calls you at home and at work, sends little notes or cards, and generally intrudes on your life in ways you never imagined.

You also must weigh the risks, both to your marriage and to yourself. The majority of men and women who report their affairs were of minor consequence to their marriages describe those liaisons as shallow and short-lived or enduring but emotionally limited, in other words, low emotional-involvement affairs. Some of these people also have marriages that are emotionally limited. When people get involved in highly emotionally charged affairs, they report conflict and pain upon discovery or separation.

A casual affair may coexist with marriage, but an intense amour competes with it. Are you prepared for the outcome should the extramarital relationship become more intense? On any level, affairs can be disruptive, but they can also be constructive or exhilarating and rewarding. Even if the liaison is casual, the experience may have a strong impact on you and your marriage. These consequences run the gamut from destructive to enhancing.

One of those consequences may well be mistrust. Once you have broken the bond of intimacy between you and your spouse, you may discover that you don't trust him or her anymore than you trust yourself. You may wonder, is my spouse cheating on me, too? Affairs can contribute to the unraveling of the fabric of a relationship by sowing those seeds of mistrust.

Should you have an affair or not? Only you can answer that question; it's hoped after you've answered several others.

2. *My lover is becoming too involved in this relationship. (Or I am.) What can I do?*

Often a person comes to the conclusion that one lover's involvement in the affair has become more "intense" than the other's. Perhaps one lover cares more than the other or finds the relationship more important in his or her life. If one is single, the chances of this being true increase. Whatever the causes, an inequity of emotional involvement exists. This situation can seem threatening to a lover who wants a low emotional-involvement affair that won't threaten the marriage or other committed relationship.

At this stage, pulling back from the affair is the best course of action. Cut down on meetings and phone calls. Perhaps even take a vacation from each other. If the more intense lover can't cope with the reduced involvement, the other is left with a choice between getting out altogether or staying in an affair that is increasingly likely to produce feelings of guilt, resentment, and anxiety—as well as put the primary relationship at greater risk.

3. *Should I leave my spouse for my lover?*

According to several studies, only about one out of ten people having an extramarital affair marry their lovers. The consequences of divorce are frequently as hard on the person who seeks it as they are on the other partner. Divorce can lead to financial hardship, emotional distress for children, problems with extended families, embarrassment, and the discomfort or sadness that accompanies any loss. In addition, the difficulties of starting over with the new partner may be greater than anticipated.

Divorce is sometimes the best choice for a couple, but not one that should ever be made in anger or haste. See a counselor before leaving your spouse. And take all the time you need in making a decision. Don't be hurried by an impatient lover.

4. *How should I handle my partner's affair?*

First, try not to say anything you really don't mean. Threatening to get a divorce, for example, when you have no intentions of doing so only puts you in a weak position.

For some couples, a temporary separation provides an important "time-out" period. The difficulty in separation lies in how it is used. Often, rather than employing this brief separation constructively, a spouse is attempting to punish or "teach the [expletive deleted] a lesson." A pattern of outburst and withdrawal frequently ends in illusory resolution with the apology of the wandering mate accepted by the aggrieved partner.

Whether your mate goes with you or not, see a therapist. You need to work through a process of grieving that will probably include blaming and self-pity. And you will need to learn how to reestablish communication with your partner. If the marriage is to be healed, the betrayed spouse will have to work through feelings of resentment and animosity before he or she can examine the problems that may have led to this tear in the marital fabric.

Does your partner want to heal the relationship? The affair will almost certainly have to be ended. A new monogamous sexual agreement between the two of you is the secret to reestablishing trust.

Finally, should you leave? That depends on whether or not you want to rebuild your marriage or even accept it on nonmonogamous terms, not on what friends or family tell you to do or what you feel inspired to do in hurt or anger or as an act of revenge. Sometimes a deceived mate's anger and an adulterous mate's guilt combine to end a marriage neither partner really wanted to end.

5. Can an affair ever be good for a marriage?

Extramarital sex in our society is fraught with difficulties, dangers, and risks. The time commitment, emotional investment, deception, and lying, as well as the decreased attention and affection to one's spouse that may occur frequently lead to several negative effects. These include: erosion of communication, trust, and security; the stimulation of destructive jealousy and the heightening of feelings of inadequacy; and the rapid and agonizing deterioration of a shaky marriage. Even solid marriages can be adversely affected by affairs.

But, in some cases, affairs do enhance a marriage in the following ways:

- Lessen the feelings of resentment frequently found within the constraints of long-term marriages.
- Remove the burdens of sex and companionship from a spouse who may be exhausted, ill, preoccupied with other matters, or simply not in the mood.
- Increase the warmth and excitement of one spouse, thereby stimulating the other.
- Provide a diversion or temporary respite from marriage difficulties. This can bring a new perspective or tolerance to these problems.

- Assist a person to discover new dimensions of his or her own sexuality and personality including (for women) orgasm, which may then be experienced with the husband.

- Help an unsatisfactory marriage to remain intact when there are other good reasons to continue the marriage, such as children, finances, an established home base.

- Allow persons to remain (or become) warm individuals despite cold marriages.

- Provide additional passion, tenderness, and stimulation for a person experiencing a good marriage.

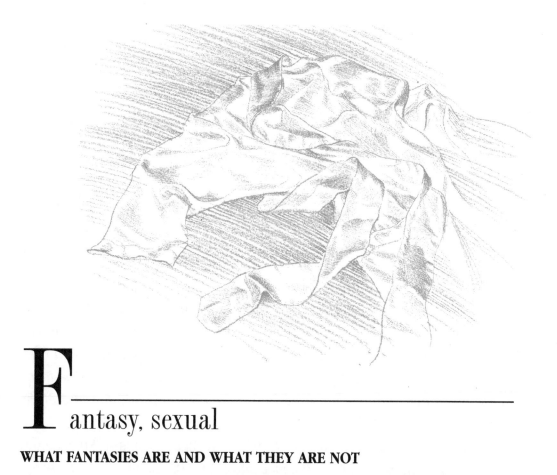

Fantasy, sexual

WHAT FANTASIES ARE AND WHAT THEY ARE NOT

Sex is said to take place largely in the brain. And fantasy is a mental aphrodisiac. Researchers believe that sexual fantasy is a nearly universal experience among women as well as men. Sometimes fantasy is a conscious process, but often it is not. A sexual fantasy may be, for example, the fleeting thought a man has when he sees an attractive woman and wonders what her breasts look like beneath her blouse or the long romantic scenario of seduction and lovemaking that a woman uses during masturbation or anything in between those points. Like scenes from favorite movies, some fantasies are enjoyed again and again.

Recent studies indicate men and women now have fantasies that are more alike than they were 15 or 20 years ago. Sex journalist Nancy Friday reported on this new phenomenon in her book, *Women on Top*. Women's fantasies, she noted, have become more graphic and overtly sexual and aggressive.

A fantasy is not necessarily a sexual wish. In fact, few people want to act out their fantasies. For example, imagining being forced to have sex is not the same thing as wanting to be raped. Typically, the forced-sex fantasy signifies the desire to enjoy sex without feeling guilty. Some fantasies may be bizarre, even violent. The occasional violent fantasy is generally not cause for concern. Often-recurring fantasies are rooted in early childhood arousal experiences, though you may not be able to recall any incident that seems related. A man who fantasizes lovemaking with much older women may have experienced his first feelings of sexual arousal as a small child being bathed by an older female caretaker.

EXAMPLE

"I am naked on a tropical island, alone with my husband's best friend," says Annie. "I can see him in my mind kissing me, stroking my body. He can almost make me come by kissing me. But he takes his mouth away from mine and moves it down my body. I tremble as he approaches my clitoris. The fantasy is so real I can feel the warm sand on my back and hear the waves of the sea."

Annie's fantasy ends in the last of a prolonged series of tumultuous orgasms. She and her lover are euphoric and sated. But when the good feelings subside, they are replaced by guilt.

"I feel as if I'm cheating on my husband with his best friend," she says. "Sometimes I have this fantasy when I'm at work. I go home and make passionate love to my husband, but is it him or another man inspiring me? Does it mean I don't love him? And worse, I have occasionally had fleeting thoughts of this other man during lovemaking. I would never really cheat on my marrage. Or, I don't think I would. The fantasies scare me." ■

Many people feel guilty about having sexual thoughts or fantasies. These feelings may have been fostered by religious teachings or parental messages about sex being "dirty" or other negative cultural messages. Some people feel guilty because they fantasize doing things that they consider wrong or immoral, such as committing adultery or engaging in a homosexual or sadomasochistic encounter. In Annie's

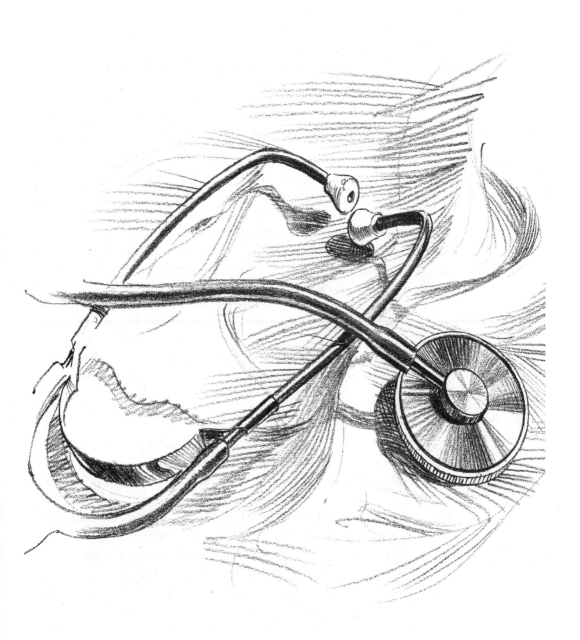

case, the guilt stems from her belief that she is somehow "cheating" on her husband in her head when she has erotic thoughts about his friend. That is not true at all.

Rather than feeling guilty about your fantasies or worrying about what they mean, enjoy them unless—and this is not likely—they are more than brief escapes from reality and do truly prohibit intimacy within a relationship.

WHY THEY'RE GOOD FOR YOU AND WHEN THEY'RE NOT

Sexual fantasies serve many useful purposes. They enhance masturbation, create a mood conducive to lovemaking, sometimes facilitate orgasm by blocking out intrusive worries or concerns, and allow us to explore "taboo" activities that arouse without actually participating in them—from affairs to sadomasochism (S/M). Indulging in fantasy is a way of widening your sexual experience without taking any risks. Even fantasizing during intercourse is not unusual or necessarily indicative of a problem in the relationship.

Not all fantasies, however, are benign. Recurrent violent fantasies can be indicative of deep-rooted emotional problems. People who cannot become aroused or reach orgasm without utilizing the same fantasy every time may also have some intimacy issues or other problems. If a fantasy really troubles you, talk it over with a professional.

The Top Ten Sexual Fantasies

1. Making love with someone other than one's regular partner, the most common fantasy for men and women.

2. The forbidden partner—someone from another race or class, a relative, a friend's spouse.

3. Multiple partners, typically sex with one's partner and another person. (For men, this "two-women fantasy" is a favorite.)

4. The romantic fantasy—sex in idyllic surroundings such as a Caribbean beach. (More common for women than for men.)

5. Spontaneous encounter—such as the "zipless fuck" popularized by author Erica Jong in *Fear of Flying*, in which strangers meet on a train, for example, and fall upon each other in the nearest sleeping compartment, their clothes simply melting away.

6. Forced sex—sometimes called "the rape fantasy" and actually common to both genders.

7. "Taboo" sex acts, such as having sex in a public pool or spanking one's partner.

8. Exhibitionist (or voyeuristic) fantasies, in which one is having sex while being watching or watching someone else have sex. (A common version of this fantasy for men is watching a spouse make love to someone else.)

9. Homosexual encounter.

10. Sex with a celebrity.

SHOULD YOU SHARE OR ACT OUT SEXUAL FANTASIES WITH YOUR PARTNER?

"I have a very active fantasy life," says Rob. "In a favorite scenario, I imagine my wife with another woman, then the two of them with me, making love in every way possible. I'd like to tell my wife about these fantasies. What do you think? Would hearing about them excite her or even make her want to try a threesome?"

That depends on how comfortable she will be with the idea of her husband making love to two women in his erotic dreams—and how likely she will be to want to make it a reality. Maybe she will find his thoughts exciting, and maybe she will be offended or made jealous by them or even find them disgusting. Sometimes sharing fantasies and acting them out can add excitement to a relationship. Consider your partner's feelings carefully before you share. Many people prefer to keep their fantasies private, too. Sharing them, and especially acting them out, can rob them of their power to arouse.

If you want to try acting out a fantasy:

- Write six scenarios each. Be as wildly imaginative as you like but limit the actors to the two of you.

- Together, pick from the lists something that both of you find exciting. Don't pressure your partner to try something he or she finds distasteful, embarrassing, or uncomfortable.

- Adapt the scenario for the real world and give it a try.

Some form of fantasy is essential to heighten the pleasures of lovemaking. When couples don't enjoy each other anymore, one of the areas they should examine is their fantasy lives. What changes have taken place in their fantasies—both private and shared—as their relationship became less satisfying? The answer to that question may tell them a lot.

*H*ere's a recipe for some mouthwatering lovemaking: Stock up on some special treats so you can have them at hand when you feel hungry for each other. If you don't need to use condoms, buy yourselves some whipped cream, smooth peanut butter, chocolate sauce, maple syrup, and bananas. If you aren't yet mutually monogamous, you can use any fresh fruit, honey, jellies, syrups, or powdered sugar—these won't damage a latex condom. You can apply any of these foods to your lover's delicious body and nibble, suck, lick, and chew them off.

You may want to have your love banquet right in the kitchen, because it's going to be messy. If you have a long enough counter, remove the toaster and the food processor and put down a few towels. If you'd prefer a softer surface, strip your bed and use an old sheet. If the weather's good, and you have a patio with some privacy, you can have a picnic outside.

Eating food off your partner will sensitize your taste buds, your tongue, your teeth, and your mouth. When you lick food and skin at the same time, you get a whole different flavor. You have to be very gentle, especially around the vulva and clitoris, and around the penis and testicles. But you'll find, as you consume and caress at the same time, that your awareness is heightened. Your senses of taste, smell, sight, and touch are all intensified.

Let's start with an appetizer, perhaps a nicely mashed avocado. Using your fingers or a chip, you can put a dollop of bright green fruit right on your partner's belly. Start with the chip—taste its salty goodness and then swipe some guacamole and put it in your partner's mouth. Then you can feed yourself, right from the source. Make your lips conform to the muscles of your lover's stomach—enjoy the way they ripple as you graze.

To clear your palate, you might want a drink. Take a fresh orange and squeeze over your lover's breasts. Lap the juice from her nipples, then you can both squeeze what's left in the orange right into each other's mouths. It might also be fun to take a spray canister of whipped cream and shoot a dab in between your toes (prewashed, of course), and let your partner suck each one clean.

The main course might be a swipe of peanut butter on the top of your partner's hip. You'll find it gives you resistance as you draw your tongue across it and get your lips working on the smooth flesh as you gobble up the tangy spread.

Dessert is a cannoli, a crisp shell that can be fitted around the penis and crunched off (very carefully!) and the cream which can be applied to nipples or vulva and then slowly licked off.

Don't count calories! You'll work off the extra pound or so as soon as you take a shower and throw yourselves into bed, sated with food but not yet with love. ■

Fear, overcoming

Sometimes fear prevents a couple from experiencing the kind of exciting, satisfying sex life they dream of having. The fears that get in the way of sex are often ones not recognized or articulated. If you are afraid of heights or spiders or public speaking, you know you suffer from that fear. Fear of passion is not so easily identified.

Such fears keep people from reaching erotic heights as surely as if they were physically constricted from doing so. A person who is held back sexually by fear may blame his or her partner for imagined failures. He or she may look for circumstantial or technical reasons why lovemaking isn't good.

Often if one partner is crippled by fear, so is the other, though not necessarily by the same fear. Fear leads to protective behavior that makes it difficult to be intimate and vulnerable in a relationship. Most fears tempt us to create an avoidance pattern that keeps the beliefs that fed the fear from being challenged and eventually transformed. If you have created a "fear story" about something and avoid the something, you keep the story intact. But, if you confront the situation, you have opportunity for new experience, especially with the help of your partner.

The Five Fears to Overcome for Great Sex

1. *Fear of intimacy.* For some people, intimacy is associated with early memories of an overly involved or protective parent. They may subconsciously believe they will lose their own identity if they become too close to a partner in adult life. And they may believe the partner's demands will become overwhelming if they get too close. People who fear intimacy protect themselves emotionally rather than becoming vulnerable.

2. *Fear of being rejected.* Men fear being laughed at sexually, especially if they experience performance failure. Women typically fear abandonment. Both men and women sometimes fear that a partner would reject them "if she/he only knew the real me." They censor their words and feelings to protect themselves from rejection.

3. *Fear of losing control.* Some people hold on to control because they fear losing themselves in passion. They may even worry about how they will look and act if they were to let themselves experience intense sexual arousal. Others fear losing power to their partners if

they surrender. For whatever underlying motive the controller holds on to personal power in a relationship, he or she is probably also holding back sexually.

4. *Fear of becoming overly sexual.* Some people are afraid they won't remain faithful to their partners if they allow their sexuality to bloom. They feel the need to keep safe by not becoming too sexually attractive. Sometimes people gain weight as a means of keeping themselves unattractive to co-workers, friends, and strangers. Consequently, they limit their pleasure for fear that too much would lead them to lose control.

5. *Fear of hidden desires.* He may secretly want his wife to ravage him. She may fantasize having sex in a public place. They are afraid their desires are wanton or not appropriate to their gender so they stifle those feelings. Often by stifling highly charged desires or fantasies, the baby is thrown out with the bathwater. Sex interest is depleted.

My simple but not necessarily easy formula for overcoming fears:

- Acknowledge the fear.
- Share it with your lover.
- Face your fear rather than avoid it.
- Talk sense to yourself before, during, and after exposure to your fear. Don't allow the old story to continue. Develop a new, revised, more reality-based explanation.

Fellatio

(see Oral Sex)

Fetishism

Fetishism is the dependence on a body part or inanimate object for sexual arousal and ejaculation. This is predominantly a male behavior. Though little research has been done on fetishism, it is believed to be one of the most common yet least often discussed sexual phenomenons. But it is difficult to say with accuracy how widespread such behaviors are. Typically, the fetishist comes to the attention of sex therapists or researchers only when his marriage is threatened by his behavior, his sexual functioning is impaired because his fetish has become difficult to obtain, or his behavior has led to legal problems.

Shoe and foot fetishes are among the most common perhaps because shoes and feet are on eye level of little boys who often play on the floor. Other fetishes include lingerie, long hair, and garments made of latex, rubber, or leather, sometimes worn by the man himself or by his partner. (When a man is sexually aroused by dressing in women's clothing, he has a transvestic fetish or is, in popular terminology, a transvestite.) Some fetishists make collections of the desired object, high-heeled leather boots for example. While many men may find these body parts or objects arousing, the true fetishist can become aroused *only* by the fetish.

No one knows exactly why some men develop a fetish. Dependence on the fetish for arousal is probably acquired during childhood (see Lovemap and Paraphilia) and often manifests itself as early as adolescence. When he is young, a man may be able to achieve erection and ejaculation by fantasizing the fetish object. Over time, his need for the presence of the object will most likely grow more pronounced.

EXAMPLE

"Martin won't make love to me unless I've had a pedicure or will leave on my high heels in bed," said Angela about her husband of ten years. "I know it sounds almost funny, but it isn't. We never have spontaneous lovemaking. It always has to be choreographed around my feet. We hardly ever have sex anymore, because I can't stand to have it this way."

Angela was humiliated by Martin's needs. In the past, she'd made excuses for his behavior, then blamed herself for not being attractive enough or good enough in bed to compel him to abandon his fetish for her. Now she had stopped blaming herself and excusing him. She also gave him an ultimatum: Seek help or agree to a divorce. ■

A fetishist rarely seeks treatment unless his partner insists. He will continue to live with the fetish as long as she will accommodate him because, however uncomfortable it may be for both of them, that is less painful than trying to change. Once he does agree, as Martin did, to pursue sex therapy, what can he realistically expect to happen?

The fetishist has no other way to become aroused than through his fetish. In treatment, he learns to expand his repertoire. He will always be aroused by feet, but he can learn over time to also be aroused in other ways. Through a combination of controlling his fantasies by gradually replacing images of the fetish with more acceptable ones and practicing standard sex therapy techniques with his partner (see Sex Therapy), he can learn to become aroused and ejaculate without the fetish.

"The therapy worked pretty well for us," Angela says. "In the beginning of therapy, I wore high heels for him, but I added sexy lingerie. Then we took off the heels. Eventually, over about a year's time, he got to the point where he could make love to me without lingerie or heels."

If an obsession with a body part or object dominates your sex life, you should seek help. But don't worry if your sexual repertoire includes elements of "kinky" sex play. An occasional urge to suck a woman's toes or a keen appreciation for sexy lingerie or an interest in shopping from a leather-clothing catalog—none of these things represent problem behavior. The desire to experiment during sex is the mark of a creative lover, not a fetishist.

Flirting

In these politically correct times, flirting has become almost an endangered practice. Women are afraid of encouraging unwanted sexual advances. Men are afraid of being labeled "sexual harassers." Both genders take the heightened awareness of sexuality from the workplace into their social lives—a sad state of affairs.

Flirting is a lighthearted form of communication between the sexes. It may not be appropriate between boss and subordinate, but neither is it totally inappropriate between co-workers who are both friendly equals and attuned to each other's meanings. Certainly flirting has its place in the social world, even between men and women who have commitments elsewhere.

Where is the harm in letting another person know he or she is attractive and appreciated, with no demands or expectations either stated or implied? Flirtation is nothing more than that. It may lead to a date or a relationship or it may be merely a pleasant way of testing our own sexual appeal and acknowledging the appeal of others.

EXAMPLE

"I lived outside the U. S. for nearly twelve years," said Bill, a diplomat recently reassigned to the State Department in Washington D. C. "When I last worked here, men and women had a casual rapport. There was some harmless flirting going on in the office. It made people feel good. I had one of those crushes never meant to go anywhere on a married co-worker. She would ruffle my hair when I got a fresh haircut. I would tell her how beautiful she looked. I'll bet our little harmless exchanges revved up her engine a little and her husband benefitted from that.

"Now in Washington everyone behaves like we're in a private school run by monks or nuns. I found myself taking that carefully nonsexual attitude home with me. I'd go to a party or a happy hour at the neighborhood bar hoping to meet someone I could get to know and ask out—but I'd be held back by my attitude.

"Then this wonderful woman from Paris flirted shamelessly with me one day in a restaurant in Georgetown; and I remembered how things were supposed to be. I'm myself again, outside the office that is. I like paying court to women and seeing them glow with the attention; and I like getting it back, too. Flirting feeds the soul." ■

When I shared Bill's story with a group of men and women in their twenties through forties, many of them told me they had forgotten—or never known—how to flirt. Many of them had misconceptions about flirting, equating it with sexual innuendo or physical touching. Flirting is largely carried on through eye contact, body language, and light verbal bantering that has gentle sexual undertones.

If you don't know how to flirt, start using your eyes more. When you see someone you'd like to meet at a party or in a pub, look at them until they look back at you. Don't drop your eyes or look away once contact has been made. Smile. Women who have engaged a man in this way often toss their hair back or sweep it off their foreheads with one hand. These hand and hair gestures are inviting to men. Then they may lower their eyes and look up at him which emphasizes long lashes. Both sexes indicate their receptivity to the other by open body language. Arms and legs crossed, for example, are typically viewed as signs of discouragement.

You don't have to be adept at the humorous double entendre to flirt. Tell someone how nice he or she looks but try to say it in a personal way. "That shade of peach silk compliments your face," or "I love the way that jacket fits across your broad shoulders."

Just keep it light. Flirting is supposed to be fun and frothy, like dessert.

The Five Rules of Flirting

1. *Be wary of flirting on the job.* You can't always predict who will be flattered by the remark and who will report you for harassment.

2. *Make eye contact while you flirt.* The other person is less likely to misinterpret a remark if you do.

3. *Keep your comments above the waist.* Flirting is a nongenital activity which makes it fun and safe for everyone, even the very married.

4. *Use touch sparingly.* In the office, touching is not a good idea. But in social situations, touch the other person's had or arm lightly to emphasize a point while you're speaking. In advanced flirting, run a finger down his or her cheek, stroke your thumb across the other's hand, brush a leg under the table with your foot.

5. *Be subtle.* Hold her gaze a moment longer than necessary. Lower your voice when you talk to a man in noisy room so he will have to lean forward to catch your words. Be witty if you can be.

Foreplay

(see also Kissing, Noncoital Sex, Oral Sex, Romance)

"Foreplay" describes the sexual activity that takes place prior to intercourse. Most sex authorities find the word mildly objectionable, because it implies that everything else is but a warm-up for intercourse, the main event. That puts a lot of pressure on a man to have an erect penis and reinforces the narrow definition of sex as intercourse. "Loveplay" is a better term.

Traditionally the period of lovemaking known as foreplay has been considered something a man has to do for a woman to get her as ready for sex, that is, intercourse, as he presumably always is. In reality, men, especially as they age, both need and want more of the touching, kissing, stroking, and loveplay that precedes and accompanies intercourse. Women need to recognize that their partners will both require and enjoy much more erotic touching as they get older. The truth is: Men are not always "ready" for intercourse; and for both genders, getting there is more than half the fun.

EXAMPLE

Lydia and Ramon call themselves "foreplay experts." Sometimes they begin making love hours before they both get home from work. She may leave a note in his pocket alluding to her plans for that night. He may call and leave a message on her voice mail with some ideas of his own.

"During the day we both become aroused just anticipating the lovemaking," Lydia said. *"When we get home, we like to take a long bath or a shower together. Lathering each other and later drying each other off are sensual experiences. We play this little game called sneak a peek. When I am out of the tub, I bend over drying my hair so Ramon can catch a glimpse of my genitals from the rear.*

"When we go into the bedroom, we slowly caress and tease each other, increasing the anticipation until we just can't bear it before he ever enters me." ■

Seven Tips for Hotter Foreplay

1. *Remember that sex begins in the brain.* Start thinking about lovemaking hours in advance and share your thoughts briefly and graphically with your lover if you can. Quick calls and brief notes don't intrude into the work day, but they can be powerful erotic stimulants. Send a single rose to his or her office.

2. *Pay attention to romantic details.* Set the stage for love in little ways, making sure the room is warm enough, the lighting is right, and so forth.

3. *Go slow.* Begin by kissing and caressing each other's bodies, but not the sex organs. Start, for example, by kissing fingers and toes and moving gradually to breasts or testicles.

4. *Give her an orgasm, manually or orally.* Many women are not orgasmic during intercourse. Some women who are multiply orgasmic are far more likely to have the second or third orgasm during intercourse if they've already had one or more. During manual stimulation of her

genitals, use the same kinds of strokes she does during masturbation and at the same speed.

5. *Pay attention to his other erotic zones.* Women often go straight for the penis. Many men have sensitive nipples, scrotums, and perineums. If he cannot tolerate too much stimulation of his penis without wanting to have intercourse, spend more time on these other areas.

6. *Experiment with varied touch.* In "spiders' legs," a French love game, only the fingertips and fingerpads touch the lover's body hair and occasionally the skin, with the lightest touches possible. A Chinese game, the spring butterfly, uses the point of a paintbrush. With the lover's eyes closed, take the brush and, imagining it a butterfly, have it skip across the body, landing lightly here and there.

7. *Experiment with different rhythms.* Arouse your partner, then back off. By "teasing," you increase the level of arousal. Your partner never knows if you will continue stroking or stop and change the pattern. His or her excitement is increased by the anticipation.

Frequency of Lovemaking, and how to increase

(see also Desire, Disparate [overcoming]. Obstacles to Sex)

Many couples want to have sex more frequently than they do. If two people want to make love more often, why don't they? Often increasing the frequency of lovemaking is simply a matter of reawakening sexual energy that has been dampened by the demands of life. In the early days of a relationship, the sexual energy level is high, no matter how busy the couple is.

As time goes by, the flow of energy diminishes. Some people consider this inevitable. They look back at the intense and frequent lovemaking they once shared as if it had happened in a former life. Maybe it isn't possible to be young again, but it is possible to increase the frequency of lovemaking.

EXAMPLE

"I felt as if I had come to the edge of a canyon," Edward said. "I had been so used to logging long hours at the office that I'd almost forgotten I once had *a personal life. When things slowed down in my work, I wanted to feel alive agin sexually, but the feeling seemed to be gone. It just wasn't there.*

"I blamed my wife Janice for that," he continued with a rueful smile. "She wasn't arousing me. She wasn't initiating sex. It had to be her fault. When I complained to her, she shocked the hell out of me by saying she wanted sex more often too but I wasn't arousing her. I wasn't initiating sex. She blamed me for the lack of lovemaking in our relationship."

After that frank discussion, Edward and Janice realized that, as in other areas of life, a passive approach to sexuality isn't an effective way of getting what you want. Rather than waiting for the other to reawaken their sexual energy, each took steps to get the feeling back on their own.

"Sometimes you have to do something to feel something," Edward acknowledged. ▪

Instead of wishing you had sex more often, start doing something to make that happen.

✐ix Sexual Energizers

1. *Dress sexy.* The way we dress delivers a message about us. I know that seems obvious—and cliched—but people do overlook the obvious every day. While complaining that she wasn't gettting enough sex, Janice was wearing faded and tattered flannel pajamas. What kind of signal were those pajamas sending to Edward? Dress to feel sexy— even before you enter the bedroom. Select styles and colors that flatter you and make you feel desirable. If you can dress for success, you can dress for sex too.

2. *Get in shape.* Yes, I've said this before, but it bears repeating. If you have difficulty mastering the self-discipline for a regular exercise program, try working out with a partner, perhaps your mate. You'll be astonished at how much sexier you feel and look when you are in good physical condition.

3. *Write sex letters.* Correspond with your partner, even if you live together and never travel separately. Write down your sexual feelings and fantasies. Be very graphic in your descriptions. Sex letters are a turn-on for both the writer and the reader. If you have difficulty putting your thoughts and feelings in writing, borrow someone else's words and adapt them. Use sexy novels and poems as inspiration.

4. *Think sexy.* Watch erotic films. Read erotic novels. Notice and admire the sexy people around you. Make a list of your turn-ons. Your imagination is your most potent sexual energizer. Use it!

5. *Create romantic rituals.* Send flowers on special days. Give affection, both physical and verbal. Plan regular dates and mini vacations as often as you can afford them. Romantic rituals are simple but powerful ways of reconnecting with those feelings of attraction and passion.

6. *Practice enlighted self-interest.* Make love to yourself first. That doesn't mean: Be selfish and go for your own pleasure at the expense of your partner. You are entitled to seek pleasure as long as you are responsive to your partner's efforts to do the same. You are also responsible for teaching your partner how to please you. The enlightened self-interest approach to sex will probably increase pleasure for you and your partner and leave you both wanting more sex more often.

G Spot

(see also Hot Spots, Orgasm, Positions)

The G spot, named for physician Ernst Grafenberg who rediscovered it in the 1950s, is located inside the vagina on the upper wall, an inch or two behind the back of the pubic bone. When stimulated, this area swells and, in some women, produces a pleasurable response that, in a few women, leads to an orgasm. Reaction to stimulation in the G-spot region varies greatly among women. Some are sensitive, others are overly sensitive, while still others report very little sensitivity at all.

Individual differences and response patterns vary so much that no woman should feel pressured to find her G spot and then reach orgasm this way. If you do want to experiment with G-spot stimulation, relax. Consider it a treasure hunt. You may not find the treasure you had in mind, but the hunt can be a source of amusement.

WHAT WOMEN SAY ABOUT THEIR G SPOTS

From a 30-year-old single woman:"I can't find my G spot if I have one. I've explored, my boyfriend's felt all around the area. We've both searched. Nothing! I don't think I have sensitivity there."

From a 40-year-old married woman:"I have terrific orgasms when my husband stimulates my G spot. I climax in a spurt of fluid! It's astonishing."

And from a 35-year-old divorced woman:"I think I have found the spot or rather my boyfriend has. It gives me pleasure when he strokes it, but nothing extraordinary. The G spot is not the next clitoris. Sometimes it takes me a while to feel what he's doing with the G. Now, when he strokes my clitoris, I know!"

 **ow to Stimulate Her G Spot**

1. Lie face to face. You should both be relaxed and no more than mildly aroused.
2. With his palm facing him, insert his lubricated index finger and middle finger into her vagina.
3. Push gently in the outer third of the vagina's top region until you find the sensitive place, a rougher patch than the surrounding skin.
4. Using your fingers make the come hither gesture, stroking the spot.
5. If she feels the urge to urinate, stop. Try later with an empty bladder.
6. To stimulate her G spot during intercourse, experiment with positions. Some women report the rear entry position most effective.

Gender Role Expectations

Even in our relatively liberated times, most American boys and girls are brought up in divergent ways, taught different skills, rewarded for diverse acts. There is little argument that some personality traits appear more dominant in one sex than the other. As adults, most of us feel pressure to conform to the expectations socially prescribed to our genders. Just as certain clothing is deemed appropriate for men and women so are certain behaviors. These sex roles prohibit men from wearing dresses and women from playing football. Gender role expectations can sometimes enhance relationships, but they can also constrict people sexually.

From Hercules to James bond, the heroic man is presented as impenetrable. Witness some discriminating reactions to male and female children: A shy little girl is considered cute, a shy boy is thought a sissy. Girls and women are allowed to show physical signs of affection toward each other and cry openly in each other's arms. Boys and men are not. Rather than seeing themselves as full human beings capable of versatile roles, many men and women have confined themselves to one-dimensional roles: Mother, father, leader, follower, and so forth.

Though that is changing, women have been expected to play a more passive role sexually than men. An aggressive woman can be seen as threatening or intimidating. Conversely, a sexually passive man may be called a wimp or suspected of being a homosexual. Until recent years, women weren't expected to initiate sex—or, for that matter, enjoy having it.

Couples who can bend the gender roles experience a wider range of behavior, sexual and otherwise.

EXAMPLE

❝I had a hard time learning how to be sexually assertive," Theresa said, "because I was afraid the men in my life would think it was unfeminine behavior. I would not be the one to say I wanted to make love. I would not orchestrate the lovemaking the way men did.

"Early in my thirties I began to relax my ideas about how a woman should behave sexually. Partly this comes from having more confidence now and partly from my boyfriend. He likes to playact in bed. Sometimes I am the aggressor and sometimes I am the virgin being pursued by him.

"The games have really helped me to loosen up, to expand my ideas about how I should be."

Theresa and her boyfriend have found that alternating between breaking the gender rules and following them in exaggerated form increases their arousal and adds spice to their sex life. They have become more complete lovers. ■

*T*he Three Keys to Becoming a More Complete Lover:

1. *Step out of role.* When we confine ourselves exclusively to either "masculine" or "feminine" behavior, we impose restrictions on our actions and feelings—thus limiting our sexual potential. Lifting those self-imposed limits increases your range of sexual satisfaction. To do that, spend several days "reversing" roles with your partner. A man should try being seductive, cuddly, passive. A woman should initiate sex and take the lead in lovemaking.

2. *Get personal.* This will probably be harder for men than women. Male relationships often revolve around activity, both in work and social settings, and are deficient in intimate exchanges. Try personalizing statements. Begin with "I feel..." and describe some emotion that you are experiencing, such as sadness, joy, disappointment, excitement. Elaborate on the feeling by saying, for example, "When you initiate sex, it makes me feel wanted."

3. *Show Interest.* Take an interest in each other's activities. A woman, for example, might learn the basics of football and attend some games with him, while a man might accompany her to step aerobics class. People are more giving in bed if their partners are interested in their lives outside the bedroom.

Guilt, overcoming

Guilt is said to be a peculiarly human emotion. This feeling that we are doing something we shouldn't be doing and furthermore deserve punishment for doing is first experienced in early childhood. Typically the activity producing guilt also affords us some pleasure or gratification. Few pleasurable activities make people feel more guilty than sex.

Sex guilt has its roots in the sex-negative messages of parents, teachers, and religious and other authority figures. Children are warned that touching their genitals is "bad." They are told that sex is dirty and leads to dire consequences, such as unwanted pregnancy, disease, shame, and disgrace. Some children aren't told specifically that sex is "bad," but they are taught to distrust pleasure on nearly every level. Complicating the situation, sexual behavior does need to conform to an ethical standard in which acts such as incest are deemed morally wrong.

Some people believe that sex guilt protects them from having indiscriminate affairs. And for some, a little guilt makes sex more exciting. They enjoy themselves more when they're feeling a little naughty. For most people, however, guilt is an inhibiting factor, preventing them from masturbating or fantasizing joyously and from letting themselves be truly free with their partners.

Overcoming guilt takes a little time. You must first believe that you deserve pleasure. When you start to feel guilty while masturbating, for example, stop and tell yourself, I deserve to find pleasure in my own body.

WHAT PEOPLE SAY ABOUT GUILT

From a 38-year-old man: "*I always enjoyed sex, but felt guilty afterward. I wondered if what they'd told me in Catholic schools was true. Could I go to hell for doing this with a woman who was not my wife? For feeling this good? I was torn between my faith and my physical yearnings and cravings.*

"*I wish I could say all the guilt disappeared when I got married, but it didn't. Now I feel guilty about my fantasies, about wanting my wife to wear racy clothes and do certain things to me. I haven't told her about the guilt. She wasn't raised Catholic and wouldn't understand.*"

From a 35-year-old woman: "*I feel guilty when I masturbate. I'm in a relationship, and masturbating seems like taking something away from him. Admittedly, I didn't feel quite comfortable about masturbating when I wasn't in a relationship either.*"

And from a 25-year-old woman: "*I feel guilty only about taking so long to reach orgasm. It doesn't seem fair to my boyfriend to expect him to keep going and going and going until I come. Sometimes I stop him before I come because I feel so guilty, but he insists he wants to finish and that makes me feel worse. Most of the time, I fake an orgasm so he won't feel bad and I won't feel guilty.*"

Besides reminding yourself that it is not sinful to find pleasure in your body, here are guidelines to consider: ■

$\mathcal{T}$hree Suggestions for Overcoming Guilt

1. *Talk the talk.* Engage close friends who have healthy attitudes toward sex in conversation. Allow yourself to be influenced by their views. Take those views to other friends who are inhibited by guilt and gently and sensitively reinforce your new beliefs by discussing them with these friends.

2. *Walk the walk.* Practice (rather than avoid) behaviors you know are pleasurable and healthy so that you can become more comfortable with these behaviors.

3. *Actively challenge your internal guilt messages.* Rather than accept old beliefs, question them. Why is this bad? Whom am I hurting? What's wrong with pleasure?

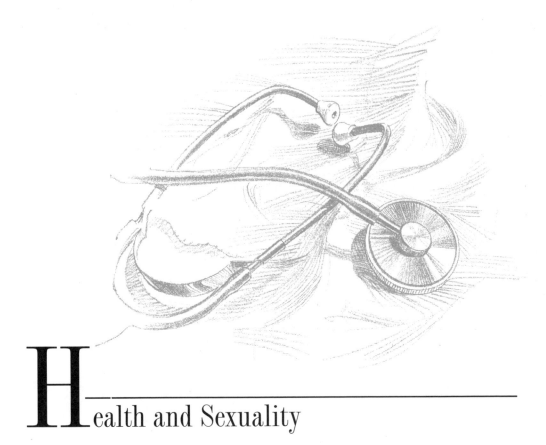

Health and Sexuality

(see also Illness and Disability, Hormones, Medications, Menopause, Orgasm)

The components of good health are exercise, proper diet, adequate rest, preventive medicine, and psychological, spiritual, and sexual well-being. Health affects our sexuality just as sexuality affects our health. Sex not only feels good, it's good for you. According to many research studies, lovemaking and orgasm boost circulation, improve skin tone, strengthen the immune system, release tension, and promote psychological health. Sex has been shown to relieve the minor pain of headaches and arthritis and other complaints, possibly because the brain releases endorphins, the body's natural painkillers, during orgasm. In women, regular sex can prevent some of the unwelcome changes to the vagina accompanying menopause, such as dryness and slackened muscle tone. In men, good cardiovascular health is a factor in achieving and maintaining firm erections. Some studies even indicate that sexual intercourse is good for your heart.

In my practice I have found that people report enjoying everything—including sex—more when they improve their general level of fitness by becoming more active and eating simpler foods. Healthy people are also far more likely to remain sexually active in later years. Numerous studies have linked physical activity in seniors to sexual activity. In taking care of your body, you encourage the positive mind-body effects of sex. A recent California study, for example, found that people who exercise regularly reach orgasm more easily and more often than people who don't engage in physical activities.

A healthy sex life, either through masturbation and fantasy or with a partner, is essential to good health, and vice versa. Health and sexuality are so intrinsically linked that the best prescription for good sex might well be exercise and a healthful diet. In fact, some diseases such as high blood pressure and diabetes have both a negative impact on sexuality and some causal relationship to diet and exercise.

What people say about sex and health

From a 40-year-old man: "Since I lost weight and have stopped eating heavy foods, I feel younger, more virile. I look better and feel better. My libido has increased and my responsiveness during sex is much more intense."

From a 45-year-old woman: "I started taking dancercise classes six months ago because I felt fat, out of shape, and had no energy. Now I feel sexier, more vibrant. I have more energy and find myself having more sexual fantasies and better orgasms. It's not a new lover. I'm still with the same guy but enjoying him so much more!"

A 35-year-old man said: "I was worried about my loss of libido. I blamed my wife, I blamed myself. My doctor suggested I cut back on the beer, get some exercise, and eliminate some of the other fats from my diet. I did and lost 17 pounds and regained my virility. When you eat a heavy meal in the evening and then sit in front of the TV with a beer, you're killing your libido."

Four Health Steps for Enhancing Sexuality

1. *Get a thorough physical before starting a diet or exercise program.* Ask your doctor for guidance on what activities are best for you. Also get specific diet suggestions, including recipes.

2. *Start with moderate exercise you can easily build into your day.* Walk instead of driving. Take the stairs, not the elevator.

3. *Involve your partner in efforts to build a healthier lifestyle.* You will both benefit from the changes. And you're more likely to stick to a program if you have his or her support.

4. *Don't accept your own excuses.* You're tired, tense, rushed. No time to eat right or exercise? Not true. Exercise is energizing. Cooking light takes no more time than cooking heavy.

Homosexuality

"Homo" in Greek means "the same." Homosexuality is the term for a sexual orientation toward members of the same sex. In our culture, the word "gay" conveys the same meaning. Often homosexual men are labeled "gay" and homosexual women are identified as "lesbians."

Researchers have not yet determined what causes homosexuality, though evidence increasingly points toward a·genetic predisposition. Homosexuals and bisexuals come from as many different backgrounds as heterosexuals and often grow up in families with heterosexual siblings. Studies of children raised by homosexual parents show they are no more likely to grow up homosexual than are other children.

Depending on the study cited, anywhere from 3 to 10 percent of Americans may be homosexual. That is a significant number of people. Yet the stigma attached to homosexuality in this society remains powerful. In some states, sexual activity between same-sex couples is still against the law. And the laws and practices of many states make it difficult for such couples to own property jointly, adopt children, or name each other as beneficiaries on insurance policies.

Because of these attitudes, many people who have had homosexual experiences in their youth harbor guilt. Others fear that such an experience or a random fantasy indicate they are secret homosexuals. Some people actively repress their homosexuality in an effort to lead lives conforming with social, family, or religious standards.

If you feel confusion or guilt about your sexual orientation, talking to a therapist will help.

The Five Questions Most Often Asked by Heterosexuals About Homosexuality:

1. *Am I gay?*

Having fantasies about same sex experiences is not by itself an indicator of homosexuality. Neither is childhood or adolescent sexual experimentation with someone of the same gender. A man can be effeminate and a woman can exhibit many so-called masculine traits without either being gay.

If you are attracted to and aroused by members of your own sex and not of the opposite sex, you are gay.

2. How do I know if a man is a repressed homosexual?

Women sometimes believe a man is secretly gay if he doesn't want to have sex with them. Repressed homosexuality can seem like a good explanation for any form of sexual rejection, from the indifference of a man who excites you to a sexless marriage. Men have the right to say "no," too.

On the other hand, a man's complete lack of interest in making love to his chosen female partner or any other woman might be an indicator of repressed homosexuality. It's certainly a sign that something is wrong.

3. Should I tell my partner about a past homosexual incident or a recurring fantasy?

How likely is your partner to be accepting and understanding? Some relationships are enriched by this kind of shared intimacy. Others are not.

Learning about a childhood incident probably would not be as threatening to a partner as hearing about recurring fantasies. Some people are jealous of their partner's fantasies anyway. If you want to share this information to relieve your guilt, maybe you should just absolve yourself.

4. How do homosexuals make love?

The major difference between heterosexual and homosexual love-making is the obvious one: No penis/vagina penetration. Contrary to popular myth, not all male homosexuals engage in anal sex and not all female homosexuals insert dildoes and other objects into the vagina.

Homosexuals enjoy the full range of kissing, caressing, and oral and manual stimulation of genitals. According to studies, lesbians most often reach orgasm during lovemaking via mutual masturbation and gay men through fellatio or mutual masturbation. They have the same patterns of desire, arousal, orgasm, and resolution as heterosexuals.

5. Can a homosexual fall in love with someone of the opposite sex and change his (or her) sexual orientation?

Women who develop crushes on gay men fantasize "saving" them from their homosexuality. Men imagine themselves being the one man with such great erotic power that lesbian lovers will turn from each other toward him. And sometimes homosexual men and women share the fantasy. They long to be "turned around" by a member of the opposite sex for whom they feel love or admiration.

In reality, sexual orientation isn't something we choose like a clothing style. If you are unhappy about your sexual orientation, therapy can help you gain understanding and self-acceptance. Unhappy about someone else's sexual orientation? No amount of love or seductive wiles will enable you to turn that desired homosexual in your direction.

Hormones

(see also Desire, Menopause)

The types and amounts of sex hormones present in our bodies play important roles in sexual desire and functioning. Before birth, all embryos are exposed to estrogens, the "female" hormones, through the mother's blood. In female fetuses, the estrogen stimulates the development of female sex organs. However, if the fetus is male, the "male" hormones, particularly testosterone, cause male sex organs to develop. Though male and female hormones are present in each sex, the predominant hormone in each gender causes the continued development of sex organs in puberty and influences reproductive functioning. Testosterone is responsible for sexual desire—or sex drive or libido—in both sexes.

As we age, men have less significant hormonal changes than women do. While there is a gradual decline in male testosterone production, most men continue to produce testosterone, sperm, and semen until the end of their lives. In women, the hormonal changes are more dramatic. Estrogen levels drop off precipitously during menopause.

Reduced levels of estrogen have important health implications for women, ranging from vaginal dryness to osteoporosis. Also, recent studies indicate that women are more at risk for heart disease following menopause, probably as a result of estrogen deficiency. Whether or not women should take estrogen supplements (hormone-replacement therapy) has been much debated, with advocates citing benefits to heart and bones and detractors pointing to a slightly increased risk of cancer in women taking HRT. Each woman must make her own choice after evaluating the research and in consultation with her physician.

Testosterone replacement for both men and women is a relatively new way of treating flagging libido. A significant deficiency in testosterone greatly reduces sexual interest and responsiveness. Men typically report an increase in sexual functioning as well as increased desire when normal hormonal balance is restored. Women receive much smaller doses of the hormone, now available in a skin patch for both men and women. Whereas estrogen replacement corrects vaginal dryness and atrophy that affect sexual functioning, testosterone rekindles only desire.

Is hormone replacement for you? If there is no other explanation for low desire and blood tests show low levels of testosterone, it may be. A physician should check blood levels before prescribing. If there is not a true deficiency, added testosterone won't help. Even if blood levels indicate treatment, a small percentage of men will not respond. They include heavy smokers, the morbidly obese, and some men who have damaged blood vessels and nerves in the penis from diabetes or other causes. Talk to your doctor.

EXAMPLE

"I was looking forward to retiring at age 60 for a lot of reasons," said Ben, "including the chance to enjoy a second honeymoon with my wife, who retired from her job too. When the time came, I wasn't as interested in sex as she was. The truth is I hadn't been interested in a few years, but I'd blamed that on my work. When I retired with no financial worries, I ran out of excuses."

Ben mentioned his problem to his internist, who brushed it aside. Many physicians are not comfortable talking about sex with their patients, and some accept the stereotypes about age and sexuality. Ben made an appointment with another doctor.

"This man didn't treat me as if I were too old to be thinking about sex," Ben said. "He ran some blood tests, found I was deficient in testosterone, and prescribed Testoderm, a scrotal patch. Within several weeks, I noticed an improvement in my mood, energy level, and level of sexual desire. My relationship with my wife is much improved." ■

Hot Spots

(see also G Spot, Orgasm, Positions)

Many men and women have a number of "hot spots" that, when stimulated, produce extremely pleasurable sensations and often orgasm. I prefer to consider these sometimes elusive places *areas* rather than distinct *spots*, because they are not exactly magic buttons.

Following are the areas and suggested ways of stimulating them.

The Five Hot Areas

1. *G spot.* A small mass of tissue on the front wall of the vagina, approximately one third of the way up. See page 107 for directions.

2. *U spot.* Unlike the G spot, the U area—for urethral canal—has received minimal press since its discovery as a source of sexual pleasure was reported in 1988 by a professor of physiology at Northwestern University Medical School. The urethral canal is found in the front wall of the vagina with its orifice about an inch behind the clitoris, directly in front of the vaginal opening.

   ■ It's a good idea for the woman to begin her exploration by stimulating the small area around the urethral opening on her own. If it feels good to her, she or her lover can provide the same manual stimulation to her during intercourse. Some women find the area particularly sensitive if the bladder is near full.

3. *The F spot for men.* The frenulum can be found by running a hand along the underside of the penis. It is that loose section of skin from the edge of the top of the penis, the coronal ridge, to the beginning of the penal shaft, where the skin is smoother and tighter. This area is highly sensitive to touch in most men. In fact, some men find they reach orgasm too quickly if the area is positioned in certain ways during intercourse so that it receives unusually intense stimulation.

   ■ Stimulate the frenulum by stroking it up and down. Vary the pressure and speed of movement.

4. *The R spot for men.* The R area is the raphe, the line along the center of the scrotum. The skin on the scrotum is very sensitive, similar to lips around the vagina. Integrating the frenulum and scrotum into a man's response cycle can help take the focus away from the head of the penis orientation many men have.

   ■ Stimulate the raphe by gently running fingertips along it.

5. *The AFE zone.* The anterior fornix erogenous zone is located on the upper vaginal wall between the top of the G spot and the back of the vaginal barrel. Discovered by a Malaysian sexologist who runs a clinic in Kuala Lampur, the AFE Zone may be the next G spot. Even women who do not experience intense pleasure report that stroking the area produces greater lubrication.

- Stimulate it first by sliding a finger up and down the area. Then move from the AFE to the G Spot and back again. Stroke the AFE area in clockwise, then counterclockwise motions.

Hysterectomy, effect on sexuality

(see also Aging, Illness and Disability)

WHAT HAPPENS TO A WOMAN'S SEXUALITY FOLLOWING A HYSTERECTOMY?

In a hysterectomy, a woman's uterus and sometimes her ovaries and fallopian tubes are surgically removed. Recent research indicates that the operation has been unnecessarily performed on many women, particularly in cases of fibroid tumors that often either do no harm or respond to other forms of treatment and shrink or disappear following menopause. If your doctor advises a hysterectomy, get a second opinion before submitting to surgery. Sometimes, of course, hysterectomy is unavoidable.

Some women who were plagued by pain or discomfort and heavy bleeding or other problems feel tremendous relief after having a hysterectomy. They find that sex after surgery is better than it was before. Other women report a loss of sex drive.

Some of the fears and concerns women have about life after a hysterectomy are groundless. Removal of the reproductive organs does not cause weight gain. (Only consistently taking in more calories than you expend in energy causes weight gain.) A woman does not lose her ability to have intercourse after surgery either.

Other concerns are valid. I am not convinced that we know all there is to know about the impact of hysterectomy upon a woman's sexuality. Some researchers believe the uterus, which continues to produce hormones in small amounts after menopause, plays an unrecognized hormonal role in sexual functioning. We do know that removal of the ovaries and the loss of the estrogen they produce leads to menopause, with attendant symptoms often including thinning of the vaginal walls, a decrease in the ability of the vagina to lubricate, and general loss of sexual desire. These symptoms can be alleviated by hormone-replacement therapy.

EXAMPLE

To correct a heavy bleeding problem, Karen had a total hysterectomy, which includes removal of the ovaries and fallopian tubes. Afterward, she experienced an array of symptoms including loss of memory, loss of sexual desire, inability to lubricate, the reduced ability to feel emotions of any kind, depression, and others.

"My doctor said I was imagining these things," she said. "He told me those were old wives' tales and gave me a pamphlet describing how much better life was after surgery. Then he gave me the estrogen patch, which he said would solve the lubrication problem—apparently the only problem of any consequence he thought I had. The patch did help somewhat, but I was still depressed, disinterested in sex, and particularly bothered by memory problems."

Reluctant to go back to her doctor with the same complaints, Karen kept silent. She faked an interest in sex and pretended to take as much delight in life as she had in the past. Not until nearly a year after her surgery, when she met Jean, who'd also had a hysterectomy, did Karen decide to see another doctor.

"My hysterectomy was the best thing that ever happened to me," Jean told her. "I had fibroids so large that they distended my uterus, causing my bladder to leak almost constantly. My periods lasted more than half the month. I felt like I was going to die if I didn't get some relief."

Her doctor removed her uterus but not her ovaries. He also put her on hormone-replacement therapy, carefully monitoring the dosage through period blood tests.

"I'm having the best sex of my life now," she said. "The orgasms feel a little different from the way they had. I always felt an orgasm in my uterus, and now

that isn't possible. But the sex is good. I never have to worry about bleeding while making love. For the first time in years I can be spontaneous."

Karen made an appointment with Jean's doctor. He put her on a stronger estrogen product, which has alleviated many of her symptoms, including depression and memory loss.

"I feel like a year of my sexually active life was taken away from me," Karen says. "Now I know that I didn't need to lose my ovaries, maybe didn't even need the hysterectomy. My surgeon didn't fully inform me of the options or the risks involved. He dismissed the problems I had afterward as being more or less in my head. But my sex life is finally improving." ∎

If you, or your partner, are suffering from loss of sexual desire following a hysterectomy, take the following steps immediately.

ℋow to Handle Post-Surgery Loss of Libido

1. If your doctor dismisses your complaints, see another doctor.
2. Insist that a doctor explain treatment options including all benefits and risks of estrogen-replacement therapy. Even if your doctor takes the time to educate you, consider it a beginning. A lot is at stake. Go to a library and continue your education before making your decision. Look into alternative options, such as increasing soy in your diet. A high soy diet as is the case in Asian cultures increases estrogen levels naturally.
3. Ask about androgen (testosterone)-replacement therapy, too. The ovaries secrete up to half of a woman's supply of androgen, the male hormone that is responsible for libido in both sexes. The uterus also produces androgen.
4. Should loss of libido and depression persist after treatment, talk to a therapist.

Illness and Disability

(see also Recovery)

Many chronic illnesses and/or their treatments and some disabilities can interfere with sexual functioning. Among these are diabetes, hypertension, heart disease, arteriosclerosis, endometriosis, ovarian cysts, and others. Some illnesses affect sexual behavior indirectly. When a man or woman feels ill and debilitated or is in pain, he or she is not usually interested in pursuing erotic matters. Other illnesses are not only psychologically demoralizing, they have damaging effects on sexual functioning by virtue of direct impact on the mechanisms (vascular, neurologic, or hormonal) that are necessary for sexual responsiveness.

Just as illness may influence our sexuality, feelings about sexuality influence our zest for living, our self-image, and our relationships with others. Yet physicians and patients often hesitate to talk about the sexual ramifications of illness, medication, or disability. I find that health issues consistently ignore female sexuality. For example, women diabetics may be more prone to vaginal infection, and, in advanced stages diabetes can cause loss of sexual sensation. Yet most information on the impact of diabetes on sexuality is related to men's erections.

If you are suffering from a long-term illness or disability, don't get discouraged. A healthy lifestyle can prove beneficial in any disease process. You can significantly improve your health by the choices you make, including the choice to enjoy pleasurable touching with your partner, which is always possible, regardless of the physical circumstances or medical history.

EXAMPLE

Barb was injured in an automobile accident at age 40. Confined to a wheel chair, she was frequently depressed. For two years she wouldn't allow her husband, Sam, to touch her in a sexual way. In fact, she would no longer sleep in the same bed with him.

"I miss the close physical contact with her terribly," he said. "I want to hold her, kiss and stroke her, and have her touch me."

"I don't want to be too near him," she said, "in case I have an accident with my bladder. I would die if that happened."

Finally, Barb consented to see a sex therapist with Sam because she was afraid he would leave her if she didn't. First she learned how to empty her bladder completely by pressing on the pubic area with the palm of her hand. That ensured she would be dry for at least 30 minutes and enabled her to overcome the initial huge hurdle to reestablishing intimacy with her husband.

Barb may have no feeling below the waist, but she has a lot of sensation in her breasts, back, arms, shoulders, face, neck, mouth. Sam is able to give her a great deal of pleasure by stroking those areas; and she, in turn can pleasure him with her hands and mouth. After they began sleeping in the same bed together again, Barb's depressions grew less severe and frequent. ∎

Seven Steps to Restoring Sexual Responsiveness

1. *Talk to your physician frankly and openly.* Get the best medical advice you can on the physical aspects of sexual interaction in your case. Include your partner in the discussions.

2. *Don't hesitate to consult a sex therapist.* Most physicians have not been trained in sexuality. Nor are they experts in dealing with personal psychology and relationship issues.

3. *Don't react to illness or disability by withdrawing into yourself.* Fear of burdening others, shame, and anger about being ill can isolate a man or woman. Share your feelings.

4. *Think about sex.* Read erotic stories, watch videos. Indulge your fantasies.

5. *Masturbate.* By exploring your own sexual feelings without concerning yourself about your partner, you can rediscover your sexuality.

6. *Be affectionate.* Even if you do not feel up to having sex, do not withdraw from physical expressions of affection. During times of stress, you and your partner need physical contact, kissing, hugging, cuddling, holding hands.

7. *Have a positive attitude.* When you do make love, don't worry about functioning. The attitude you take about your sexuality is far more important than any physical limitation you may have.

Impotence

(see also Recovery)

Even young men may have experienced a time where they wanted an erection and didn't get one or, more likely, lost one at some embarrassing moment. That lack of response in an organ men expect to be robust and ready is confusing and frustrating. The culprits are usually food, drink, exhaustion, illness, medication, stress. By age 40 nearly every man will have had a bout of impotence, the failure to get and sustain an erection for lovemaking. In some men, the problem is ongoing rather than situational. While chronic impotence is rare in young men, it is not something that naturally occurs with age either.

Except for the spontaneous orgasms that occur during sleep, erections begin in the brain as a response to real or fantasized stimulation. The brain tells the nerves to provide a chemical signal to the feeder arteries; which send blood into the chambers of the penis to create an erection. In the chronically impotent man, either the signal doesn't get sent, or, more likely, blockages in the arteries prevent the blood from filling the chambers.

The majority of chronic impotence cases have contributing physical causes, with prescribed medications accounting for many of them. Most age-related impotence is the result of reduced blood supply to the penis. The cause may be heart disease, high blood pressure, or some other factor that narrows the blood vessels in the penis or groin. Treatment may be as simple as a change of lifestyle: exercise, stress control, cutting down on dietary fats, reducing alcohol consumption, and quitting smoking.

A wide range of medical interventions are available for men who do not respond to lifestyle change. The penile implant, a surgical prosthetic device, is inflated by a pump placed in the abdomen, allowing a man to get an erection whenever he wants simply by pushing a button. Even safer and less invasive are vacuum constriction devices, in which blood is pumped into the penis and a rubber band at the base of the penis constricts the shaft, trapping the blood in the penile erection chambers. Vasoactive drugs can also be injected into the penis to enhance circulation. Other simpler and less cumbersome remedies are being developed all the time. There are more options for treating impotence today than ever before, yet fewer than one sixth of the nation's estimated 30 million affected men seek help.

Even thinking about sex can become painful for the man whose erection problem has become frequent or chronic. He feels self-conscious and inadequate. His partner, having been taught that an erection signals desire, is also confused and distressed. She probably thinks he no longer finds her attractive. It is not uncommon for a man to begin avoiding his partner and she him.

Not surprisingly, talking about this situation with a doctor can be distressing. Until recently, doctors and therapists believed that most impotence was psychological in nature, compounding the difficulty for the patient. In some cases, impotence is psychological. One episode may have escalated into a chronic problem. Worry about being impotent causes a man to be impotent; and the cycle of failure feeds on itself.

EXAMPLE

Ray, aged 49, came to therapy for help after experiencing nine months of increasingly frequent episodes of impotence. Eileen, his wife of 20 years, was puzzled and hurt by his inability to make love to her. Ray had run through the gamut of excuses: too tired, too much to drink, too much to eat, too late, and so forth. She wasn't accepting them anymore.

"I don't think he finds me attractive now," she said. "I feel old and dumpy. I've tried everything to arouse him and nothing works."

Ray did have contributing physical causes: high blood pressure, overweight, a smoking habit, and a fondness for high-fat meals accompanied by several glasses of wine. In a meeting alone with the therapist he revealed something else that had bearing on his problem.

"Eight months ago at an out-of-town business conference," he said, "I met an aggressive woman who wanted to have sex with me right there. I'd never done anything like that before. We went upstairs to a private room and attempted to have intercourse on the floor. I became excited and erect, but for the first time in my life, lost my erection and couldn't get it back. Nothing she did brought me back to life."

Ray was greatly distressed by this experience. He wasn't proud of himself for being unfaithful to his wife; and he was humiliated by his sexual failure. He told himself it was an impulsive, uncharacteristic act and tried to put it out of his mind. Then he lost his erection with his wife one night and couldn't get it back again. The cycle of failure had begun.

He broke the cycle by taking the following steps. ■

*F*ive Steps a Man Can Take to Restore Sexual Function

1. *Remind yourself that every man sometimes experiences an uncooperative penis.* Don't let one or even several episodes convince you that you're impotent for life.

2. *Focus on what you can do to please your partner.* Lovemaking is not dependent on an erect penis. You can bring her pleasure orally and manually.

3. *Let your partner know this isn't her fault.* She needs to be reassured that you find her attractive. Communicate clearly that your erection difficulty does not reflect your feelings for her.

4. *Make healthy lifestyle changes.* Once a man enters his forties, he can't live a sedentary life and eat and drink unwisely without suffering some consequences.

5. *If the problem persists, consult a medical doctor and/or a sex therapist.* You need to rule out or treat medical causes. You may also need help from a therapist in dealing with insecurity and anxiety the problem has created.

ℱive Steps a Woman Can Take to Help Restore a Man's Sexual Functioning

1. *Don't blame yourself.* His erection difficulty has nothing to do with you. Your insecurity will only make him feel worse than he already does.

2. *Be understanding but don't be too solicitous.* Think how you feel when you are embarrassed, humiliated, or feeling inadequate. Empathize, without fussing over him.

3. *Don't analyze him or the relationship.* He doesn't need a critical evaluation now.

4. *Don't keep trying to get him erect.* Let him pleasure you. Hold him, kiss, stroke, and caress him. Ignore his penis.

5. *Encourage him to get help.* If the problem is chronic, he needs to see a doctor. The two of you would also benefit from sex therapy.

Infertility

Infertility—the inability to conceive when conception is desired—has been increasing in the United States in the last two decades. Widespread STDs and the trend toward later parenthood (when fertility naturally declines in women especially) are contributing factors to the rise. After a couple have been trying to get pregnant for a year—or less, depending on their ages—they may have fertility tests done to pinpoint the problem. Then they may elect one of various forms of infertility treatment, ranging from drugs to expensive technologies such as in vitro fertilization.

The impact of infertility and infertility treatments on sexuality is tremendous. Passion is regulated by charts and timetables. Massive doses of hormones to stimulate development of eggs in women causes pain and discomfort, mood swings, bloating, and weight gain. Anxiety and depression coupled with feelings of inadequacy sometimes beset the man who is told his sperm count is low or the woman whose eggs aren't fertile. Both men and women find the process of trying to conceive under laboratory conditions dehumanizing and decidedly not erotic.

Sexual relations that were once spontaneous and pleasurable become perfunctory at best and traumatic at worst.

EXAMPLE

"Sex became a chore after Roger and I started trying to get pregnant," explained Marie. "We never expected to have difficulty conceiving. When we did, we found ourselves faced with all these directions on how and when to have sex. Lust flew out the window."

Added Roger: "I was feeling like less than a man after the doctors told me I had a slightly low sperm count. When I needed Marie's comfort the most, I was deprived of it. She wouldn't let me near her unless the timing was right."

After eight months of trying unsuccessfully to conceive a child, they felt sexually deadened and emotionally estranged from each other. Is there any way out of the infertility trap? Yes, but you have to be creative.   ∎

Five Ways to Make Sex Hotter While Trying to Conceive

1. *Pretend your doctors are your parents.* Remember what it was like when you were a teenager discovering your sexuality behind your parents' backs? Indulge in noncoital sex on a day when you're not supposed to be having sex. Fondle each other whenever you get the chance. "Cheat" and have "unofficial sex" on a chastity day.

2. *Change the location and/or the time of lovemaking.* If this is Tuesday and you're supposed to have sex, do it on the kitchen floor at dawn.

3. *Change positions.* Women do get pregnant when not in the missionary position.

4. *Pretend you're dating and "sex day" is the day you plan to have sex for the first time.* Be romantic. Court each other. This is no time to stop sending flowers and leaving love messages on the voice mail.

5. *Be sensual.* On days when you aren't having sex, give each other massages and back rubs. Build up the anticipation for lovemaking.

Intercourse

(see also Ejaculation, Erection, Kegels, Orgasm, Positions)

Americans like to quantify sex. Surveys frequently ask, "How often do you have sex?" Intercourse is implied in the phrase "have sex." Men also like to know "How long should it last?" and "How soon should I be able to have intercourse again?" The answers to those questions vary with the polls, surveys, and studies, with "having sex" once or twice a week the most frequent responses. The period of active thrusting probably does not last more than a few minutes for most men. Young men may have a refractory period—the time required for the penis to become erect again—of several minutes while a senior citizen might require several days. That time period varies from one man to another and within the same man depending on circumstances. Frequency of intercourse or any other form of sexual activity is an individual matter. You shouldn't strive to meet a norm or feel inadequate or oversexed if your numbers don't match the latest ones reported.

Are you having sex if you don't have intercourse? In our society where intercourse—penis inside vagina—is considered the main form of lovemaking, many people would answer "no." The joys of intercourse for both sexes include intense physical stimulation and a sense of intimacy and closeness not found in quite any other way. Even women who do not achieve orgasm during intercourse usually enjoy the feeling of having their partner inside them. But sex is much more than intercourse. A couple can have sex without inserting penis into vagina.

Equating sex with intercourse has disadvantages. First, it causes people, especially men, to rush through everything they consider "preliminary." Also, it puts a lot of pressure on the man to have an erection and on the woman to reach orgasm that way. Intercourse requires contraception unless pregnancy is desired and in non-monogamous relationships a condom to prevent the spread of STDs. The act may require more physical energy than an ill partner has and may be medically inadvisable during part of some pregnancies and certainly for several weeks following birth. Men and women can enjoy intercourse a lot more if they take the pressure off, demythologize the act, and view it as one of many ways to make love.

EXAMPLE

"I always liked sex," Charlene said, "but I rarely had an orgasm during intercourse. The problem with men is they want to have only intercourse as soon as the relationship gets to that point where you do it for the first time. I prefer lovemaking in the early days of an affair before I let a man 'go all the way' as my mother would say. I spent a lot of happy nights in college, especially, with men who kissed, stroked, fondled, and caressed me all the way to heaven and back. Sometimes I lied and said I was a virgin just so they wouldn't pressure me as much to move on to intercourse."

Married less than two years, Charlene was dissatisfied with her sex life. For her husband, "sex" equaled intercourse, and "foreplay" had become a form of shorthand he expected her to pick up quickly. Often she faked an orgasm "for the sake of his ego" and also "to make me feel like more of a woman." A narrow focus on intercourse can set up this pattern in a relationship that began with uninhibited and varied lovemaking.

"I love feeling him inside me," she said, "but I want more than that."

After several months of silent unhappiness, she told him how she felt. He hadn't realized how much his lovemaking style had changed with marriage until she spoke up. When she told him she wanted more kissing, stroking, fondling, and oral lovemaking, he readily agreed to meet her needs.

"Our sex life is a lot better now for both of us," she said recently. "I should have shared my feelings with him sooner." ∎

Seven Ways of Enhancing Intercourse

1. *Vary the thrusting pattern.* Most men don't think about their thrusting pattern. As soon as they enter the woman, they begin thrusting in a rapid and vigorous manner with even strokes, often quickly accelerating as they reach climax. Intercourse would last longer if they alternated deep thrusts with shallow ones. Sensations for both partners are also heightened by varying the pattern.

2. *Vary the speed of thrusting.* Slow down. Speed up. Slow down again. Varying the speed, like varying the pattern prolongs and intensifies the experience.

3. *Don't always finish what you start.* Most men enter a woman and continue thrusting to climax. If you pull out before climax is imminent and make love in other ways, you can resume intercourse later. The experience lasts longer, and the climax delayed feels stronger.

4. *Touch her clitoris during intercourse.* Most women need additional clitoral stimulation to reach orgasm during intercourse. Encourage her to masturbate herself or do it for her, using the techniques she would use.

5. *Alternate positions.* Moving from the missionary position to the female superior position, for example, changes the coital dynamics. The sensations are different; and again the lovemaking lasts longer.

6. *Practice delaying techniques.* See page 74 for the techniques men use to prevent premature ejaculation. They can also be used to prolong intercourse.

7. *Do your Kegels.* Directions for both sexes on page 141. Strong pubococcygeal muscles give men better control over the ejaculatory process and help both men and women achieve stronger orgasms.

Intimacy

(see also Communication)

WHAT IS INTIMACY?

Women often complain about men's failure, or inability, to be intimate partners with them. They mean: He doesn't listen, he doesn't talk about his feelings. Men often assume that intimacy is what happens when you have sex with someone and don't understand why women fail to recognize what an intimate act lovemaking is. "Why do I have to talk about my feelings when I'm showing them?" they may ask.

Why do men have more trouble expressing their feelings and listening closely to their partner's shared confidences than women do? Little boys are rarely encouraged to be as open about their feelings as little girls are. As they grow into men, they are rewarded for keeping their feelings to themselves, for not crying when they are hurt, or not admitting to fear when they feel it. When a woman comforts a friend after a loss such as a break-up, she listens to the other person pour out feelings and provides tissues as needed. A man in the same situation takes his buddy out, not to listen, but to help him forget by avoiding the subject altogether. After years of this kind of socialization, men find themselves in close relationships with women who want them to show their emotions.

Though they have learned to express (or not express) their feelings in different ways, both men and women want deeper intimacy in relationships. They seek closeness, caring, and mutual nurturing. When sex occurs within such a relationship, both men and women find it more psychologically and emotionally satisfying than sex in a less close, committed, or intimate relationship.

Sometimes women have problems with intimacy, too. They may have been raised in a family where emotions were suppressed, not expressed. Intimacy blockers for either sex include unrealistic expectations, intolerance, fear of closeness, duplicity.

EXAMPLE

"I show her how much I love her in every way possible," said Matt, a 45-year-old executive whose wife, Cindy, had just shocked him by asking for a divorce. "She says I don't pay enough attention to her or show her enough affection. We have a great sex life. I've knocked myself out to provide a good lifestyle for her and the kids. I don't understand what the problem is."

Matt assumed that working hard to buy the luxuries he wanted his family to have was proof of his love for his wife. In addition, he helped support her aging grandmother and had loaned her nephew the money he needed to attend college. He did those things, he said, out of love for his wife.

"After 22 years of marriage, I feel as if I don't even know him," Cindy said. "We never have real talks. He says he loves me only when we're having sex. I want a deeper communication than I have with him."

Matt agreed to see a therapist with Cindy because he didn't want a divorce, not because he really thought they needed help. But once they were in therapy, he began to understand what Cindy meant when she said, "I feel as if I don't know you," and "We never talk." For her part, she was able to recognize that Matt was showing his love every day by supporting his family, spending time with her, making love, taking care of her grandmother.

"If I didn't love you," he told her, *"I would have quit my job, bought a sailboat, and headed for the South Pacific years ago."*

In a short time, they had deepened the level of intimacy in their relationship. Instead of a divorce, they took a second honeymoon. ∎

ℋow to Overcome His (or Your) Fear of Intimacy

1. *Accept your partner as he (or she) is.* Understand that he considers his actions to be signs of his feelings. Sometimes men and women seem to be speaking in different languages, hers more verbal and his more action-oriented. Look for the meaning in what he does.

2. *Use positive reinforcement.* He may not speak about emotions as eloquently as you do. Respond positively to him when he shares his feelings, no matter how awkwardly he expresses them.

3. *Acknowledge his fear—and sometimes your own.* Men, and women too, can be afraid of losing respect of the partner or losing power in the relationship if they reveal secret fears, desires, anxieties. Intimacy requires that you open yourself up to the other person. Intelligence demands that you acknowledge there is risk inherent in doing so.

4. *Recognize that change takes time.* He may want to share his feelings with you, but he will still need time to learn new ways of behaving.

Jealousy, sexual

(see also Trust)

Sexual jealousy, one of the strongest human emotions, grows out of the fear that another person will threaten the exclusivity of a romantic relationship. Sometimes the fear is irrational and fleeting. Often in a new relationship, people are temporarily insecure and so afraid of losing what they have only just found that they see cause for jealousy when there is none. Almost everyone has experienced an attack of jealousy in a new relationship or when a new person—in the office, the neighborhood, the social circle—seems to pose a threat to an established relationship because of his or her good looks, availability, and other obvious charms. Most of us quickly see our unfounded jealousy for what it is and let go of it.

Sometimes the fear of losing the loved one is both irrational and chronic. Often described as "blindly jealous" or "insanely jealous," a person with this problem may suspect his or her partner of flirting if a smile is exchanged with a friend or co-worker or even of having an affair on equally flimsy evidence. Someone who is always jealous—especially when the feelings are expressed in angry or violent ways—will kill the relationship without the help of a third person. It also needs to be said that, in some cases, constant jealousy is understandable. If one partner repeatedly violates an agreement of sexual exclusivity, how else can the other feel?

When not extreme and omnipresent, jealousy can serve a useful function: protecting the relationship. Perhaps one partner has become complacent in the relationship. When someone else takes a perceived or real interest in the beloved, the complacent partner snaps to attention. It's then hoped that jealousy will lead to a dialogue between the couple that causes them to examine their behavior and make positive changes.

Both men and women experience jealousy. Men may more often express their feelings in angry shouting and women more often express theirs in tears, but an individual man or woman might behave in either way. Either a man or a woman may also choose to shut out his or her partner emotionally or to "fight fire with fire" by striking up a flirtation of his or her own.

If sexual jealousy is an issue in your relationship, get it out in the open. Talk to your partner and really listen to what he or she has to say. Unresolved issues such as this one can erode trust.

EXAMPLE

"I don't like to go to parties because my husband always finds the most attractive woman in the room and talks to her," said Gail. She and David have been married eight years and are the parents of a six-year-old son, Jeremy. "It happened last weekend. Around midnight, I was tired and eager to go home. Jeremy had been sick for most of the previous week, so I was feeling a little uneasy about him.

"David was sitting on the sofa next to some young and attractive woman. I positioned myself so that I was able to make eye contact with him, but he ignored me. I tapped my foot impatiently. When I had his attention, I motioned to the door with my head.

"Well, little Miss Clairol sitting next to him caught my eye and threw her head back, letting her hair fall freely in a provocative manner, as if to say, 'He's with me, Mrs. Mom!' And she was right, the bitch! He was with her. When I finally spoke up, he put me off. We stayed at the party another 30 minutes, David engrossed in conversation with her the whole time."

According to Gail, that was not the first time David had ignored her at a party while he focused his attention on a young and attractive woman. Does she suspect him of having affairs? No, but she "doesn't like the way he always manages to find the prettiest woman in the room."

David said, "Gail is too territorial. I don't care who she talks to at parties. The point of going out is talking to other people. In public, Gail never takes her eyes off me, which is a lot more attention than she pays to me at home. She would like us to go through life joined at the hip. I think we need a little breathing room."

In the past, Gail and David "handled" her jealousy in a typical way. She cried and accused him of being attracted to other women. He apologized for making her jealous, swore he had eyes only for her, and made love to her. Now they are talking calmly and openly about her jealousy, looking for its root causes and exploring ways of accommodating both their needs in social situations.

They are taking the following steps to defuse jealousy. ■

*F*ive Steps to Defusing Jealousy

1. *Examine the behavior of both partners.* What triggers feelings of jealousy? Is one partner misreading the situation? Would better communication dispel the jealousy?

2. *Examine your own feelings.* If you are the jealous person, ask, "Is jealousy a natural response to my partner's behavior or am I insecure?" And, if you are the other partner, ask, "Do I secretly enjoy my partner's jealousy? And if so, why?"

3. *Look for the causes.* You've identified your feelings. Now, why do you feel this way? Is one person chronically jealous? Does he or she have valid reasons for feeling insecure in the relationship? Is jealousy used as a means of controlling a partner's behavior? Could jealousy be an expression of your own hidden desire to violate the agreement of sexual exclusivity?

4. *Find ways of making the jealous partner feel more secure in the relationship without making the other person feel controlled.* Behaving in a more romantic way toward your partner might help. (See Romance.) The jealous partner may also have to take some responsibility for achieving inner security. Maybe you feel your partner looks at others because you've gained weight, dropped your personal grooming standards, become dull. Make yourself more attractive and interesting.

5. *Put things in perspective.* A spouse who flirts at parties in front of you but is faithful to his or her marriage vows is not the worst partner you could have.

Joy Break

The joy break is the antidote to those stresses that can sap all the joy from life if we let them. Joy breaks are brief sensual/sexual interludes.

Ask your partner to join you in planning a joy break at least once a week. The possibilities are endless.

- Soften the lights, put on some music, and dance with each other in the nude.
- Take a candlelight bubble bath.
- Deliver a rose to your partner at work.
- Have breakfast in bed.
- Make plans for a getaway weekend, even if you can't afford to take the trip now. Enjoy the planning.

What if your partner won't plan a joy break?

Don't get mad. If your partner won't reciprocate, continue planning the joy breaks on your own. Still no reciprocity? Talk it over. Find out what obstacles are standing in the way. Some people simply feel foolish or silly in organizing such activities. Can you negotiate a reciprocal agreement that he or she will accommodate you in this way and you will cooperate in an area important to him or her?

"John thought it was silly at first," said Carolyn. "Then, after he came home from a difficult day, I rubbed the back of his neck in a very sensual way. It brought a smile to his face. I told him, 'This is your joy break for the day.' He got the message.

"The next day at the office I found a love note from him in my purse. The following week he called me at work just to talk—something we hadn't done in a long time. Our phone conversations had been reduced to exchanges of information about who was running what errands. Just chatting like we had in the early days was very exciting to both of us."

Enjoy the joy breaks even if your partner won't get involved in the planning process.

*M*ake reservations, but don't tell her. Instead, agree to meet her in the hotel bar for a drink after work. When she walks in and asks for you, the maitre d' will hand her a note with a key to the room, which you've given him in advance. It says, "This key will open the door to an erotic evening you won't want to miss. Follow your heart upstairs. I can't wait."

The room is dark as she enters it. You come up behind her and take her around the waist, kissing her from behind. The adult channel is playing on the TV across the room, and she can catch a glimpse of two naked people playfully chasing each other across a tennis court. It's funny and sexy at the same time.

Take some silk scarves out of your pocket and tie her hands behind her back, then take another and cover her eyes, whispering that you have a wonderful surprise for her. You open the bottle of wine you've ordered from room service, and she can hear the pop of the cork. You pull off the coverlet and turn down the sheets—she can hear your hand gliding across the smooth cotton and imagine your fingers doing the same to her.

Guide her into the bathroom where you have already turned on the heating lamp. The room is toasty, and as you begin to touch her softly through her clothes, you can feel how excited she is. Kneeling before her, reaching under her skirt, you run a wooden back brush or a loofah sponge (whichever the hotel has provided) up the length of her legs. As you teasingly remove her shoes, then her pantyhose, then her underpants, you kiss her stomach and thighs, listening to her moan softly.

You open the sample bottle of body lotion on the counter and massage all her crevices, from her toes to her waist. When she is thoroughly lubricated, take your hands off her, leaving her in a state of high desire. Just talk now, describing her incredible body, the sheen of her skin, and how turned on she gets you. Tell her how exciting you find making love to her away from home.

Bring her to the bed and hold the glass of wine so that she can sip from it. If it spills, so much the better—you can lick the excess off. Remove her blindfold and untie her so that she can take off the rest of her clothes and yours too.

For a while, you lie together just touching hands, watching the onscreen couple who are now lying in a hammock, swaying softly together as they interlace their legs and arms. The rhythm of their movements is too tantalizing to ignore, and soon you two are locked together, ignoring everything in the world except the sound of your beating hearts and quickened breath.

Now it's your turn to wear the blindfold. Amazing how each touch of her hand or mouth is heightened when you can't see. As she kisses your elbow, feel the hairs rise on your arm; as she runs her nails lightly down your back all the way to your buttocks, enjoy the chills that make you feel even warmer inside.

"What would you like me to do to you?" she asks.

"Never stop touching me," you tell her ardently, stopping her mouth with your kiss. She slides down and places your penis between her breasts. The room spins wildly. ■

Kegels

Developed by Dr. Arnold Kegel in the 1950s, Kegel exercises were originally meant to strengthen the pubococcygeal (PC) muscle in women who suffered from a post-childbirth weakening of that muscle, a condition that often leads to urinary incontinence. As women reported their experiences with the exercises, the doctor discovered the connection between pubococcygeal muscle tone and increased vaginal sensitivity. Because these muscles are used during intercourse and contract during orgasm, strengthening them makes lovemaking more pleasurable for women, and orgasm feel stronger or more intense. Men also benefit from performing Kegel exercises, which both strengthen the muscle and improve blood flow to the pelvic region. By strengthening their pubococcygeal muscles, they can sometimes slow down the ejaculatory process and feel stronger sensations during ejaculation and orgasm.

What men and women say about their PC muscles

From a new mother in her late twenties: "I discovered the erotic benefits of PC muscles after my gynecologist prescribed post-childbirth Kegel exercises. I have stronger orgasms than I had before thanks to those muscles!"

A 40-year-old woman says: "I use my love muscles to grasp my husband's penis tightly during intercourse. I can make him come by fluttering those muscles around his penis. I can intensify my orgasms by clenching and releasing the muscles repeatedly as soon as I feel the first contraction. I can even hold him inside me after he has gone soft. Strengthening my love muscles has changed the way I make love."

And from a 35-year-old man: "I discovered my PC muscles after reading an article in one of my wife's magazines. I can't believe how much better lovemaking is now that I have developed them. I can delay orgasm by clenching the PCs and when I do come, the feeling is more intense. Why didn't I start exercising these muscles years ago?"

How to Exercise Your Love Muscles

1. *Locate the pubococcygeus (PC) muscle, part of the pelvic floor in both sexes, by stopping and starting the flow of urine.* Practice this stopping and starting several times to become familiar with the PC.

2. *Start with a short Kegel squeeze.* Contract the muscle 15 or 20 times at approximately one squeeze per second. Exhale gently as you tighten only the muscles around your genitals (which includes the anus), not the muscles in your buttocks. Don't bear down when you release. Simply let go. Do two sessions a day twice a day. Gradually build up to two sets of 75 per day.

3. *Add a long Kegel squeeze.* Hold the muscle contraction for a count of three. Relax between contractions. Work up to holding for ten seconds, relaxing for ten seconds. Again start with two sets of 20 each and build up to 75. You will be doing 300 repetitions a day of the combined short and long and be ready to add the *push out.* After releasing the contraction, push down and out gently, as if you were having a bowel movement with your PC muscle. Repeat: *Gently.* No bearing down.

4. *Now create Kegel sequences that combine long and short repetitions with push outs.* After two months of daily repetitions of 300, you should have a well-developed PC muscle. You can keep it that way by doing 150 repetitions several times a week.

Kinky Sex

(see also Anal Sex, Fetishism, Paraphilias)

"Kink" is a subjective term and thus difficult to define. Sometimes it is used as a pejorative word identifying the sexual behaviors of someone else, not *us*. Often "kink" merely describes sexual behavior less inhibited than that of the stereotypical "average" couple.

Twenty-five years ago oral sex and masturbation, which are part of most people's sexual repertoire, were frequently labeled "kinky." Though people surely masturbated as often as they do now, few openly admitted to doing so; and the practice was not condoned by teachers, preachers, even therapists. Today "kinky sex" is generally considered to include those practices outside foreplay, intercourse, masturbation, and oral lovemaking—practices such as fetishism and cross-dressing, bondage, spanking, exhibitionism, S/M (short for sadomasochism), and perhaps heterosexual anal sex, which is probably more mainstream than the others.

How common is kinky sex? Anywhere from 10 to 30 percent of the population may have experimented with one form of kink or another at least once. Some experts believe that sex has gotten kinkier in the past decade and attribute the change to several factors, including the desire of couples to spice up their monogamous relationships through sexual game playing and the prevalence of kinky images in the media, such as light bondage and leather clothing.

Light kink can be just another way of adding variety to one's sex life. Some people have a greater need for variety than others; and some people enjoy experiencing the strong sexual sensations associated with bondage, spanking, and other behaviors. More exotic forms of sex play can be incorporated into an erotic life that includes tender and emotional episodes of lovemaking. If sexual practices cause pain or humiliation or become obsessive—the only way you can become aroused and reach orgasm—they are cause for concern. And, of course, no one should feel coerced by a partner into doing something he or she does not want to do.

EXAMPLE

"We were the couple who did it in the bathroom at college parties," said Shelley. "Len and I need to push the limits sometimes to keep the sex hot in our relationship."

Married fifteen years, Shelley and Len consider themselves "erotic explorers." Their lovemaking runs the gamut from "soft and sweet" to "intense and a little rough." They occasionally enjoy anal sex, bondage, and spanking.

"We like to role-play sometimes," Shelley explained. "One of us might be feeling submissive and want to be the bad boy or bad girl and be punished by Mommy or Daddy. Being turned over a knee and spanked a few times is exciting. We couldn't tell you why. It just is."

Their favorite kinky sex game is "tie and tease." One partner ties the other's wrists and ankles with silk scarves. The bound partner is repeatedly teased to the edge of orgasm, brought back down, and teased again.

"We have the most explosive orgasms this way," Shelley reported. "Being bound is like being on vacation. You aren't responsible. The other person is in charge of providing the pleasure. But there is excitement in both roles. Being in charge has an erotic kick all its own." ∎

The Five Most Common Forms of Kinky Sex Play

1. *Heterosexual anal sex.* (See Anal Sex.) This has to be practiced with care and only with full consent.

2. *Bondage.* Using silk scarves or ties or Velcro restraints (purchased in sex-toy stores or catalogs), loosely bind your partner's wrists and/or ankles. Then stimulate him or her sexually. The object of bondage is to prolong the arousal phase of lovemaking for your partner, thus creating a stronger orgasm when he or she is "allowed" to come.

3. *Spanking.* A few light swats on the rear with hand or the back of a hairbrush is very arousing for some people.

4. *Light S/M.* More theater than pain, S/M games are erotic power plays. One partner plays the dominant, who "controls" the erotic action and administers light pain, physical or psychological or both. The other partner, the submissive, receives, for example, the velvet covered whip across the buttocks or the order to kneel and kiss the dominant's genitals. As in all plays, costumes are a major part of the production. Gear includes leather, fishnet stockings, very high heels, garter belts, even masks.

5. *Exhibitionism/voyeurism.* Some couples shoot videos of themselves making love and watch them later to get excited all over again. Other couples delight in having sex in semi-public places such as their backyard. In one game, a woman might dress in a revealing outfit and wait for her partner in a bar. Obviously, the rules of common sense apply.

Kissing

Done well, a kiss can be one of the sexiest exchanges between lovers. A kiss is usually the first intimate physical contact with a new lover, making it the first erotic impression, the introduction to the physical being of another person. A kiss leads the way to knowing the other with our body rather than just with our minds.

Some people find kissing the most intimate erotic act. Prostitutes rarely kiss their clients, reserving mouth-to-mouth contact for their personal lives. Often men and women engaged in low emotional-involvement affairs exchange only the most perfunctory of kisses. Not wanting to be kissed by your partner can be a signal of trouble in the relationship.

Prolonged and passionate kissing is also very arousing, particularly to women. The mouth, like the genitals, is rich in nerve endings. A few women can reach orgasm through kissing alone. And some people, again particularly women, believe they can tell a lot about a person's lovemaking style by their kiss alone.

Kissing is no place to let your lovemaking skills get rusty. Yet many people do just that in long-term relationships. A lackluster love-life can be rekindled with a good kiss.

What men and women say about kissing

From a 20-year-old woman: "A kiss that is wet and soft is a glimpse at vulnerability. It is an invitation for more."

A 38-year-old man says: "I remember a particular kiss as one of the most passionate experiences of my life. We were listening to Dvorak's Symphony Number 8 in G major. We began kissing and just kept at it through the entire symphony, merging into each other, mouth to mouth, breathing as if one, tongues flirting, and just taking in marvelous sensations. I felt as if I were seeing her through her lips. When our mouths parted, I felt no less satisfied than I would have if we'd been having intercourse."

And from a 30-year-old woman: "I know if a man is going to be a good lover or not when we share the first passionate kiss. If he pushes a fat, flabby tongue straight into my mouth, I don't want to go any further with him. But if he first licks and nibbles and sucks my lips and tongue, I do."

$\mathcal{S}$ix Essential Kissing Tips

1. *Start with a kissable mouth.* Brush before lovemaking whenever you can. If you can't brush, suck on a breath mint before you kiss.

2. *Tease with your lips.* With mouth slightly open, lips firm but not rigid, begin the kiss in a light, playful way.

3. *After touching lips softly, pull away.* Lightly lick or suck your partner's lips. Alternate this tongue play with gentle kissing.

4. *Let your partner's mouth extend the invitation before entering.* When she/he is ready for a deeper kiss, his or her mouth will fall open. Don't force your tongue inside.

5. *Vary the pace of your kissing.* To keep the kiss stimulating, move from slow to urgent, hard—but not too hard—to soft.

6. *Learn the art of the French kiss.* A French kiss is *not:* insert tongue, push hard down throat. Use your tongue lightly to explore your partner's mouth. Run it over his or her lips, teeth, tongue, and the moist recessed areas inside the mouth. With the tip of your tongue, trace the inside of your lover's lips and around his or her tongue. Thrust your tongue lightly and quickly in and out of your partner's mouth.

Lovebites

A popular form of sexplay is the love bite. More a gentle nibble than a true bite, it was so commonly practiced in ancient times that the Hindu erotic writers composed lengthy lists of where and how hard to "bite." In his landmark study of sexual behavior, Kinsey reported that 50 percent of people surveyed felt at least some arousal from being nibbled during lovemaking. In our time, some people, particularly the young, prize "hickeys," marks left typically on the neck by overzealous lovers who actually create the bruised effect by sucking rather than biting.

Most effective love bites really are a combination of light nibbling, sucking, and licking.

What people say about lovebites

From a 41-year-old woman: "I like it when my husband makes a growling noise and nibbles the insides of my thighs. Maybe this sounds silly, but it really turns me on."

A 30-year-old man says: "I like having my nipples bitten, but not hard. I can get an erection from my partner sucking and biting my nipples, even if I've just ejaculated. It's as if there's a hot wire running from my nipples to my penis."

And a 29-year-old woman says: "Biting and being bitten during sex is a primal experience. I like to graze my lover's testicles with my teeth and have him graze my genitals with his teeth. But the teeth should never sink in. That would hurt. There's a thrill in feeling the edge of someone's teeth against your most sensitive parts."

The Five Best Spots to Love Bite

1. *Ears.* Nibble the fleshy lobes. Then run your tongue inside the ear.
2. *Neck.* Nibble and suck the neck, and don't forget the nape.
3. *Fingers and toes.* The extremities are often neglected during love-making. Suck. Occasionally take a small nibble while sucking.
4. *Nipples.* Don't forget his nipples. Many men have sensitive nipples but are afraid to ask for stimulation there.
5. *Genitals.* More sucking and licking than nibbling here. Be very gentle. Teeth should graze, not sink in. If your partner flinches or pulls away, sheath those teeth!

Lovemaps

WHAT IS A LOVEMAP?

Both the term and the theory behind it were created by famed sex researcher John Money, Ph.D. He discovered that patterns of arousal are formed in childhood when the brain develops a lovemap through interactions with parents, other adults, and peers. Early experiences you may not even remember are placed on the map. As an adult, the kinds of sexual activity you prefer and the partners you choose as well as your paths to arousal are all influenced if not determined by this lovemap in the brain.

Everyone has a lovemap. According to Money, some people have "vandalized" lovemaps, often as the result of childhood abuse of one form or another. Their arousal patterns cause them to become, for example, foot fetishists who are aroused only by feet or shoes, or sadomasochists who need to give or receive pain to become aroused—or perhaps people who are unable to find pleasure in sexual activity. In extreme cases, those with vandalized lovemaps act out in violent ways.

Most of us, however, have lovemaps that predispose us to find, for example, petite redheaded women or tall blond men attractive. It is helpful to understand not only your own but also your partner's predisposition for certain lovers or particular ways of making love. With knowledge, you can find ways of increasing arousal.

EXAMPLE

Cynthia sometimes thinks that Allen married her for her long, shapely legs. A self-confessed "leg man," he can rarely resist the temptation to look at another pair of beautiful legs when they are out together. He favors lovemaking positions that emphasize her legs. All this attention paid to legs makes her uncomfortable.

"Allen likes to do it missionary style because he likes to feel my legs wrapped around his body," she says. "But I don't have orgasms often in that position. I like to be on top. When I'm not, I feel stifled."

"No matter what position she's in, she's passive," Allen complains. "Yes, I like to feel her legs around my waist or neck, to pull back and see them as I'm making love to her. If she really lost herself in passion in some other position, I wouldn't object."

When pressed, Allen can trace his love of legs to early childhood memories of his long-legged young mother and her friends, women who were often dressed in shorts or bathing suits because the family lived in southern California. Perhaps he's right about the origins of his love of legs. Establishing a lifelong arousal pattern, Allen may have experienced erections while playing on the floor surrounded by all those female legs.

Cynthia's earliest sex memory may also help explain her sexual passivity.

"I was nine or ten and staying with my parents at my grandmother's house," she says. "It was summertime. My mother's mother had made up a bed for me on the sun porch. I could hear my parents having sex—he was grunting softly

and the bed was squeaking in the guestroom—so I tiptoed to the window and peeked inside.

"There was just enough moonlight shining in the windows for me to see them. He was on top of her with the sheet pulled up to his shoulders. She wasn't making any noise. I was afraid I would get caught so I tiptoed back to my own bed. In a very short time, the noise stopped. She never did make a sound." ■

Maybe Cynthia's mother was inhibited by making love in her own mother's house or maybe she was sexually inhibited most of the time. Whatever the reason for her passivity that night, it left a place on Cynthia's lovemap. Did this one experience determine her sexual responses for life? Of course not. The lovemap is more complicated than that. And now that Claudia sees how the incident may have impacted upon her present behavior in bed, she's able to dilute its influence on her.

Any couple can probably improve their sex life by learning about their lovemaps.

Three Steps for Creating a New and Positive Lovemap

1. *Each make a private assessment of your personal lovemap.* Use the following questions as a guide, but don't be limited by them:
   - Describe the first explicit sex scene you actually witnessed in person. Can you see how that incident still has influence on your arousal and responses?
   - What do you know or surmise about your parents' sexuality?
   - What forms of childhood and adolescent sex play did you have with others?
   - Describe your childhood sweethearts. Have you formed adult relationships with people who have similar characteristics?
   - What can you remember about your early masturbation experiences?
   - How and when did you lose your virginity?
   - When did you have your first orgasm? Describe the experience.

2. *Share your assessments.* Can you see how both lovemaps might have been created? Now that you have more understanding about how preferences developed, can you find ways of helping each other build on the old maps and make richer new ones?

3. *Each let the other know in very specific terms how you would like lovemaking to change.* Complete the following sentences to get started:

- To arouse me, I would like you to _____.
- To bring me to the point of orgasm, I would like you to _____.
- When I am having an orgasm, I would like you to _____.

Lubrication

(see also Desire, Hormones, Menopause)

Vaginal dryness, the failure of the vagina to lubricate when a woman is sexually stimulated, is typically associated with aging, or worse, with frigidity. Approximately 60 percent of women over 40 have some problem with dryness; and about 35 percent of women under 40 do at one point or another in their lives, making this a not strictly age-related issue. If a woman does not produce adequate secretions during arousal, lovemaking can be painful for both partners. As a result, they may avoid sexual contact; and prolonged avoidance can cause problems of its own, including male impotence. For women who do not produce sufficient lubrication, prolonged, frequent, or vigorous intercourse can cause chafing and irritation to the vaginal walls and urethra and perhaps lead to bladder infections.

The causes of vaginal dryness are varied. Some women do not produce copious amounts of lubrication at any point in their lives, regardless of how aroused they are. Some may produce adequate amounts of lubrication for ordinary lovemaking, but become dry during a prolonged session. Other women may experience dryness due to fluctuating hormone levels during their menstrual cycles. In the second half of the cycle, the body produces less estrogen. Vaginal dryness is, of course, one of the symptoms of menopause, when the body's production of estrogen dramatically declines. Certain medications, including antidepressants, oral contraceptives, and fertility drugs can cause dryness, as can the use of latex condoms without a lubricant.

There is also a psychological component to lubrication. Fear and anxiety can inhibit lubrication. In some cases, a woman may feel arousal, but find her body is not responding for psychological reasons. She may have some ambivalence about the relationship. Or she may not be lubricating simply because she is not being sufficiently aroused by her partner.

A woman can feel as if her sexuality is in doubt when lubrication is a problem. And a man can feel the same way about his sexuality when he consistently "fails" to arouse his partner to lubricate. Before vaginal dryness becomes a relationship issue, look at possible physical and psychological factors, as well as remedies.

EXAMPLE

"We are at a stand-off sexually," said Claudia about her marriage to Greg. Both in their thirties, they have been married for two years and have a one-year-old son. "He wants to have intercourse every day. In the beginning of our marriage, I accommodated him. With the demands of my job and the baby, I just don't want it that often. Now I find that I don't lubricate enough to make sex enjoyable, and that makes him angry too."

Greg said, "Claudia is never in the mood for sex. After the baby was born, she pleaded headaches and fatigue though we have live-in help. I think she's frigid. Nothing I do can get her excited anymore."

Claudia countered the charge of "frigidity" by calling him "a lousy lover." Her vaginal secretions, or the lack of them, had become another fighting issue in their marriage. When medical tests showed no physical reason for her dryness problem, each became more vehement in criticism of the other. ∎

Claudia's vaginal dryness was clearly psychological in origin. When they began working on their relationship in therapy, the situation improved. Now communication between them has improved and they have learned how to make compromises centered around the issue of their disparate desires.

Four Steps to Take in Relieving Vaginal Dryness

1. *Get a check-up.* Tell your doctor that vaginal dryness is a problem. Could medications you're currently taking be a causal factor? Do blood tests show insufficient estrogen production? Is estrogen-replacement therapy indicated?

2. *Talk to your partner.* If physical causes have been ruled out, the two of you need to look at other possibilities. Are there hidden unresolved issues in the relationship? In your own attitudes about your sexuality? Is your partner failing to arouse you?
3. *Use a lubricant.* Choose one of the water-soluble products made specifically for this purpose. Oil-based lubricants can damage condoms, block the pores in the vagina, and incubate a vaginal infection.
4. *Have more sex.* Studies have shown that regular sexual activity, including masturbation, encourages the vagina to produce more lubrication.

Marriage (and/or Monogamy), spicing up

(see also Boredom [sexual], Extramarital Affairs, Calendar [romantic], Communication, Intimacy, Joy Break, Romance, Trust)

Many people find their greatest emotional and sexual satisfaction within a committed relationship. The state of being "in love" may be temporary, lasting anywhere from six months to two years, but it is replaced in good relationships by a deeper, more solid kind of love. Most couples accept that the fever pitch of courtship cannot be sustained indefinitely. In the best marriages, there are sexual peaks and valleys, the peaks often coinciding with periods of increased intimacy. A good way of improving the sex is deepening the intimacy. Truly great sex, of the lasting variety, is more likely to happen within a committed emotional relationship than outside one.

In marriage, or in any other long-term monogamous relationship, sex can easily become routine, perfunctory, predictable, even dull, but it doesn't have to be that way. After a couple have been together for some time, they may complain that the excitement is missing or the "thrill" is gone. What's missing is the aura of anticipation, the

155

sense of intrigue, the willingness to take the time and effort to surprise and delight each other.

The married couple know when they are going to have sex and more or less how they are going to have sex and how it will turn out for each of them. With exclusivity comes security and stability and a dulling of the erotic edge that keeps one awake wondering what the beloved is doing on the nights they aren't together making passionate love. You can recapture some of this edge, without losing security and stability, and bring something new into an established relationship, but you have to get rid of that old attitude first.

Marriage does not have to be the sexual equivalent of a bland but nutritious meal. If yours is, toss in some spice.

EXAMPLE

"Jennifer and I have been married for six years," said Bob. "Sex is very comfortable. We are mostly in agreement on issues such as frequency and oral sex, but we don't have much variety in our lovemaking beyond oral sex and intercourse. I don't want to have an affair, but increasingly I crave some excitement.

"There are things I wouldn't suggest doing with Jennifer, like talking dirty in bed. Something about marriage makes it hard to have nasty sex."

Prompted by a discussion they were having about a friend's affair, Bob finally expressed his desires to Jennifer. Was she shocked and hurt to discover that her husband occasionally wanted "nasty" sex?

"Women get bored too!" she retorted. "I didn't want to hurt Bob's feelings, but I often felt like he was rushing through lovemaking to get to the end. He wasn't putting the same kind of thought and energy into pleasing me he once did. We don't have any sexual problems, but we don't have very hot sex either."

With effort, any couple can expand the erotic boundaries confining their relationship. ■

The Five Steps to Rekindling Marital (Monogamous) Sex

1. *Eliminate performance goals.* Stop thinking you have to make love a certain number of times a week or have an orgasm or more than one orgasm every time. Creativity and spontaneity do not thrive in a goal-

oriented setting. (See the following list for creative lovemaking suggestions.)

2. *Think dirty.* Are you censoring your fantasies and desires because you think your partner would be offended by less than wholesome sex? You may be surprised.

3. *Surprise each other in nonsexual ways.* Meet her for dinner wearing a bow tie. Send him flowers. Do something unexpected, even out of character, and see how your partner reacts.

4. *Be playful.* Have a snowball fight. Feed each other cookie dough. Inject a note of youthful exuberance into every day, no matter what your age. Then carry that sense of play into the bedroom.

5. *Experiment sexually.* Make love in a new position—and don't be embarrassed to laugh if it's awkward. Try a sexual technique you read in a book or saw on a video. Agree not to make love in the same old way for a week.

Beyond Bubblebaths and Lingerie—Twelve Less Obvious Ideas for Reviving a Tired Sex Life

1. Play a game of strip monopoly.
2. Unplug the TV.
3. Dance nude by candlelight.
4. Make love blindfolded.
5. Give your partner a pedicure.
6. Write each other an erotic poem.
7. Sneak off to the kitchen to feel each other up during dinner at your parents' house.
8. Feed each other an entire meal, including mashed potatoes, with your fingers.
9. Have a conversation about sex in which you talk about fantasies without asking, "Did you ever really try that with someone else?" or "Do you fantasize doing that with someone else and not me?"
10. Schedule a risqué rendezvous, a date for making love in the backseat of the car, in his or her office after hours, or someplace else.
11. Rent a costume when it's not Halloween. Wear it to seduce your partner.
12. Have a picnic in bed. Chinese take-out, wine, and candlelight. Eat it in the nude.

Marriage, open

In an "open" marriage, both partners agree to have outside lovers. Sexual nonexclusivity in marriage is not a new idea though the term "open marriage" is a product of modern times. In some cases, the partners openly discuss their lovers with each other, while in others, they don't. Most couples who live this way have established some ground rules, which typically limit the emotional involvement either partner will have in an outside relationship.

The survival of an open marriage depends on both partners being able to have sex without emotional commitment and being able to maintain the delicate balance between their life together and their lives apart. Can that be done? Obviously, some people can live this way. Probably most can't. But, with the divorce rate at nearly 50 percent, an argument can be made that many traditional marriages don't work either.

Sometimes one partner proposes an open marriage as a transition between marriage and divorce. He or she may be unwilling or unable to make the emotional commitment monogamy requires yet isn't ready to lose the security and stability of the marriage either. The other partner, perhaps fearful of being left alone, may reluctantly agree to the new terms. In that scenario, the most likely outcome is separation.

EXAMPLE

"We were married for less than a year when I found out Dick was cheating on me," Kaye said. "He told me that he loved me but couldn't be faithful to any woman for the rest of his life. I was in agony. I loved him so much and couldn't imagine my life without him. He suggested an open marriage and reluctantly I agreed.

"It was only open on his end for several years. I went through periods, especially after our son was born, when I accepted the situation pretty well. I didn't ask questions. He kept his word about not letting outside affairs take him away from me or our child. But sometimes I really suffered the torments of hell wondering if he was with someone and who she was. A few times I cried and screamed at him, demanding he tell me all the details. He wouldn't."

After ten years of marriage, Kaye's end of the relationship opened up too. She met a man on a business trip and had a brief affair.

"It was liberating," she says. "I had a few more affairs and then I began to worry about STDs, both from the men I was seeing and from the women I knew my husband saw. Finally, I knew this wasn't the way I wanted to live and I told Dick I wanted a divorce. He was devastated. He even promised to stop seeing other women. I don't know if I believed him or not, but it didn't matter anymore." ■

What should you do if you or your partner wants an open marriage? Ask yourselves the following questions. Examine the answers carefully, perhaps with the help of a therapist.

The Essential Open Marriage Questions

1. Can you separate sex and love?
2. Are you good at keeping your emotions in check?
3. Are you well educated on how STDs are spread and their symptoms? Are you willing to assume the health risks and responsibilities of non-monogamous sex?
4. If you have young children, have you considered how your extramarital relationships might affect them?
5. Are you equally capable of handling an open marriage?
6. Has jealousy ever been an issue in your relationship?
7. How stable and secure is the relationship?
8. How will you handle the situation if an outside lover becomes a threat to your marriage?
9. Have you fully explored your motivations with your partner for wanting an open marriage?

Marriage, sexless

Approximately 10 to 15 percent of married couples have sex only a few times a year or not at all. Some are older adults who have abandoned lovemaking for physical or psychological reasons, many of them not necessarily impediments to sex. (See Aging, Hormones.) But a substantial number of people who live in sexless marriages are couples in the prime of life, from their twenties to their early fifties. They look like other couples and probably treat each other with courtesy, even affection, in public.

Their reasons for withdrawing sexually are diverse. Some couples have lost all desire to make love, perhaps as the result of repeated performance problems. (See Desire.) In the most common pattern, the couple has let buried anger and hidden resentments stifle their sexual urges. They don't know how to deal with their anger or communicate their feelings or change their behavior. In some cases, deeply held negative beliefs about sexuality have poisoned one or both partners' attitudes. Two people who think sex is "dirty" and shameful may be able to squelch all erotic thoughts and feelings after the heat of courtship has subsided.

If you can't remember the last time you made love or, worse, the last time sexual energy passed between the two of you, sex may be disappearing in your marriage.

EXAMPLE

"I never did feel the earth move," Tanya said. "When we were dating, we were very passionate about each other. We had a lot of stimulating foreplay and oral sex, but I never had an orgasm. In the first year of our marriage, we continued to have that same kind of passion but again I never had an orgasm."

Married seven years, Tanya and Dwayne, both in their late thirties, haven't made love in almost two years. While they both profess love for each other, they have stopped all sexual touching. Furthermore, they don't even talk about sex.

"I wonder if I'm normal," Tanya admitted, "if we're normal. I wonder if Dwayne still finds me attractive."

When pressed, Dwayne acknowledged the same doubts and fears.

"Our desire for a child drove us to see a therapist," he said. "In the therapist's office we acknowledged that neither of us knows how the other thinks or feels about the subject of why we haven't had sex in two years. Is it too late? Can we have sex again after all this time?" ■

In Dwayne and Tanya's case, the lovemaking had stopped because she had been continually frustrated by her failure to reach orgasm. Rather than telling him she was dissatisfied and exploring ways of his giving her pleasure, she withdrew. Hurt and confused, he also withdrew. Couples who have lived without sex in their marriage are often embarrassed about making an overture toward each other. But the good news is that it is never too late to start making love again.

Five Steps for Putting Sex Back in Your Marriage

1. *Talk*. If you don't talk about it with each other, and preferably with a sex therapist, the situation won't change.
2. *Understand the problem*. Couples must acknowledge the other's dissatisfactions before they can understand why they've stopped reaching out sexually.
3. *Separate the nonsexual issues from the sexual ones*. These types of sexual impasses don't get better with time. A sexual problem like this one can't be solved by itself. What are the reasons for anger, resentment, withholding?
4. *Treat dysfunctions*. Some sexual dysfunctions require medical attention, but most can be treated in sex therapy.
5. *Teach each other new sexual techniques*. You can learn how to give each other pleasure. Open the lines of communication and talk about what you want, what feels good, and what doesn't.

Massage, erotic

Erotic massage is tactile stimulation in the form of caressing, fondling, cuddling, embracing, and stroking. The aim is to give sensual and sexual pleasure that is different from the goal of a regular massage, relaxing stiff muscles and reducing body tension. Practically every sexual relationship could be improved if the partners occasionally took the time to give each other an erotic massage. In addition, it is a useful tool in helping couples with sexual difficulties overcome their anxiety about physical contact. Such nondemand (no performance pressure) touching is part of the sex therapist's standard prescription.

There is a hunger for body contact within all of us. Research has shown that babies suffer impaired development if they are not touched. In adults, the need to be touched varies in intensity from person to person and in the same person from time to time, but it is present in all of us. Yet touching is often neglected in relationships. Too many of us have been programmed to avoid touching or to confine it to a few permissible circumstances such as sex, athletics, casual greetings, and aggressive expressions.

Couples who minimize physical contact—exclusive of sexuality—are in danger of losing their emotional link to each other. If they ignore their desire for tactile contact for a long time, they may even lose sexual desire. Touch hunger will eventually evaporate if not fulfilled.

EXAMPLE

"Jane and I were too busy for sex," says Mack. "After a few years of being too busy to make love more than once or twice a month, we were afraid we were going to lose interest in sex altogether and that scared us."

Both in their mid-thirties, Jane and Mack were married for five years when they talked to a sex therapist about their concerns. He helped them develop a plan for getting back "in touch" with each other that fully restored their sexual relationship within several months. Part of their prescription was to give each other an erotic massage once a week but not on the same day. That encouraged them to focus solely on the pleasures of either giving or receiving.

"At first it seemed too artificial to schedule time together for touching one another," he says. "It didn't seem romantic, it seemed more like a duty. But when we thought about it, we realized appointments for erotic massage made a lot of sense because Jane and I are so busy.

"This was like dating again. I liked thinking of it that way. When we did get together the first time it was awkward. Not until our third massage date did we really relax and start to have fun. Now this is part of our routine. We really get a lot out of it.

"Erotic massage has helped me focus on the sensual side of our relationship. It has enriched our love life." ■

Six Steps to an Erotic Massage

1. Use a small amount of scented oil, baby oil, or lotion—warmed in your hands—and lightly massage your partner all over, backside first, using a combination of the following strokes:

- *Gliding.* Let your hands glide over the surface of your partner's body in large movements. Make the long strokes flow into each other. (This is particularly effective on back, chest and breasts, buttocks, and spine.)
- *Kneading.* The pressure should be not as deep as you would use in giving a regular massage. If done with the right pressure at the base of the neck and top of the back, kneading can relieve tension while arousing.
- *Spider walking.* Use your fingerpads as lightly as if they were spider legs to walk all over your partner's body. Barely touch, not tickle, the skin's surface.

2. Use your hair, mouth, and breasts to stroke your partner's body.

3. Massage the buttocks using kneading strokes and finish with light teasing strokes up and down the crack between them. If your partner likes this, continue the stroking down to the anus. Massage the perineum. Ask him or her to turn over.

4. With one hand massage the front of your partner's body using one of the preceding strokes, and with the palm of the other hand begin massaging breasts or chest and nipples. Alternate the palm rubbing with gentle squeezing of the nipples. Massage both breasts, or chest, and both nipples at once.

5. Make slow trips up and down your partner's body between nipples and genitals.

6. Separate your partner's legs. Stroke the inner thighs. Move up to the abdomen and back to the inner thighs. Caress the genitals with one hand while simultaneously massaging abdomen, chest, or thighs. Your partner's desire and level of arousal dictates how far you take genital massage.

Masturbation

Masturbation is self-stimulation of the genitals for pleasure. Our Victorian ancestors considered masturbation a form of self-abuse, a waste of vitality, a destroyer of relationships, a sin. They believed that youthful masturbation retarded the growth of sex organs and resulted in moral, mental, and physical weakness. Shame, guilt, and sorrow accompanied the practice for most people.

The legacy of our ancestors still clouds our thinking; and some people still believe that self-pleasuring is evil. It is not. Nor is it a threat to a relationship as some perceive it to be, unless one partner chronically masturbates while withholding sex from the other. Even in marriage we have the right to enjoy our own bodies without feeling as if we're "cheating" on a spouse.

Masturbation is one of life's little pleasures, a way of experiencing our sexuality that is risk-free and should be guilt-free too. For men and women alike, it provides sexual release when no partner is available and teaches us how our bodies respond so that we might share that information with our lovers. Women who masturbate without guilt are more likely to be uninhibited lovers and to feel comfortable enough to touch themselves during intercourse when they need extra stimulation to reach orgasm. Men who masturbate without rushing through the experience learn to appreciate their own sensuality and how to gain some control over the ejaculatory process.

Masturbation is an affirmation of self-love. Enjoy it without guilt. You are worthy of joy and pleasure.

Top Ten Questions About Masturbation

1. *Why would my partner want to masturbate when I am always there?*

One can delight in the solitary experience of masturbation just as one does in wearing attractive clothes, taking a walk alone in a natural setting, reading a book, or listening to music. People who enjoy sex find pleasure in the full range of their sexuality, which includes masturbation. That is not a rejection of you.

2. *What is mutual masturbation?*

Two people masturbating at the same time! This is a sexy way of having safe sex. Regular partners also enjoy it as a variation on lovemaking. The visual stimulation is exciting for both partners. And there is a built-in educational factor: You learn what manual strokes arouse the other by watching.

3. *How should I masturbate?*

There are many ways of giving self-pleasure. Make it a sensual experience by surrounding yourself with music, candlelight, fragrance. Don't rush and don't forget the lubrication. Use your fingers and/or a vibrator or other sex toy. Some women masturbate by squeezing their thighs together, rubbing against a folded towel or other surface, or in the bath or shower by turning a spray of water on their genitals. Be creative. Experiment with different rhythms to see

if you can sustain the arousal phase longer and induce stronger orgasms.

4. Should I always have an orgasm when I masturbate?

There are no "shoulds" in self-pleasuring. Sometimes you may want to masturbate without reaching orgasm so you will be highly aroused for lovemaking with your partner later. Or you may want to stop short of climax to prolong the excitation period with the intention of masturbating again later. Or you may simply be not in the mood to "finish."

5. How often is it okay to masturbate?

Some people masturbate almost every day and others only once a month or less. Unless you are masturbating so often and/or in inappropriate places such as the office that the practice is interfering with your life, don't worry about how much is "too" much. Needs vary from one person to another and within the same person from one time period to another.

6. What should I do if I catch my child masturbating?

First, understand that this is normal behavior. Children as young as four or five may also have orgasms via masturbation. The majority of men and women begin masturbating in early adolescence.

What should you do if you inadvertently catch your child in the act of masturbating? Don't act as though she/he is doing something dreadfully wrong. Explain that people don't touch their private parts in front of others—and let the subject go. Unless your child compulsively masturbates in public, there is no problem.

7. My partner wants me to stop masturbating altogether. How do I handle this?

Ask your partner to explain his or her objections. Does he or she want more lovemaking and feels cheated by your masturbating? Does he or she think masturbation is wrong? A negative reflection on his or her ability to excite and satisfy you? If frequency of lovemaking is the issue, can you work that out? If your partner's negative attitudes or fears are the problem, explain why you like to enjoy yourself in this healthy way sometimes. Your partner may have to resolve his or her own inner conflicts about self-pleasuring.

8. How can I handle the guilt I feel after masturbating?

Maybe you would feel less guilty if you thought of masturbation as another way of taking care of your body, like exercise, a healthy diet, and getting enough sleep. Masturbation is good for you, in psychological as well as physical ways. (Also, see Guilt for suggestions.)

9. *Why do I have stronger orgasms during masturbation than during lovemaking?*

This is not uncommon. (See Orgasm.) And it is no reflection on your partner's lovemaking abilities. During masturbation, you focus totally on your pleasurable sensations. Nothing distracts you. There are no concerns about pleasing a partner. Your hands do exactly what is needed when it is needed. Not surprisingly, the physical sensations of orgasm seem strong. They are undiluted by emotion.

10. *Why do I fantasize during masturbation?*

Without the presence of a partner, you become and remain aroused through visual stimulation, erotic reading material, or fantasy. (See Fantasy.) Men are more likely to use visual aides such as magazines or videos during masturbation than women are. Women more often use fantasy. Both sexes fantasize things they would not or do not want to do in real life.

Medications, prescribed, sexual effect of

(see also Aphrodisiacs, Desire, Erection, Illness and Disability, Recovery)

With more than 75 million Americans taking medication at any one time, drugs touch all of our lives sooner or later. We use them to lower our blood pressure, for heart conditions, ulcers, infections, and for aches, pains, colds, allergies, and to cope with stress. As we age, the probability of taking medications increases, at the same time sexual responses become more fragile and more easily thrown off by medication side effects.

Prescribed medications can have a negative impact on sexuality. Side effects of some prescription drugs include loss of desire or reduced desire, loss of responsiveness during arousal, inability to achieve erection or ejaculation, or inability to reach orgasm. Not every medication affects sexuality, and sometimes it is difficult to tell if a sexual problem has been caused by medication or by the illness itself. A middle-aged man, for example, with erection ability already somewhat compromised by the aging process, might be unable to get an erection at all once he begins taking a prescription drug. If a change in your patterns of desire and response occurred when you began taking medication, the medication may be responsible.

Compounding the problem is a vast lack of information on specific drugs and their sexual impact. Sometimes a new drug is on the market before these side effects are documented. More likely, the physician and patient are both too embarrassed to broach the subject, or the doctor fears planting the seed of dysfunction by saying, for example, "This drug may cause erectile difficulties." In some cases, a combination of drugs or of drugs and alcohol may cause sexual problems.

Drugs can interfere with sexual functioning at any age, but statistically they do so more often in the older male. Partly that's because so little research has been done on women. A drug manufacturer may list male erectile difficulties as a side effect for a particular medication and list nothing for women simply because women were not tested, not because the drug was found to produce no sexual side effects in them.

EXAMPLE

"Michael blamed his erection problems first on his job and then on me," said Suzanne. "It was very stressful for both of us when we tried to make love and he couldn't get an erection hard enough for penetration. We fought about the situation a lot."

Though Michael suffered from a variety of medical ailments and was taking several medications, they never thought to cast the blame for their sexual problem on prescription drugs.

"I did blame her," he admitted. "She quit work with our second child, and while I knew spending days at home with two preschoolers wasn't easy, I thought she wasn't trying hard enough to keep herself attractive and be seductive for me. I feel foolish about that now. Obviously, I was looking for excuses for my failure in bed."

Their mutual unhappiness drove Michael to make an appointment with a psychologist who specialized in sex therapy. The psychologist did a thorough assessment. While he noted job stress and marital discord, which could affect sexual functioning, he told Michael that one of the drugs he was taking sometimes had the effect of diminishing erectile capacity. Michael consulted his *physician, who changed the medication. Over the next week, Michael's erectile problem disappeared.* ∎

Most side effects disappear when you stop taking the medication. That's fine if the prescription is short term. What can you do if you need to take medication on a long-term basis? Use the following checklist as a guide.

The Medication Action List

1. *Be an informed consumer.* There are more than 200 drugs that according to drug manufacturers' product literature influence sexual performance or enjoyment. Antidepressants and antihypertensives (to control high blood pressure) are the leaders in this category. Read the leaflet accompanying your prescription. If you still have concerns, call the company's 800 number.

2. *Enlist your pharmacist's aide.* Ask him or her about sexual side effects. Also ask if there are other drugs used to treat your problem that don't have those side effects. And, finally, ask if your prescription when taken with another medication or food or alcohol produces these side effects.

3. *Talk to your doctor.* Tell him or her your sexual history. If, for example, the doctor knows you have a history of erectile dysfunction, she or he will try to prescribe something less likely to contribute to that problem. If you are taking other medications, including over-the-counter products, list them.

4. *Report sexual side effects to your doctor immediately.* Share what you have learned from the company's literature and from your pharmacist. Can you change medications? Do something to lessen the sexual impact of them?

5. *Don't talk yourself into a problem.* Chemical reactions vary from one individual to another. Although a prescribed medication may be known to cause sexual side effects in some individuals, it may not affect you. And sometimes the effect is negligible, a small price to pay for the drug's benefits.

6. *Don't stop medication without consulting with your prescribing physician.* Even if you suspect your medication is interfering with your sexual responsiveness, it may be dangerous to abruptly stop a necessary medication.

Mental Health, effect on sexuality

(see also Health and Sexuality, Illness and Disability, Medications)

The connection between mental health and sexuality is an obvious one: You're more likely to feel sexy when you're feeling good about life in general. Anxiety, depression, and the other little psychological ills that beset people from time to time all take their toll on sexuality. Conversely, sexual problems or lack of a sexual partner can affect mental well-being too. Sometimes it's difficult to recognize what came first, mild depression or sexual dysfunction.

Studies have shown that depressed men who are physically healthy have fewer nighttime erections than men who aren't depressed. Both sexes typically report loss of libido or inability to reach orgasm during periods of psychological illness. Often treatment for depression, anxiety, and other conditions includes medications that have side effects that include the further dampening of libido. How does someone get out of the cycle of depression and low libido?

I advise medication as a last resort—for someone suffering from moderate to severe depression, anxiety, or whatever—and then preferably on a short-term basis. You can help yourself climb out of a psychological low place by talking about your situation, possibly with a therapist, seeking and giving hugs, kisses, and other signs of affection, eating a healthful diet, and exercising more. Exercise is, in fact, one of the best ways to elevate mood. Studies have shown that even moderate exercise releases mood-enhancing chemicals called endorphins in the brain.

If you're feeling blue, reach out to the people in your life and get more active.

EXAMPLE

"I never felt really bad, but I never felt good either," Carla said in describing the "mild bout of anxiety and depression" that gripped her last year. "I cried more easily, had less energy, and less patience at work and at home with the kids. When I lost interest in sex, my husband Marty lost patience with me."

Friends had a lot of suggestions for her, including schedule a weekend ren-dezvous alone with Marty, set aside more time for herself and perhaps take a class at the community college, get a makeover. None of these were bad ideas and any one of them might have lifted another person out of a low spot. Carla opted to join a gym.

"I was about 30 pounds overweight and very out of shape," she said. "The gym immediately did two things for me. It gave me a place to be alone doing something just for me. And it gave me the impetus to take off the weight, get back in shape. I had lost myself under those 30 pounds."

Like most people who significantly change their lives, Carla found this behav-ior change led to others. She confronted Marty about the problems in their rela-tionship, problems they had either been ignoring or handling by having "the same old fights."

"A year later I have a renewed body, a renewed marriage, and a revitalized sex life," she said.

When the blues have led to the sexual blahs, take the following steps. ■

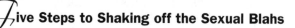 **ive Steps to Shaking off the Sexual Blahs**

1. *Talk.* To your partner, friends, a therapist. Get help identifying and strengthening the underlying attitudes and beliefs that are consistent with being in a good mood.

2. *Improve your diet.* Consult a nutritionist or a doctor who under-stands nutrition for guidance on diet and vitamin supplements.

3. *Show and seek affection.* Hug the kids. Kiss your spouse. Pet the cat. Studies have shown that physical affection, even between humans and animals, elevates mood.

4. *Get physical.* Exercise. If you're out of shape, get a check-up before embarking on a work-out program. Walk. Go dancing.

5. *Put the* as if *principle to work.* Most of us wait to do something—in this case, have sex—until we feel something—in this case, desire. Rather than waiting to feel sexual, initiate some form of lovemaking. Every time you do something, the feelings and ideas consistent with that behavior are reinforced. It's as though the act recharges the feel-ings. Start making love and you may find yourself feeling the desire to continue.

I'm exhausted. I could really use a good soak," Kathleen told Jay when she got home from work. She kissed him lightly and went into their bathroom, where she turned on the taps and stripped off her clothes. She poured in some bath oil and stepped into the warm, rushing water.

The door opened behind her. "Mind if I join you?" Jay asked. He leaned over the edge of the tub to kiss the soft skin under her right ear and she latched on, throwing an arm around his neck and pulling him toward her. His blue denim workshirt was soaked when he leaned away. "Hey!"

She splashed the water up at him, completely soaking him. In mock anger, he stripped off his clothes, and she pretended to be shocked as he dove for her. The water sloshed on the floor and she turned off the faucets so that they could dunk each other.

Jay poured shampoo into his palm and massaged the bubbles into her long red hair. Then he let his soapy palms move down her neck and shoulders, and he inscribed circles of bubbles around her full breasts. He let his other hand roam further down so he could stroke her soft pubic hair.

Kathleen grabbed the bath mit and poured some more bath oil into it. Starting with his muscular thighs, she worked the mit higher as she looped the cloth around his testicles and back between his legs. She played with him, decorating the tip of his now erect penis with soap, then gently dusting it off, then applying more soap more vigorously.

Jay pulled her to her feet, releasing the catch so that the water would start to drain. "Got to get all this soap off," he said, turning on the shower sprayer. He adjusted the nozzle so that three powerful streams of water issued forth, and he held her so that her back was flush against his chest and he directed the water on her breasts, her belly, and her vulva. He told her to spread her legs, and as she did so, the water spurted up into her, creating such a wave of pleasure that she buckled against him. He turned the nozzle again, giving her a fine mist, and trickled it between her rounded buttocks. She pulled the sprayer out of his hand and turned it on him, raising his arms to wash between them, tickling his ribs, and finally switching on one hard stream of water and running the sprayer along the length of his penis and up toward his ass.

They clung to each other as they stepped from the tub and wrapped up in one big bath sheet, pulling another over their wet heads. They wriggled together for a moment, not really getting dry, but just enjoying the sensation of skin on skin.

Jay sat her down on the edge of the tub and picked up one foot, letting the drops fall from her toes into his mouth. He cupped one breast as she drew him closer. The room was steamy, but not only because of the hot water. They got down on the floor and lay on the bathmat like two dolphins at play, rolling around until they were partly dry.

"Suppose I dry off the tub and throw in some towels and pillow? It might work," she said, though he seemed skeptical.

They had just as good a time dry as they had wet. ■

Menopause, effect on sexuality

(see also Aging, Body Image, Desire, Hormones, Hysterectomy, Lubrication)

Menopause is clinically defined as the point at which a woman has not had a period for one year. In the popular literature, the term is used to indicate the months or years before, during, and after the cessation of menstruation, a time when a woman is likely to be affected by a group of physical and psychological changes. Some of those changes impact on her sexuality.

About 85 percent of women experience some symptoms of menopause including hot flashes, night sweats, and vaginal dryness due to plummeting estrogen levels. When estrogen levels drop, the flow of blood to the vagina may also decline, resulting in a decreased sense of pleasure. The severity of symptoms varies greatly among women. Some lose the desire for sex, which may be only partially due to hormonal changes and symptoms such as vaginal dryness (which is easily remedied.) They may have negative attitudes about aging and body image. They may have a partner who has those attitudes or have difficulty finding a sexual partner. A woman who has the opportunity for regular sex in a good relationship is more likely to remain sexually responsive than one who doesn't.

While most women will notice some difference in sexual responsiveness after menopause, these changes are not necessarily all bad. Many women get through menopause with minimal discomfort and find that sex is better after they no longer need worry about contraception. Women who have had heavy or prolonged periods also find menopause liberating. Everything about life, including sex, seems more enjoyable to them. There are benefits, sexual and otherwise, to growing older.

My experience suggests that as with everything else, how you were before will be a major factor in how you are after menopause. If you never enjoyed sex, menopause is a good excuse to close shop. If you love to make love, you will fare just fine during and after the menopause years. There are, of course, other factors that play a major role in sexual desire and responsiveness, such as your attitude about aging, the strength of the relationship you have, and your level of health and self-esteem.

EXAMPLE

❝I began to notice some changes in my sexual responsiveness coinciding with the physical changes I began experiencing prior to menopause," said Sue, a 50-year-old divorced artist. "I don't lubricate as quickly or as fully as I once did. My libido is not as robust as it was. This bothered me because I've always enjoyed sex. I didn't want to lose my sexuality in my fifties."

Sue talked to her gynecologist about her concerns but found him abrupt and glib.

"Perhaps he wondered why a single lady my age would have any interest in sex at all," she said. "I knew from talking to other women that I was not alone in my concerns. Where do women like us go for help?"

Sue wisely decided to look for another doctor, someone who could give her the information she required as well as the support she felt she needed for her sexuality. After studying the pros and cons, she chose hormone-replacement therapy, which alleviated vaginal dryness. With that, her interest in lovemaking returned.

"I'm involved with a man in his late fifties," she said recently. "Our grown children might think we are past the point of making love, but they would be wrong. We have a very satisfying sexual relationship. Menopause is not the end, and it can be a new beginning."

If you are experiencing changes in sexual responsiveness with menopause, take the following steps to restore your erotic equilibrium. ■

𝓔ight Steps to Maintaining Sexual Responsiveness During and After Menopause

1. *Keep sexually active.* Remaining sexual either with a partner or through masturbation can help minimize some of the vaginal changes that occur with menopause. Frequent sexual activity also boosts estrogen production. The phrase "use it or lose it" applies here.

2. *Practice Kegel exercises.* (See Kegels.) This rhythmic contracting and relaxing of the pelvic-floor muscles helps maintain muscle tone. Good muscle tone reduces the possible loss of pleasurable sensation in the genitals.

3. *Give yourself time.* It may take more time for you to become aroused or to respond to sexual stimulation. The vagina may not lubricate as quickly as it once did. Don't push your partner away if your response isn't as fast as it once was.

4. *Choose a healthful lifestyle.* Good physical and mental health becomes more critical to sexual functioning as we age. A lot of the problems, sexual and otherwise, we attribute to aging could be avoided by a more healthful lifestyle, including regular exercise.

5. *Consider hormone-replacement therapy.* Evaluate the risks and benefits by researching the subject and talking to your doctor.

6. *Use a lubricant.* Sometimes all a woman needs is a water-based lubricant to feel as sexual as she did in her youth. You may want to use a lubricant containing hormones on an ongoing basis, not only as an aide to intercourse or masturbation.

7. *Take vitamins.* Evidence indicates that 400 units daily of vitamin E helps reduce symptoms of vaginal atrophy and dryness. Talk to your doctor.

8. *Eat soy products.* Soybeans contain phytoestrogens, which have been shown to strengthen and lubricate vaginal walls. Soy flour, soy milk, tofu, and other soy products can be found in health-food stores and some supermarkets.

Menopause, male

(see also Aging, Desire, Erection, Hormones, Impotence)

Strictly speaking, the word "menopause" does not apply to men. They do not experience a universal shutting down of their ability to procreate as women do. Many older men do, however, have a decline in virility that corresponds with a decline in their production of testosterone. Some European researchers refer to this as the "viropause." However it is described, the response is more gradual than menopause in women, does not affect fertility, and does not happen to all men.

The term "male menopause" has been increasingly used in this country to describe a pattern of behavior also sometimes referred to as the "male midlife crisis" when a middle-aged man experiences erectile difficulties and responds to them by behaving in age-denying ways. In the stereotypical case, he leaves his middle-aged wife for a much younger woman and starts a second family. Not all men can afford to do this, of course, even if they were so inclined; and sometimes today the middle-aged wife is the one who seeks the divorce and finds the younger partner.

The "crisis" in midlife is often one of self-esteem. A man may be at the height of his earning power when he has his first episode of penile failure. The dissonance between his achievements in the world and in the bedroom can be disturbing. Or, he may be coming to the realization he's never going to reach his life goals or be facing employment problems due to corporate downsizing or similar factors. In that case, a bout of temporary impotence can loom very large in his mind. Whatever his professional situation, he, like women his age, is coming to terms with a changed appearance and a sense of declining physical attractiveness. All this and a faltering penis too? For some men, the combination is deadly to the libido.

Interestingly, men are less likely to talk about their "menopause" or crisis than the women in their lives are. Women complain about their partner's depression, moodiness, lethargy, loss of libido. As is the case with midlife women, men in good relationships with understanding partners fare better than others do at midlife.

EXAMPLE

"My husband, Dan, went into a tailspin when he failed to get the promotion he was expecting," said Elizabeth. "He got the bad news a few weeks after his fiftieth birthday. Worse, the job went to a man ten years his junior. He was devastated. And he viewed this as his last chance to make it to the top."

Dan had been experiencing some erectile difficulties before losing the promotion. He had admitted to Elizabeth that his inability to get the rock hard erections of his youth troubled him. More than once he had told her, "I wish I could be the man I was for you again." Her reassurances seemed to mollify him until his crushing professional defeat.

"He became impotent the day another man got his job," she said. "For six months, we did not have sex. At first I was understanding and solicitous. Then I blamed myself for not being attractive enough and I tried hard to seduce him. When my efforts failed, I was hurt and angry. We fought. I accused him of hav-

ing an affair and he retaliated by saying I was looking for an excuse to have one of my own. It was ugly."

Dan and Elizabeth went to see a sex therapist because she threatened to leave him if they didn't. In therapy he confronted his issues about aging and lack of achievement. The therapist also sent him to a physician who put him on testosterone-replacement therapy. Within two months, Dan and Elizabeth were making love again. Both feel their marriage is much stronger now. ∎

If you are middle aged and feeling uncertain about your virility, there are steps you can take to ease this passage of life, whatever you choose to call it.

Ten Steps to Alleviating the Male Midlife Crisis

1. *Don't blame your partner.* If there are issues in your relationship, deal with them. A new partner will bolster your ego. The sex will seem better because new love is invigorating. But the cycle of erectile difficulty and self-doubt will eventually begin again.

2. *Accept that some change in sexual performance and responsiveness is inevitable.* Not all change is bad. On the plus side, older men can make love longer. And it's hoped that they know better how to please their partners.

3. *Adopt a healthier lifestyle.* I know I have said this repeatedly, but I cannot overemphasize the importance (to women as well as men) of nutrition and exercise in maintaining sexual function as we age. A lot of men's problems are caused by sedentary lifestyles, overweight, alcohol, fatty foods, and smoking.

4. *Consider testosterone replacement therapy.* Talk to your doctor. Read on your own. Come to a decision that is right for you based on medical input and your research.

5. *Improve your self-esteem.* When you're feeling good about yourself, you find it easier to give and receive sexual pleasure. Do what it takes to feel better about yourself, for example, through a continuing education program, body building, volunteer work, therapy.

6. *Strengthen your intimate ties.* Deepen the relationship with your partner, with children, parents, and friends.

7. *Become more sensual.* Touch more and take the time to appreciate touch.

8. *Be more romantic.* (See Romance.) Holding hands, taking walks together, writing love notes—these and many other things make you feel younger because you did them when you were young. Why did you stop?

9. *Please your partner.* You can make love without an erection. In fact, you can give your partner fantastic orgasms that will leave her limp and grateful without an erection. Doing so will make you feel potent again.

10. *Get help if you need it.* See a sex therapist if problems persist.

Myths, sexual

Many myths inhibit sexual pleasure. Ascribing to these myths keeps people from exploring their own and their partner's sexuality and learning how to become better lovers. Many of our cultural myths have their basis in religious proscriptions. While few people today believe that sex is only for procreation, many are, consciously or unconsciously, influenced by negative messages about sex passed down to them in the form of myth when they were children or adolescents.

Are any of these myths holding you back?

The Top Ten Myths About Sex

1. *Sex is "dirty."* Even people who don't use the word "dirty" often treat sexual pleasure as something shameful or suspect.

2. *Sex should be natural and spontaneous.* This no-lessons-required school of thought encourages men and women to believe there is something wrong with wanting to learn new techniques and find better ways of giving and receiving pleasure. It also leads to a Puritanical distrust of sex toys, videos, sexy lingerie, and other erotic aides.

3. *There is a "right" way to make love or have an orgasm.* For many years the debate raged over whether a woman "should" have a clitoral or vaginal orgasm. (See Orgasm.) There are many ways to make love and reach orgasm. Sex is not an exact science.

4. *Sex equals intercourse.* In Western society, oral and manual pleasuring are called "foreplay" and it isn't sex unless a penis has been inserted into a vagina. That narrow view of sexuality causes many couples to stop making love during times when intercourse is not possible or feasible.

5. *Sex is a man's responsibility*. Many women still expect men to pay for dates, earn more money, and assume responsibility for initiating sex and bringing her to orgasm. That kind of thinking limits her as much as it does him.

6. *Men are always ready and always want to have sex*. Men are never supposed to say "no" or be allowed not to be in the mood when she is. And, of course, she can't show him tenderness or affection unless she wants sex because he won't be able to control himself. This view of man as sexual animal is demeaning to both sexes.

7. *Sex requires an erection*. A man can give and receive a great deal of pleasure without ever becoming erect. Even intercourse is possible with a semi-erection.

8. *Sex must end in orgasm.* Some women aren't lying when they say they can enjoy lovemaking even if they don't reach orgasm. Particularly as men age, they too can be content with a lovemaking session that does not include orgasm or ejaculation. And, some people deliberately make love without orgasm to intensify the orgasm they will have the next time.

9. *Women have to be in love to enjoy sex*. The corollary of that myth is this piece of "advice" modern women give each other: Sex is wrong unless you're in love. This myth inspires women to commit to a relationship with a man just because they've had sex with him.

10. *Women who love sex are promiscuous*. Our society distrusts women who love sex. They are cast as "whores" while women who have less interest in sex or even difficulty reaching orgasm are seen as today's "madonnas." It is possible to love sex and be highly selective in choosing partners.

Noncoital Sex

(see also Foreplay, Massage [erotic], Oral Sex, Safe Sex)

Noncoital sex is lovemaking without penetration. There are times when it makes medical sense, such as late in pregnancy, during recuperation from childbirth, surgery, or an injury, or while being treated for an STD. Couples who are new to each other sometimes find this a good way of easing into a sexual relationship. And having an alternative plan in case the condom box is empty is always a good idea.

Some couples also practice occasional noncoital sex as a method for creating greater desire for intercourse. By withholding penetration on one night, for example, they set the stage for powerful intercourse the next night. The man is able to get a stronger erection. Both partners may feel their orgasms are more intense than usual.

Lovemaking is an erotic menu filled with many possibilities. Creative lovers don't limit themselves to foreplay and intercourse.

E X A M P L E

"We don't always need penetration to have exciting sex," explained Sharon, and her husband, Joe, nodded his head in enthusiastic agreement. "Sometimes I want Joe to make love to me the way he did when we were teenagers. I don't want him to penetrate me."

Joe and Sharon, in their early forties, have been married for 20 years. They were childhood sweethearts who kept the romance alive during separations while each attended college in a different state and later worked in different cities. And they are still keeping the romance alive.

"People say that sex inevitably gets boring after a few years, because they don't put variety in their lovemaking," Joe said. "sharon and I get a thrill out of making love on the sofa without penetration. We feel like we're kids again, doing something illicit in the den while her parents are asleep upstairs."

Sometimes they masturbate each other or have oral sex or she may squeeze his penis between her thighs or breasts while he thrusts to climax. They massage each other with oils.

"Last night we flirted and teased each other, then writhed around on the floor fully clothed, rubbing against each other until we both came," Sharon said. "Some of our hottest times together aren't in the bedroom and they aren't about intercourse." ■

Five Ways of Having Sex Without Penetration

1. *Outercourse*. Partners can partially undress if they choose, but the underwear stays on. They caress and rub against each other. Sometimes called "dry humping," outercourse as an occasional game can make people feel young again.
2. *Mutual masturbation*. (See Masturbation.) Couples can masturbate each other or watch each other masturbate.
3. *Cunnilingus and fellatio*. (See Oral Sex.) Many people consider cunnilingus and fellatio an integral part of foreplay. Oral lovemaking can be more than the preparation for intercourse. It can stand alone.
4. *Femoral intercourse*. He puts his penis between her thighs with the shaft between the labia, but not inserted into the vagina. She squeezes

her thighs together as he thrusts. Some women find this particularly exciting, especially if the head of his penis brushes her clitoris as he thrusts.

5. *Intermammery intercourse.* (See Breasts.) He places his penis between her breasts as she holds them together, and thrusts. Some couples also enjoy placing his penis in her armpit. This is more commonly practiced in Europe where women do not shave their armpits.

Overcoming Obstacles to Good Sex, daily

What are the daily obstacles that come between you and your partner and a rich, rewarding sex life? Kids, lack of energy and/or time, work problems, money worries, and all the tension generated by life's minor irritations such as mechanical breakdowns, traffic snarls, and visiting relatives.

EXAMPLE

"Someone once said, or should have said, that life is 90 percent maintenance," complained Bruce. "It damn well is. We don't have much time for doing anything enjoyable or relaxing, let alone make love.

"Where can I find the time to be romantic with my wife? The baby is asthmatic. I hear him wheezing at night. It scares the death out of me. I'm always tired. She's always tired. Time or energy for lovemaking is not there.

"With both of us working, every second at home counts. And we both have to take work home, though we promise each other we won't. If it's not work, it's the kids. Sex is almost nonexistent." ▪

No one who has experienced the demands of life in a two-career family with children would say that finding time for a great sex life is easy. It isn't. You simply have to make the time and create the mood. Spontaneity grows out of leisure. How many people in today's world have the luxury of a lifestyle that nurtures spontaneity?

Twenty Suggestions for Overcoming Daily Obstacles to Sex

1. *Become more self-indulgent.* When people have a lot of responsibilities, they begin to feel guilty about taking any kind of pleasure, from a long hot bath to an afternoon at the movies—an attitude that is certain to affect sexuality. Luxuriate in small pleasures.

2. *Schedule one hour a week for just the two of you.* Maybe you'll choose to make love or maybe you'll take a long walk or lie in each other's arms in front of the fireplace. No pressure.

3. *At least once a week give each other a ten-minute massage.* The recipient picks the area to be massaged.

4. *Instead of watching television at night before falling asleep, do something else.* Play a board game or read out loud. One couple keeps a chess set under the bed. They may only play for 10 or 15 minutes, but the activity brings them closer together than watching the tube.

5. *Coordinate bedtimes.* Go to bed at the same time at least one or two nights a week.

6. *Do not discuss issues that are likely to lead to angry exchanges in the hour before bedtime.* Your grandmother was right when she gave you that tried-and-true piece of marital advice: Don't go to bed mad.

7. *Have a real dinner together at least once a week.* If you can afford to go out alone, do so. Otherwise, plan one leisurely meal at home, serving the dishes the kids don't like.

8. *Learn how to stop negative thoughts.* When you can't stop thinking about the irritations and injustices of the day, make yourself stop. Each time you have a negative thought, hit the pause button on the mental VCR. Replace it with a positive thought.

9. *Set your clock for midnight love.* Set your alarm for 90 minutes after you fall asleep—when the body's first sexual sleep cycle begins. Take

a shower together and make love. Yes, you're skeptical, but try it anyway.

10. *Set your clock for an hour earlier.* Make love in the morning when the male testosterone level is at its highest.

11. *Exorcise bedroom ghosts.* The ghosts of former spouses and lovers sometimes move into the bedrooms of couples who are feeling stressed and distant from each other. Banish those fleeting sexual thoughts of the other man or woman.

12. *Recognize deep anger and depression.* Both can dampen libido and may require professional help.

13. *Stop worrying about frequency.* Every couple lives through periods when sex is less frequent for a variety of reasons. If the quality is good, don't worry about the quantity.

14. *Give each other permission to be someone else.* Have you become trapped in your roles—parent, jobholder, caretaker of aging parents, and so on? Play like children. Pretend for the night that you are characters from a favorite book or film or even fairy tale. A new role may set your libido free.

15. *Come out as a married couple.* If your kids are old enough to understand, tell them you love each other and make love and need to have your privacy respected. When the bedroom door is closed, they shouldn't intrude.

16. *Deal with the issues of aging parents in a caring but realistic way.* Involve siblings or your own children in the caretaking as much as possible. Do what you can for parents who need parenting and don't feel guilty for investing emotional energy into your own marriage and family.

17. *Keep work out of home life as much as possible.* If you must bring work home, set it aside for the first and last hours of the evening. Discourage business associates from calling at home.

18. *Reevaluate your spending habits and financial goals if money is a constant problem.* Serious money problems have a negative impact on a couple's sex life. Buried resentment over money issues may be a contributing factor to the no-time-for-sex syndrome.

19. *Masturbate—but not to orgasm.* A little self-arousal in the morning, for example, can lead to lovemaking that night.

20. *Find a reason to be grateful every day.* Get in the habit of appreciation. Instead of dwelling on the faults of your spouse, children, coworkers, parents—give thanks for the happiness they bring into your life.

Oral Sex

Oral sex is the stimulation of a partner's genitals by mouth or tongue. The practice is called "cunnilingus," when the genitals being stimulated are female and "fellatio" when the genitals are male. According to most surveys and research studies, the overwhelming majority of Americans have both received and given oral sex in their lifetime. Often these activites are part of foreplay because they typically increase arousal. For some women, cunnilingus is the primary means of being orgasmic during lovemaking. Both men and women find physical and psychological pleasure in the giving and receiving of oral sex.

Many people consider oral sex a more intimate act than intercourse. Technique is probably more important here than it is in other forms of lovemaking too. For these reasons and others, including hygiene issues, some people may be a little reluctant to perform or receive oral sex, particularly with a new partner.

Men generally report a somewhat greater comfort level with both receiving and giving oral sex. In fact, they often tell researchers they want more of it than their partners do. Why the discrepancy? Women still internalize more negative sex messages as they are growing up than men do. Receiving cunnilingus may seem "selfish" to them. They are more likely to believe that their genitals produce offensive odors than men are. And they may believe that giving oral sex is degrading or that receiving it puts them in a position of extreme vulnerability.

Increasingly, the ability to give and receive oral sex is an important part of lovemaking. Many men and women now expect it as part of foreplay; and some men also like to give their partners an orgasm this way before intercourse so they can be sure of satisfying her. One partner's reluctance or refusal to participate in oral lovemaking can cause tension in a relationship.

EXAMPLE

"Jim wants to get married, and the only thing stopping me from saying, 'yes,' is oral sex," said Connie. "He will gladly receive it, but he never returns the favor. Jim is not a selfish person in other ways, so I can't understand his attitude about this. I moved from hinting to openly asking for cunnilingus. He *said it's something he just can't bring himself to do because it doesn't seem manly.*

"I love him, and he is everything I would want in a husband and father of my children. But this one issue stands in the way. I can't see committing myself to a man who won't do this for me."

When Jim understood that his refusal to perform cunnilingus was going to cost him the love of his life, he consented to talk to a sex therapist about the problem. His reluctance was not based in a deep-seated fear or dislike of female genitalia, but in performance anxiety. As a young adult, he'd been told by a woman as he was performing cunnilingus on her that he didn't know how to do it right. She'd roughly pushed him away from her. He hadn't tried again with her or anyone else.

Once Connie understood the basis for Jim's behavior, she was supportive and encouraging, and he discovered that mastering cunnilingus with a willing and helpful partner was not difficult at all. ■

*H*ow to Get a Reluctant Partner to Give and Receive Oral Sex

1. *Understand where the reluctance is coming from.* Is your partner motivated by religious or other prohibitions, fear of performance failure, a general dislike of anything "messy," or other factors? Talk about his or her feelings calmly. Often talking about our prejudices and fears with an understanding and nonjudgmental person helps dispel them.

2. *Get clean.* Bathe or shower together as part of foreplay. Consider a pubic trim. Some men find trimmed pubic hair very attractive and less intrusive during cunnilingus.

3. *Use learning aides.* Videos can be both instructive and exciting. Screen them before viewing with your partner to be sure you've selected those that give a clear view of oral sex being performed and make it look like fun for both parties.

4. *Find a position that is both physically and psychologically comfortable.* Some men feel humbled by your kneeling at his feet, for example, or women by your kneeling between her legs. Let the reluctant partner choose the position.

5. *Be patient.* Give your partner time to warm up to the idea. When he or she does try oral sex, be encouraging and generous in your praise.

The Six Steps for Performing Cunnilingus

1. *Set the mood.* Don't go straight for her genitals. Lightly massage the area between her navel and pubic hair. Then stroke her inner thighs.

2. *Get into a comfortable position.* The two primary positions for cunnilingus are:
   - The woman lying on her back with her legs drawn up and spread, the man lying between her legs, his arms under her legs, his hands gently supporting her buttocks. A pillow under her buttocks can help put her in position for him to stimulate her clitoris and labia.
   - The man on his back, the woman kneeling over his face with one leg on each side. A pillow under his head can provide more comfort for him.

3. *Master the basic strokes, flick, lick, and suck.* Begin by gently stroking the labia minor from the vagina to the clitoris with the tip of your tongue. Circle the clitoris with the tip of your tongue. Run it down the sides of the clitoris. Flick your tongue lightly back and forth across the tip of the clitoris, then across the shaft. Suck the clitoris by placing your lips on either side of it and gently pulling in. Some women also enjoy having the labia sucked.

4. *Use a combination of strokes, and vary the pressure and speed in licking, flicking, and sucking.* Don't use your teeth. Let her responses determine whether you should increase pressure and speed.

5. *Add manual stimulation.* Use your fingers to stimulate her vagina as you perform cunnilingus.

6. *Never blow air into the vagina.* Air bubbles can find their way into the bloodstream and, in rare cases, lead to death by embolism.

Three Tips for Receiving Cunnilingus

1. *Clench your sphincter and PC muscles periodically.* This enhances the experience for most women and also pushes the vaginal lips forward to meet him, much like returning a kiss.

2. *Place one or both of your hands on his head.* You can give him direction by gently pulling his head toward you or pushing it away if you want more or less pressure.

3. *Move your hips in time to his movements and moan when he gets it right.* That increases your excitement and reinforces his efforts.

What Women and Men Say About Cunnilingus:

From a 33-year-old woman: "I like the mobility and sensitivity of the tongue against my clitoris. The ongoing lubrication is also a plus. The tongue can do things that the fingers and penis can't do."

A 28-year-old woman says: "I like the sensations of being touched directly on my clitoris by his tongue and lips. They are much more gentle and exciting than his fingers. I feel open and vulnerable to him during cunnilingus and completely accepted by him too."

And from a 40-year-old man: "There is no better way to know a woman than to perform cunnilingus on her. It is the most intimate sex act. I love the way women smell and feel, the way that slick skin moves under my tongue when they're excited. I feel like a powerful lover when I give a woman an orgasm this way."

The Six Steps for Performing Fellatio

1. *Set the mood.* Start by licking and sucking his nipples if they are sensitive. Kiss and lick a path down to his genitals. Gently caress his penis and scrotum.

2. *Get into a comfortable position.* There are many positions for fellatio, but this one gives a woman a greater sense of control.
   - He lies on his back. She kneels at his side, her knees at right angles to his hip.

3. *Master the basic strokes, flick, lick, and suck.* Flick the head of the penis quickly with the tip of your tongue. Flick up and down the shaft. Lick in long strokes up the shaft. Use swirling licks around the head of the penis. Stretching your mouth so that it covers both rows of teeth, suck the head of the penis. If you can master it, swirl your tongue around the ridge while you suck.

4. *Use a combination of styles and vary the pressure and speed of flicking, licking, and sucking.* Let his responses guide you. To prolong the experience, take your mouth away from his penis if he is close to ejaculating and lick his scrotum or thighs, or lightly bite his nipples.

5. *Add manual stimulation.* While you are performing fellatio, fondle his testicles. Or while sucking the head of the penis, use your hand to stimulate the shaft. Generally, men prefer firmer pressure than women realize they do.

6. *Pay special attention to his sensitive places.* (See Anatomy, Hot Spots.) Most men find the corona, the ridge between the head and the shaft, especially sensitive to stimulation by flicking.

*T*hree Tips for Receiving Fellatio

1. *Keep your word on the swallow issue.* If you are not in a monogamous relationship, her swallowing your semen is not a good idea. Wear a condom during fellatio. And if your partner does not like you to ejaculate in her mouth, don't. Stop her before that happens.

2. *Control your thrusting.* Let her set the pace. Vigorous thrusting can be uncomfortable for her, both physically and psychologically.

3. *Show appreciation.* Don't stifle your moans. Afterward, be tender and loving.

What Women and Men Say About Fellatio

From a 43-year-old woman: "I like fellatio. It's fun and it gets me very excited. But I'm not wild about swallowing semen. It tastes bitter."

A 31-year-old woman says: "I enjoy fellatio as part of lovemaking. I don't like it when it becomes the main focus, when it's what a man wants me to do for him. I have a problem about what to do with the semen with a new partner. I don't like to swallow it, but I'm too embarrassed to spit it out."

From a 50-year-old man: "My wife, who is five years older than I am, says this is something she doesn't care to do for me even though I enjoy going down on her. She admits this is selfish on her part but expects me to understand. I don't. When I have strayed within the marriage, I have been motivated by the desire to receive oral sex."

And from a 29-year-old man: "I love oral sex, both giving and receiving. The best lovers I've had have all loved oral sex. Each woman does it a little different. If she loves it, she's going to do it well."

Orgasm

WHAT IS AN ORGASM?

The French call it le petit mort, the little death. The roots of the word "orgasm" include the Greek "orgasmus," meaning to grow ripe, swell, be lustful, and the Sanskrit "urg," meaning nourishment and power.

Romance novelists describe it in "earth-moving" terms and sometimes refer to it as a "climax." Poetry and aesthetics aside, an orgasm is a series of rhythmic contractions triggered by intense physical and psychological stimulation and typically lasting 3 to 20 seconds, with intervals of less than a second between the first three to six contractions. Some people on some occasions may continue to experience these genital spasms for a minute or longer.

Orgasm is the third in the four stages of sexual arousal observed by Masters and Johnson: desire, arousal, orgasm, and resolution. Blood pressure and heart rate increase during the first two stages, reaching a high at the point of orgasm. Both men and women usually exhibit other physical changes during orgasm, including a deepening of the color in the nipple area and genitals.

Not surprisingly, orgasm has been a focus of attention in nearly every culture throughout recorded history. Numerous strategies for delaying male orgasm, accelerating female response, and enhancing orgasm in both sexes have been developed by groups as diverse as Tantric priests 5,000 years ago in India and Western sex therapists in our time. In Western society in the late twentieth century, the female orgasm is the standard by which lovemaking is measured. A man considers himself a good lover if he "gives" his partner one and preferably more than one orgasm each time they make love. A woman finds validation of her sexuality as well as pleasure in her orgasms.

Some people have their first orgasms in infancy, without even touching themselves because their bodies during the first several months of life periodically produce an excess of hormones that triggers the response. And orgasms need not end until life does. The majority of healthy older men are able to reach orgasm. Older women seldom have physical factors that would prevent orgasm though they may deny themselves the pleasure. An active sex life is the key to remaining orgasmic into old age.

Why should one care about remaining orgasmic?

Some health benefits of orgasm have been documented by researchers. Orgasm promotes cardiovascular conditioning, imparts a healthy glow to the skin, and improves overall body tone. Recent studies have shown that breast-cancer survivors who experience orgasm—through lovemaking or masturbation—recover more quickly than those who do not. Some sex therapists even recommend masturbating as a cure for insomnia. And many women report that orgasm relieves menstrual cramps and headaches.

In addition, the psychological benefits are very real. Because orgasm is experienced in the part of the brain that rules the emotions, sexual release decreases irritability and leaves you with a sense of well-being and a general feeling of relaxation.

MALE ORGASM

Like women, men experience a series of contractions or spasms throughout the genital area occurring at approximately .8 second intervals. But for men, an orgasm is almost a certainty whereas it may be a sometime event for women. In men the onset of orgasm is also more visible. The testes, which have increased by 50 to nearly one 100 percent during the arousal phase, are pulled up against the body, signaling the feeling men have of reaching "a point of no return" when the sperm is transported from the scrotum upwards to mix with the other fluids comprising semen. Men have a longer resolution phase following orgasm and ejaculation: the refractory period.

Some sexologists and a growing number of men claim that multiple orgasms are possible for those men who can separate orgasm from ejaculation. They contend that orgasm is a psychophysical experience typically but not necessarily including ejaculation. Other experts disagree. There is a general consensus, however, that ejaculation necessitates the refractory period, which can be as little as minutes in a young and virile man and as long as days in older men.

What men say about orgasms

From a 38-year-old married man: "What I love best is going to the edge and pulling back. I have the strongest orgasms when I can get right near the point of inevitability and stop, then go there again and let the feeling subside. When I get into that kind of rhythm with my wife and I finally come, it's an explosion!"

From a 27-year-old single man: "I can't imagine having sex without having an orgasm. To me, the best experience in life is coming. Sometimes it's so good I feel it exploding out the top of my head. Once I am pretty aroused, I have to have that feeling. Everything in me is straining for it. When I hear women say they don't care if they come or not, I think, 'Are you crazy?' If I couldn't come, I wouldn't have sex."

From a 45-year-old divorced man: "There is no feeling in life quite as good as having an orgasm. But there is and always has been too much pressure on men about orgasms. First, you are pressured to give your partner one. Then, as you get older and have a little trouble sometimes, you feel pressured to have one. I can enjoy the stimulation now without needing to come every time, but the woman can't deal with that."

From a 33-year-old married man: "Some orgasms are better than others, but none of them are not good. Sometimes I feel the ejaculation like an explosion, other times like a dribble, but it's always good."

Delaying Male Orgasm

"How can I last longer?" is one of the most commonly asked male sex questions.

Men often complain that they reach orgasm more quickly during lovemaking than they or their partners would like. Sometimes a man is suffering from premature ejaculation (see Ejaculation [premature]), a condition easily self-treated in most cases. Occasionally a man might experience retarded ejaculation (see Ejaculation [retarded]), a temporary inability to ejaculate or experience orgasm even when he is trying to do so.

More often, a man would simply like to make lovemaking last longer by delaying his orgasm. Or he might want to experience multiple orgasms, extended or whole-body orgasms, or stronger orgasms. There's a lot of information available on those subjects, much of it in books on Tantric sex not particularly accessible to the average reader. In the next sections are some orgasm-enhancement techniques for both sexes that have worked well for men who aren't trained in the ways of Eastern sex.

*F*our Techniques for Delaying Orgasm

1. *Vary the thrusting pattern.* Alternate deep thrusts during intercourse with shallow ones. Periodically stop thrusting altogether and remain still within your partner for several seconds or longer.

2. *The perineum press.* Practiced in China for five thousand years, this technique is simple. Before the point of ejaculatory inevitability, use three curved fingers to apply pressure to the perineum, the area

between the scrotum and the anus. Practice during masturbation because finding the exact spot and getting the pressure just right is a little tricky.

3. *Flex your PC muscles.* This technique requires strong PC muscles. (See Kegels, for strengthening exercises.) When ejaculation is imminent, stop thrusting. Pull back to approximately one inch of penetration, but do not entirely withdraw. Flex the PC muscles and hold to a count of nine. Resume thrusting with shallow strokes.

4. *Alternating stimuli.* If you are highly aroused but not on the verge of ejaculation, stop thrusting and make love to your partner manually or orally. By alternating intercourse with other forms of lovemaking, most men can delay orgasm.

FEMALE ORGASM

When a woman becomes aroused, blood flow increases to the vagina, causing lubrication and swelling the inner and outer lips and the clitoris. The contractions of orgasm are felt in the vagina, anal sphincter, and uterus. Some women report postorgasmic contractions, particularly in the uterus, up to 24 hours later. Afterward, the blood congesting the area makes a slower trip back to the rest of the body than it does in men, which partially explains why women can experience plateau and orgasm again more quickly than men do.

Between 10 and 15 percent of women never reach orgasm at all, even during masturbation. Another 10 to 15 percent achieve orgasm only through masturbation. Only approximately 30 percent of women reach orgasm through intercourse alone. Perhaps as many women have *never* reached orgasm during intercourse. Inability to have orgasm during intercourse is the second most common sexual complaint of women—behind lack of sexual desire. It is my feeling that infrequent orgasm must surely contribute to low sexual desire.

And, finally, a tiny percentage of women may experience something called a "missed" orgasm. They have the physiological signs of orgasm, including the contractions, but they don't "feel" the orgasm in their brains. The cause may be deeply rooted in the woman's psychological denial of pleasurable feelings.

The good news is that many women become more easily orgasmic as they age. The inhibitions and insecurities that can hold you back in your twenties begin to disappear in your thirties. Greater self-confidence leads to a more relaxed attitude about sex. Many women find their sexual appetites increase and their orgasms multiply in their thirties and beyond.

What women say about their orgasms

From a 33-year-old single woman who dates frequently and has had many lovers:"The best way for me to have an orgasm is to be on top. I'm on my knees and my partner is flat on his back. This way I can rock on him, with the pressure from his penis toward the front, stimulating my clitoris as well as my G-spot. I can reach orgasm in a lot of different ways, but this is the strongest and fastest."

From a 49-year-old woman married for 20 years:"The way I'm most turned on is not the way I have an orgasm. I really like intercourse from the rear entry position, but I never have an orgasm that way. Usually what I do is have a first orgasm through cunnilingus before intercourse and then a second orgasm by stroking my clitoris after intercourse."

From a 38-year-old single woman: "There have been a few times when the earth rocked, everything was perfect for us . . . but, I don't think I've ever had a 'best ever' sex experience. It would be a vaginal orgasm. Once I really came close to it. I'd like to have at least one in my life."

From a 23-year-old single woman:"Women have to cut themselves a break. Can you imagine a man agonizing over whether or not his orgasm came from the right place? I have my best orgasms when I masturbate, but that doesn't bother me at all. Lovemaking provides other pleasures."

How can a woman experience orgasm during intercourse?

1. *Change the attitudes that inhibit orgasm.* (See also Myths [sexual].) They include:
   - He's tired, or I'm taking too long . . . . I'll hurry sex along.
   - He should give me an orgasm.
   - I shouldn't have to tell him what I like.
   - Pleasing him is more important than pleasing myself.
2. *Experiment with positions to find the ones most effective for you.* (See also Positions [sexual intercourse].) Many women find the female superior position most conducive to orgasm because they can control the angle and depth of penetration and the degree of thrust-

ing. For added clitoral friction, try lowering your torso against his, tightening your legs, and rocking your pelvis against his.

3. *Use your vaginal muscles and the pubococcygeal (PC) muscle to increase physical tension.* (See Kegels for exercises to strengthen the PC muscle.) Flexing those muscles can encourage and strengthen orgasms, too.

4. *Provide additional clitoral stimulation.* Have your partner use his hand or use your own hand or a vibrator to stimulate the clitoris during intercourse.

Orgasm and Women Who Have Them Easily

Anatomy and physiology are possible factors. Some women may have a clitoris that is either larger than average or positioned so that the shaft of the penis strokes the clitoral region during intercourse. They may have learned very early how to align their bodies with their partners' bodies and move their hips so that they get that kind of stimulation. And they may have been lucky with partners whose body types mesh with their own, making all this possible.

Behavior Traits of Easily Orgasmic Women

- *They aren't embarrassed by asking for what they need or by stroking themselves during lovemaking.*
- Comfortable with both masturbation and receiving oral and manual stimulation from their partners, *they feel entitled to their pleasure.* Either they were not advised as young girls against touching themselves or they were able to screen out that as well as other sex-negative messages.
- *They freely entertain sexual thoughts and fantasies,* rather than trying to repress them out of guilt as some women do. Often they are primed for lovemaking before it begins.

These are *learned* behaviors. Being in love or in a relationship or marriage won't necessarily make a woman more easily orgasmic—though it may provide her with the warm and secure emotional environment she needs to do so. Contrary to the fairy tale, it takes more than the prince's kiss to awaken the sleeping princess.

Early experiences can make a difference in a woman's orgasmic response system, too. If your first experiences with boys were happy ones, you probably began having orgasms while making out. Delaying intercourse is good for girls for many reasons, not the least of which is this one: She's less likely to have an orgasm from intercourse than from petting. And if a girl has negative early sexual experiences, including abuse, she is more likely to have trouble reaching orgasm as an adult, even in a loving relationship.

THEORIES ABOUT ORGASM

Spurred on by popular books on the latest orgasm theories, women often question whether or not they are having the "right" kind of orgasm. Is clitoral better than vaginal? G spot better than not G spot? Are the orgasms you experience during lovemaking better than those you have during intercourse? Is the simultaneous orgasm best of all?

Stop worrying! There is no right or wrong way to have an orgasm.

1. *The clitoral versus the vaginal orgasm.* Modern psychology has moved beyond Sigmund Freud's belief that the only "mature" orgasm was a vaginal one. Some orgasms may feel "better" to you because they are more intense than others. And they may be more intense for a variety of physical and psychological reasons, including a surge of hormones or being particularly in love with your partner that day.

   Some people still believe there is a difference between vaginal and clitoral orgasms. Through extensive research in the 1960s, Masters and Johnson determined that, physiologically, clitoral and vaginal orgasms are actually the same. Whether the orgasm seems to originate in one place or another makes no difference in measurable responses and may be nothing more than a matter of individual perception. You may even be able to have an orgasm from intercourse alone—even if you are not one of the 25 percent to 35 percent of women who naturally do so—by delaying penetration until you are on the brink of climax.

2. *The G-spot debate.* In Tantric sex terminology, the "sacred spot"—which supposedly produces "better" orgasms—is the G spot (see entry), a rough patch of skin located on the upper vaginal wall. Fewer then 10 percent of women can find this place, named after Ernest Grafenberg, the German doctor who "discovered" it in the fifties. If you can locate it and if you enjoy having it tickled, great. And if not, forget about it.

3. *The masturbation-is-stronger debate.* Many people, men and women, report that the orgasms they have during masturbation feel more intense than those from partner sex. Often they—particularly

women—are uncomfortable in admitting this because they believe masturbation does not qualify as real sex. People may experience orgasm more intensely during masturbation because they are focused purely on their own physical sensations and are not distracted by the partner's needs and responses. Nor are the physical sensations of orgasm diffused through layers of emotions. Maybe this is why most people, whether they have regular partners or not, masturbate at least occasionally.

4. *The simultaneous-orgasm debate.* A few decades ago, the simultaneous orgasm was the elusive ideal. Women, especially, believed mutual climaxes were better than orgasms achieved before or after a partner had his. Mostly they faked having an orgasm when their partners did—and then felt guilty and deprived.

The simultaneous orgasm as a couple's goal is enjoying some new popularity. If you want to experience this, here is how:

The Secret to the Simultaneous Orgasm

1. Time your response cycles so that you know approximately how long it takes for each partner to reach orgasm during your most typical lovemaking pattern.

2. Assuming it takes you longer than it does him, let him stimulate you alone until you reach the point where you are the same distance away from climax as he will be when stimulation begins for him.

3. Now begin stimulating him.

Some couples find the special intimacy of simultaneous orgasm worth the effort.

MULTIPLE ORGASM

Multiple orgasms occur when a woman (or a man, which is less likely) has a second, third, or more orgasms without completely returning to the resolution phase. Sexologists generally agree that all women are capable of having multiple orgasms but estimate that fewer than 50 percent ever do. Most believe that only 10 to 15 percent of men are capable of having multiple orgasms, with far fewer actually doing so.

Different types of multiples include:

- *Compounded singles.* Each orgasm is distinct and separated by a partial return to the resolution phase.

- *Sequential multiples.* Orgasms occur two to ten minutes apart with minimal reduction in arousal between them.
- *Serial multiples.* Numerous orgasms are separated by mere seconds or minutes at most with *no* diminishment of arousal. Some women experience this as one long orgasm with spasms of varying intensity.

How Women Can Experience Multiple Orgasms

1. *Think multiple.* Women are more likely to have more than one orgasm when they are mentally prepared for lovemaking. (See preceding tips.)

2. *Oral first.* Women who experience multiples typically report having their first orgasm via cunnilingus. After an oral orgasm, they can more easily experience another than they can if the first climax occurred during intercourse or manual stimulation. One woman said, "The sensations of pleasure seem to spread throughout my genitals more easily after cunnilingus. Maybe the intensity of coming that way first is the secret."

3. *Varied stimulation.* Their other "secret" is varied stimulation. Cunnilingus is often followed by intercourse with manual stimulation at the same time. Also, they change positions frequently to get the sensations where and how they want them. You don't necessarily have to move around the bedroom like a gymnast. A subtle shift in positions can make the difference.

How Men Can Experience Multiple Orgasms

1. *Repeatedly use the perineum press.* (see page 200 for directions) Some men not only prolong lovemaking but also experience orgasm without ejaculation by repeating the technique when they are close to ejaculation, up to three or four times until they experience the sensations of orgasm without ejaculation.

    A man who has perfected this says, "It feels like orgasm *with* ejaculation, sometimes more diffuse. The big difference is I don't lose my erection afterward as I do when I ejaculate."

2. *Practice coitus interuptus.* Some men train themselves to experience orgasm without ejaculation by pulling back at the last possible second before ejaculation. They resume lovemaking when the arousal level has subsided somewhat. Practice while masturbating when you can focus entirely on your own process of arousal.

    One man says, "I began teaching myself to pull back on the brink of orgasm just to make intercourse last longer. When I was close to orgasm, I would withdraw and stimulate my wife with my hand, then reinsert my penis when I was less aroused. I found I could manipulate my arousal level that way, bringing myself higher and higher each time before I pulled out. One night after I had backed off repeatedly from ejaculating, I found myself having an orgasm without ejaculating. It was an extraordinary and intense experience. I came several times that night before I finally ejaculated, which was more powerful than anything I'd ever felt in my life."

3. *The valley, a Tantric technique.* The valley orgasm is a continual rolling expansion of the orgasm, a greatly heightened ecstasy, like a series of orgasms, without ejaculation.

- First, make love using a varied pattern of thrusting.
- Stop thrusting when you feel near orgasm.
- Delay ejaculation by flexing the PC muscle.
- Hold your partner in a close, comfortable embrace. Continue shallow thrusting.
- Each time you feel ejaculation is imminent, flex the PC muscle to halt it. You will experience the sensations of orgasm, though more diffuse, without ejaculation.

One man says, "Combining the varied thrusting pattern with the stop/start and PC clenching does produce the series of orgasms. You bring yourself close, then pull back, then increase the stimulation and pull back again, and so forth. But you really have to practice to make this happen. Your PCs have to be in shape."

The Perineum Halt—How She Can Help

You can either induce or delay male orgasm by manipulating the perineum. Yes, this is confusing. Whether you induce or delay depends in part on the man's responsiveness to the maneuver and in part on when and with how much pressure it is performed and whether you use the thumb or three fingers. Some men claim pressure on the perineum stops them from ejaculating, while others swear it induces orgasm. This is not an exact science.

You can also stop his orgasm—sometimes—by placing the tip of your index finger against his anus, pressing the rest of the finger tightly against his skin as you cup his scrotum with your hand, pulling it away from his body. This takes practice and cooperation. Don't perform it on an unwilling partner.

One woman says, "My boyfriend and I have been able to delay his orgasms sometimes using this. He says, 'Stop me,' and I use the maneuver while he pulls his penis almost all the way out of my vagina. If we do this several times during lovemaking, we can bring on multiple orgasms for him. The added bonus is that he gets to the point where he is dying to ejaculate after having orgasms without ejaculating—and he makes love like a wild man."

EXTRAGENITAL ORGASM

An orgasm achieved with no genital contact, the ultimate no-hands experience, is an extragenital orgasm. Fewer than 10 percent of women—and even fewer men—can reach orgasm simply from kissing passionately or by having their breasts (or nipples) kissed or sucked, their thighs caressed or licked, on in a few cases, just by having their ears or neck nuzzled. They are able to excite themselves through erotic thoughts and fantasies to the point where any form of physical stimulation sends them over the edge. Some women can experience an extragenital orgasm after they've had an orgasm through clitoral or vaginal stimulation. Anywhere from 10 to 20 percent of women have experienced a sleep orgasm, the equivalent of a male "wet dream."

SPONTANEOUS ORGASM

A spontaneous orgasm occurs with *no* physical stimulation at all. According to limited research, a few woman apparently can think themselves to orgasm. In her book *Women Who Love Sex,* Gina Ogden, Ph.D., not only interviewed women who claimed to have this experience but measured their physical responses in a clinical setting and proved their claims had merit. How do they do it?

In one typical scenario, the woman listened to a ten-minute guided imagery tape of sexual fantasy. Then she stimulated herself to a genital orgasm. And finally she used her own internal imagery to have a second "no-touch" orgasm.

WHOLE-BODY ORGASM

An orgasm that seems to be felt throughout the body is a whole-body—or total-body— orgasm.

A woman who has them occasionally says: "Sometimes I feel the tremors all over my body during orgasm. First my body gets taut. It's as if my breasts and nipples and vaginal walls are expanding. They feel bigger and bigger. My whole body is alive and aroused and quivering. The orgasms start in my genitals, like waves in my clitoris, my outer lips, my vagina, deep inside the walls. The waves grow bigger and spread throughout my body until I can even feel them in the tips of my fingers and my toes.

"I see colors flashing, bright primary colors. It's a transcendent experience that lifts me outside my body and puts me back down again."

Some people experience whole-body orgasms only when they have a strong emotional connection to their partners, others when they are feeling particularly sensual or sexual or both. The WBO is most likely the result of intense connection on three levels, emotional, sensual, and sexual, though this is not true for everyone. Some have whole-body orgasms only during masturbation, others only after multiple orgasms.

WHY FAKED ORGASMS?

A faked orgasm is all smoke and no fire. In surveys and research studies, women, regardless of age, background, and sexual history consistently report faking orgasms at least occasionally. Men can and do fake, though they report doing so less often than women do. They can't fake as easily as women can, of course, because semen has a distinctive scent.

Why do people fake orgasms?

1. *To end the sex in a polite way.* You're not going to have an orgasm for whatever reason and you're tired of making love so you pretend to climax to spare his/her feelings.
2. *To spare the ego.* Sometimes people fake to spare their own feelings. They don't want to admit they didn't have an orgasm, because they equate achieving orgasm with a performance goal.

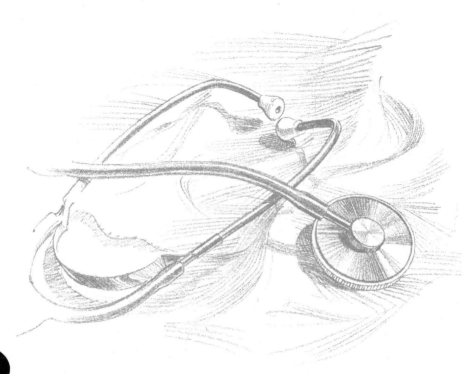

Painful Intercourse (dyspareunia)

Painful intercourse, or dyspareunia, can be caused by physical disorders, emotional factors, or both. Psychological causes include stress, physical or psychological abuse, guilt about sex, fear of sex or intimacy, anger, and deep unresolved conflict with a partner. Sometimes the problem can be resolved without treatment with the help of a loving and understanding partner, and sometimes the help of a professional is needed. In another related condition (see Vaginismus), sexual intercourse is not possible because attempts at vaginal penetration evoke an involuntary spastic contraction of the vaginal entrance.

Discomfort or pain during intercourse or upon penetration is more likely a sign of a physical disorder. Causes are numerous. They include (among others) vaginal infections, such as monilia (yeast), and STDs (see entry) including trichomoniasis, herpes, genital warts, bladder infections, vaginal dryness (see Lubrication), infections of the uterus, such as pelvic inflammatory disease, endometriosis, vaginal cysts, and even common back pain.

In many cases, the cause of pain is evident or relatively easy to determine. When it isn't, a physician will need as much information as you can provide. Note when the pain occurs—upon penetration or during thrusting—whether it is sharp or dull, lingers afterward or doesn't, and, as far as you can tell, from where it seems to be generated. Sharp and deep pelvic pain, for example, can be a sign of endometriosis, a condition in which tissue from the endometrium, the uterine lining, begins to grow outside the uterus. Pain that feels like vaginal soreness following intercourse can be caused by dryness, a condition that can be alleviated by the use of lubricants and/or hormone-replacement therapy.

EXAMPLE

“My husband, Brad, and I had both looked forward eagerly to resuming our sex life after the birth of our daughter," Amy said. "We played around with each other before the six-week deadline had elapsed, but we were careful not to let him penetrate me. When we got the medical all-clear, we had great sex—once. The next time we made love, it hurt.

"We thought we just needed to take it easy, so we did. That was fine. A week later, intercourse was painful again. This went on for a few weeks, with the pain recurring, but not happening every time. I was beginning to think it was all in my head. Brad was afraid I'd suffered some permanent damage from giving birth. We were both a little afraid to find out what was wrong."

After worrying needlessly for several days, Amy finally called her doctor and scheduled an appointment. She had a mild urinary tract infection, which flared up with vigorous intercourse, then would begin to clear up on its own when they avoided intercourse. The doctor put both Amy and Brad on antibiotics to eliminate the risk of him reinfecting her. In ten days, they were at last able to resume their sex life without pain. ∎

If you feel pain upon penetration or during intercourse, consult a physician first. She or he should perform a pelvic exam, take a detailed medical and personal history, including use of medications and your relationship with your partner, and possibly order tests as well. Should no physical cause for pain be found after a thorough examination and evaluation, you and your partner should see a therapist.

Occasionally, men can experience pain during or after intercourse too. Most often the cause is abrasion due to prolonged or vigorous thrusting, particularly if the woman's vagina is dry. The prevention is simple: use lubrication.

Paraphilias

WHAT IS A PARAPHILIA?

Paraphilias are a group of sexual behaviors that are sometimes derogatorily called perversions. The word is derived from the Greek "para" meaning "outside the usual" and "philia" meaning "love." Some paraphilias are similar to behaviors that many people do not find unusual or disruptive to personal relationships. For example (see Fetishism), many men are aroused by women wearing lacy black underwear, but a fetishist—or a man who has a fetish paraphilia—can be aroused only by women in lacy black underwear.

Erotic behavior becomes a problem when it is compulsive, destructive to relationships and/or personal mental or psychological health, in violation of another person's rights or a threat to their mental or physical health, and/or illegal, such as pedophilia, the sexual interest in children. Generally speaking, paraphilias are problems because they meet one or more of the above criteria. In psychological terms, an unusual sexual activity is diagnosed as a paraphilia when the behavior is intense, of at least six months' duration, and the person has acted upon the urges or is experiencing extreme distress while trying not to act upon them.

Paraphilias are often multiple rather than single and may be an aspect of a mental disorder such as schizophrenia or one of the personality disorders. They are almost entirely male behaviors, with the exception of masochism, a category in which men still outnumber women by 20 to 1. It is important to note that paraphilias are behaviors, *not* fantasies. Fantasizing unusual sexual situations is neither uncommon nor cause for concern.

Dr. John Money, through his research conducted at Johns Hopkins Hospital in Baltimore, has contributed much of what is known about paraphilias. The most common paraphilias involve seeking sexual gratification through the following means:

- *Exhibitionism.* Exposing one's genitals to unwilling strangers. Exhibitionism and voyeurism account for the majority of sexual offenses handled by the police.

- *Voyeurism.* Watching people in the act of undressing or having sex. Typically, these people don't know they're being observed. A true voyeur doesn't become aroused by watching a woman who is undressing for his pleasure.

- *Frotteurism.* Rubbing against or fondling a nonconsenting person.

- *Pedophilia.* Adults, overwhelmingly men, who seek physical and often sexual contact with prepubescent children not related to them.

- *Sexual sadism and masochism.* The exchange of pain for sexual pleasure. Sadists inflict pain and/or humiliation, and masochists receive pain and/or humiliation. Unlike other paraphilias, some sadists and masochists are women. Although many people switch roles, masochists outnumber sadists.

- *Telephone scatologia.* Making obscene phone calls to unconsenting adults.

- *Transvestism.* Also called cross-dressing. A man is sexually aroused by dressing in women's clothing. A transvestite may appear in public dressed as a woman or may confine his dressing to home. Cross dressers are predominantly heterosexual.

- *Incest.* Sexual relations between close relatives for whom marriage would be forbidden by law. Incest violates one of our strongest social taboos.

WHAT CAUSES PARAPHILIAS?

Researchers do not know for certain what causes paraphilias. There are, however, two general theories about the causes of male sexual compulsions:

- *Premature and traumatic exposure to sex, in the form of child sex abuse.* Approximately 75 percent of the men who are treated at the nation's leading clinic, the National Institute for the Study, Prevention, and Treatment of Sexual Trauma, in Baltimore, were victims of child sex abuse. For reasons researchers don't fully understand, when girls are abused, they are more likely to become inhibited sexually, while boys tend to act out in paraphiliac behaviors.

- *An overzealous suppression of natural curiosity about sex, for religious and other reasons.* Little boys who are taught that sex is dirty and are punished for their interest in it may become men with fetishes or obsessions. We don't think of severe repression as a form of sexual abuse, but it can be.

WHAT ARE THE TREATMENTS?

A paraphiliac needs professional help but he probably won't seek it unless a law-enforcement agency compels him to do so or his partner insists. As long as she accommodates his behavior, he probably won't attempt to change. Why not? That change is going to be very difficult and emotionally painful.

Treatment sometimes includes administering medication to relieve obsessive/compulsive symptoms, or other drug therapy that lowers the male sex drive, along with therapy. Therapists skilled and experienced in treating paraphilias are difficult to find. Contact a university or medical school that operates a sex-dysfunction clinic and ask for a referral.

Performance Anxiety

(see Anxiety [performance, male and female])

Peyronie's Disease

Though Peyronie's disease, or the "bent penis" syndrome, is fairly obscure in modern popular sex literature, it was a documented affliction centuries ago and afflicts approximately a million men today in conditions ranging from slight to severe. Named after the French surgeon Francois Gigo De La Peyronie, who published an article on the deformity in 1743, Peyronie's disease may cause the erect penis to bend into a J-shape. The deviation is caused by the growth of fibrous bands in the outer layer of the penis.

The disease develops slowly over a period of years, and the exact cause is unknown. Symptoms can include pain in the early stages. Typically penile curvature becomes evident six months after the initial pain. The curvature may stabilize or worsen. The majority of sufferers remain capable of erection, but may have difficulty in penetrating the vagina. Peyronie's disease can cause impotence.

Treatments include both medical and surgical approaches, with vitamin therapy being effective in many cases. A frequently used treatment is a combination of vitamin E and potaba, a medication that softens scar tissue. Typically, a patient is given this regimen for 12 to 24 months before surgery is considered.

EXAMPLE

"At first I didn't know what was happening," reports a sufferer. "My penis shaft gradually started to bend, forming almost a C shape. It was terribly embarrassing. I went to a urologist who told me I had Peyronie's disease. At first I nearly fainted. I figured this was the worst thing that could happen to me; I'm finished. When I calmed down, the doctor told me to take vitamin E and that the condition might clear up in time. I left the office in a daze. The happy ending is that after a year most of the curvature corrected itself with vitamin therapy alone."

If you have pain or notice the curvature developing, see a doctor. Peyronie's is a sharp curvature of the penis and should not be confused with a gradual change that occurs with age. The erect penis does tend to point upward in the younger man more so than in the aging man.   ∎

Playing Hard to Get

The classic "hard to get" ploy is based on behavior psychologists label "distance-pursuer dynamics." One partner's desirability is enhanced by a certain degree of unavailability. In show business, it's called "leave them laughing and wanting more." In courtship, the pursuer is driven to try harder when the pursued keeps her (or his) distance.

EXAMPLE

Mary kept herself more detached in the relationship than Ethan wanted. He asked her to spend every weekend with him, but she often wasn't available on the weekends at all.

"I'm busy and can't possibly see you this weekend," she told sweetly, "but I'll miss you."

Eventually Ethan proposed and Mary accepted. I don't recommend playing this "game" to force a commitment. Women and men should hold a little of themselves back in relationships, especially in the early stages.

As the relationship progresses, playing a deliberate game of distance-pursuer can add to your sex life. Melissa periodically plays "the pick-up game" with her husband of 15 years. She dresses provocatively and waits for him at the bar of an expensive hotel. He pretends to be a stranger and picks her up. She resists his attention a first, but finally succumbs. Sometimes they rent a room in the hotel.

Sometimes distance-pursuer dynamics are not fun at all. This occurs in relationships in which one partner, the distancer, is consistently withdrawn, sullen, or inhibited. The other partner, the pursuer, feels unloved, insecure, and dependent on the few crumbs of involvement or reassurance thrown his or her way. Usually, patterns such as these have been learned in childhood and are best addressed in couples therapy. ∎

Pornography

(see Erotica)

Positions, intercourse

There are six intercourse positions with each having many possibilities for variations; and no one position is inherently "better" than another. Physical limitations like pregnancy, obesity, and illness or injury restrict some people in their choices. Habit restricts most others. They have intercourse in the same position they have always done and then wonder why their sex lives seem routine and boring.

Experimenting with different positions adds excitement to lovemaking. Some positions enhance stimulation in different areas of the genitals. Some help overcome problems that may come with aging, weight gain, injury, pregnancy. Different positions offer differing levels of clitoral stimulation, visual stimulation, eye contact, G spot stimulation, and control of angle and depth of penetration for the man or the woman. And changing positions during intercourse can prolong the experience by delaying male ejaculation.

Changing positions changes the sensations of lovemaking. Why stay in one place all the time?

Advantages, Disadvantages, and Variations of the Six Basic Intercourse Positions

(Each variation changes the angle of penetration and the sensations the partners feel during intercourse.)

1. *The missionary position or man on top.* The unfairly maligned position may be the most common one for intercourse in this country. Typically, the woman lies on her back with her knees bent and legs opened outward. Some women place a pillow under their buttocks to make penetration easier or the angle of penetration more arousing. The man largely controls the speed of thrusting.

   - *Advantages:* One of the two face-to-face positions, it promotes intimacy. Partners can kiss during intercourse. It allows deep thrusting and full penetration, which is satisfying for men and women, too. If a woman is tired or slow to warm up, she can relax in this position.

   - *Disadvantages:* Too often the one position couples use exclusively or almost exclusively, it can lead to faster ejaculation. If a man is ill, incapacitated, or fatigued, he may not be comfortable in this position. And it can be difficult for the woman to move freely if the man is much heavier and does not support his weight properly.

   - *Variations:* The woman can keep her feet on the bed with her knees bent. She can wrap her legs around his waist or around his neck. He can hold her legs with his forearms under her knees. She can put her legs on his shoulders. She can pull her knees up to her chest and place her feet flat against his chest. And she can lie with her legs flat on the bed.

2. *The female superior position or woman on top.* The man lies on his back on the bed as the woman straddles him and lowers herself onto his penis. Some men put a pillow under their buttocks to raise

their hips for a more efficacious angle or easier entry. The woman largely controls the speed of thrusting.

- *Advantages:* She can get the stimulation she needs by controlling the angle and speed of penetration. Either he or she can easily stroke her clitoris during intercourse. Most men find the position visually stimulating and more conducive to controlling ejaculation than the missionary position.
- *Disadvantages:* It may be difficult for passive women to assume this position; and it may not be comfortable if a woman is tired or advisable in later stages of pregnancy.
- *Variations:* She can lean back, resting her hands on the bed or floor behind her. Or she can lean forward, resting her hands on the bed or floor in front of her. She can face the other way, toward his feet, affording him a view of her buttocks.

3. *Rear entry.* The woman is on knees and elbows, her hips elevated. The man kneels and enters her vagina from behind.

- *Advantages:* Some women report greater stimulation of the G spot in this position than in others. And some find it conducive to fantasizing. Men often enjoy the visual stimulation. Both sexes can move freely and vigorously, and at the same time each has access to her clitoris for manual stimulation.
- *Disadvantages:* Less intimate than other positions. Some women object to the connotations of the slang term "doggy style."
- *Variations:* The woman kneels at the edge of the bed while the man stands behind her. She can lie with her chest flat on the bed, elevating her hips at a steeper angle.

4. *Side by side.* The couple lie side by side facing each other. One puts a leg over the other.

- *Advantages:* Good position when both are tired but still want to make love or during pregnancy or illness. Allows slow build-up and freedom to caress and fondle each other's genitals during intercourse.
- *Disadvantage:* Does not allow a man to penetrate deeply.
- *Variations:* The spoon position, in which the woman lies on her side with her back to her partner, bent slightly at knees and waist, and the man lies behind her, also bent at the waist and knees. He enters her vagina from behind. The scissors position, in which the man lies on his right side, with the woman lying next to him on her back, her right leg between his thighs and her left leg on top.

In the scissors position, one of them can stimulate her clitoris during intercourse.

5. *Sitting.* The man sits on a bed or firm pillow with his ankles tucked under his legs toward his groin. His partner sits on his lap, her legs around his waist.

   ■ *Advantages:* Allows great intimacy and fondling of her clitoris. Visually stimulating.

   ■ *Disadvantage:* Requires some physical dexterity.

   ■ *Variation:* As he sits in position with ankles tucked, she squats beside him, then lowers herself on his penis. They sit facing each other with legs open, hers over his. She can use a pillow to elevate her for easier entry and a preferable angle of penetration.

6. *Standing.* He enters her from the rear while she is standing, slightly bent forward.

   ■ *Advantage:* Good for spontaneous lovemaking, a "quickie" position.

   ■ *Disadvantage:* Requires more physical dexterity than some couples have.

   ■ *Variation:* He enters her from the front. If a woman's vagina angles to the front, she may find this a pleasurable alternative. It helps if the partners are similar in size.

What men and women say about intercourse positions

From a 47-year-old woman: "I like the missionary position best because we can go at it better in that position than others. I move my legs from his shoulders to around his waist. Sometimes I plant my feet on either side of him or sometimes lie absolutely flat. I can thrust harder in that position. It feels different each way."

A 32-year-old man says: "If I have a favorite, it's woman on top. I like to see a woman's breasts moving over me. And I like the sense of her being in charge. But I wouldn't want to use any one position all the time."

And from a 55-year-old woman: "At different times of our life together, different positions have been 'the best' for us. Now we find the scissors and the spoon our favorites because he has had quite a bit of back trouble in the past few years. You change positions to accommodate your changing bodies."

A 27-year-old man says: "I like every position, but man on top and sitting best because I can see myself thrusting. I like to watch myself pull back and thrust. It looks as good as it feels."

Pregnancy

(see also Manual Stimulation for suggestions on how to make love during pregnancy, Noncoital Sex, Oral Sex, Positions)

HOW DOES PREGNANCY AFFECT SEXUALITY?

Some women find their interest in sex declines during pregnancy and continues to decline after the birth of the child. Acute morning sickness, negative body image, physical discomfort, exhaustion, and other factors including ambivalence toward the pregnancy and impending motherhood or toward the father—can all push sexual thoughts out of mind. Other women report feeling gloriously sexual during pregnancy, especially in the middle trimester when nausea has passed, hormones are high, and the full weight of the baby has yet to be felt.

The second trimester can be one of the sexiest periods of a woman's life. She may have an orgasm for the first time or experience multiple orgasms for the first time, even have extragenital orgasms, particularly from breast stimulation. Partly, this can be explained by vasocongestion. During foreplay, the uterus and vagina become engorged with blood and the vagina lubricates. During pregnancy, the uterus is obviously engorged, with some women experiencing greater vasocongestion than others.

Men have their own problems with sexuality during their partner's pregnancy. Some fear hurting her or the baby through intercourse; and even a doctor's reassurance doesn't completely banish that fear. A man may not be aroused by his wife's changing body and may also be ashamed of his feelings. He may feel guilty about her pregnancy, particularly if she's had a great deal of nausea or other complications. Suddenly, he is seeing his lover as a mother; and mothers have probably not been objects of desire for him in the past. Some men are more vulnerable to having an affair during pregnancy and after childbirth.

What men and women say about sex during pregnancy

From a woman in her fifth month: "I'm still very interested in sex, but my husband avoids me. I feel rejected, unattractive. I tried to rationalize that he has a fear of hurting me or the baby, but I don't really believe that's true. My doctor told him it's okay, so he knows it is. He just doesn't see a pregnant woman as sexy. That hurts my feelings."

From a man who is about to be a father for the first time: "My wife looked beautiful to me throughout the pregnancy. Yet, there was a period where I was thinking of her as a mother, not as a lover. I was not very interested in being with her sexually. She's very attuned to my feelings. When she asked what was the matter, I told her. She took it good-naturedly. We talked, and she seduced me. She became Hot Mama. After that, I couldn't get enough of her."

From a woman in her sixth month: "I know how guys feel now when they wake up with erections. I can't get enough sex. Everything turns me on. My nipples are so sensitive, I get excited putting on my bra."

From a woman in her ninth month: "Sex is different. We can't do erotic aerobics. In these last few weeks, we have kissed and cuddled and masturbated each other. Before that we were able to have intercourse. We have both enjoyed the sex, though we will be glad to get back to the place where there are just the two of us in bed, not three."

From a man whose wife is in her eighth month: "That is the baby's home now. I can't go in there. I still love my wife, but I can't make love to her. I have fantasies of infidelity, but I won't do it. She can't do it. Why should I be able to?"

HOW DOES CHILDBIRTH AFFECT SEXUALITY?

Even if the pregnancy did not interfere much with a couple's sexual desire for one another, childbirth almost certainly will. Most couples report a period of decreased sexual activity following the birth that lasts anywhere from six months to a year. Initially, physical problems cause a woman to avoid sex. Most doctors recommend a period of abstinence from four to six weeks to allow sufficient healing to take place. After that time, leaky breasts or breast tenderness, particularly in nursing mothers, and other minor discomforts may dampen a woman's ardor. But fatigue and stress for both parents are probably the biggest enemies of lust.

There may also be psychological and emotional issues. Sometimes the man feels lonely, ignored by his wife, resentful of the physical and emotional demands of the baby, jealous and left out, or confused by his new role. And sometimes the woman feels confused, pressured, or overwhelmed by all her new responsibilities, especially if she is juggling motherhood and a career.

And, finally, hormonal fluctuations play a significant role in a woman's sexual desire. The ovaries take a vacation during pregnancy because the placenta produces the hormones. Immediately after birth, the new mother is in hormone withdrawal. If she is nursing, her ovaries don't kick back in as quickly as those of the nonnursing mother, who may regain her interest in sex sooner. Often a nursing mother's disinclination to become sexual again following childbirth has a simple biological basis.

What new parents say about sex after the baby

From a new father: "Sex was great during pregnancy. Then the baby came. It's been six months now and I could count the times we've been together on one hand. I guess that's the way it is with a lot of couples at this stage, but I'm not thrilled about it. I miss the special closeness of making love."

From a new mother: "When my doctor said we could have sex again, I asked, 'Do I have to tell my husband?' I'm not ready. I may not be ready until this kid is in school."

From a mother of a two year old: "I didn't want sex, not any kind of sex, for three months after the baby. My husband didn't push it either. We were as chaste as cousins. For the next three months, we did it maybe three times. Then my mother came to stay with the baby for a weekend because she thought we needed to get away together. The first night we pounced on each other. Sex has been great ever since."

The Five Rules for Lovemaking During Pregnancy and After Childbirth

1. *Follow doctor's orders.* In some cases, intercourse may be prohibited during part of pregnancy and always for some weeks following birth.
2. *Communicate.* Don't assume you know what the other thinks or wants.
3. *Be creative.* Sex is more than vaginal intercourse. See Positions, page 209, for ways of making love during pregnancy and after.
4. *Be romantic.* Tender, romantic gestures help build and sustain closeness. (See Romance.)
5. *Be patient.* In time, your bodies and emotions will adjust to parenthood.

Premenstral Syndrome (PMS) and sexuality

The collection of psychological and physical symptoms prior to menstruation is called premenstrual syndrome or PMS. Those symptoms include, among others, mood swings and irritability, abdominal bloating and swelling in feet and ankles, breast tenderness, headaches, and anxiety. The symptoms vary in their severity in women, with most experiencing mild or minimal problems. Very few women are incapacitated by PMS. Nearly all women continue to function in their personal and professional lives throughout their menstrual cycles.

PMS may impact upon sexuality to some degree. Breast tenderness, for example, may make a woman less interested in having her breasts caressed during lovemaking. Or a woman may feel self-conscious about her body at that time of the month because of temporary water weight gain; the self-consciousness may lead to an avoidance of sex or of favorite ways of making love.

Many women report a greater interest in sex at certain points in the menstrual cycle. Sometimes an increase in desire corresponds to the time of ovulation, but not always. The premenstrual days can also bring increased erotic fantasies and desires. And sex, particularly orgasm, can alleviate tension, reduce stress, even cure the mild headaches associated with that phase of the cycle.

What Women Say About Their Cycles of Desire

From a 34-year-old woman: "I get a little bloated and edgy before my period. Sometimes I feel cranky. I also have wilder fantasies then and often the desire for harder lovemaking. I like to have my nipples squeezed a little more. I want the thrusting to be more vigorous."

A 28-year-old woman says: "My husband is in tune with my cycles of desire. He knows that I like the sex to be more romantic and soft after my period is over and really hot and heavy about midway through the cycle. In fact, he picked up on my rhythms before I realized what was going on."

And a 41-year-old woman says: "When I was first married 20 years ago, I withdrew sexually before my period. I felt fat and irritable, and I had this irrational fear of starting to bleed during sex and turning him off. My husband kept telling me that sex would cure my headaches. I didn't believe him. One night we tried it, and he was right. That changed my attitude about lovemaking before my period."

*T*hree Tips for Managing Cycles of Desire

1. *Know your sexual cycles.* Some women (and their partners) don't see the pattern in varying levels of sexual desire. Note the times when you fantasize more often or have different types of fantasies, when you desire more sex or different kinds of sex. Is there a correlation to the menstrual cycle?

2. *Use the cycles to enhance desire and increase orgasm.* Don't suppress the fantasies; use them to arouse yourself to higher levels. Plan extra time for lovemaking during your lusty periods. Try new ways of making love then, too.

3. *Tap into the healing power of sex.* When you're feeling edgy and suffering from a mild headache, you may think you're not in the mood for sex. You may be wrong. Lovemaking, particularly orgasm, will make you feel better.

Prostate Problems and sexuality

(see also Aging)

The prostate, a small walnut-sized gland at the base of the bladder, secretes fluid that nourishes sperm and helps keep it mobile. The prostate commonly becomes enlarged as a man ages. This condition, known as benign prostatic hypertrophy or BPH, rarely affects sexual functioning. Yet up to 30 percent of men diagnosed with BPH do report sexual problems. In most cases, their difficulties are caused by fear and anxiety rather than by physical disability. The average man has a lot of misinformation as well as apprehension about prostate problems.

In mild or moderate cases of BPH a man may experience frequent urination, often at night, some delay in starting a urine stream, or the sensation of a continued need to urinate after he is finished. Treatment in most cases involves medication and not surgery; and in many cases neither may be necessary at all as the symptoms go away on their own. Many of the signs of BPH and prostate cancer are the same, but BPH is not a precursor to cancer. All men over 40 should have an annual rectal exam to screen for prostate cancer. Even if cancer is detected, it is typically slow to develop and spread and responds very well to treatment.

With proper treatment and attitude, a prostate problem will not adversely affect your sexuality.

EXAMPLE

"Around my fiftieth birthday I began having some problems with my prostate," said Jerry, age 52. "I was often awakened during the night with the urge to urinate. When I got to the bathroom, I sometimes couldn't go. At public urinals I was embarrassed by my dribbling. A man doesn't feel like a man anymore when he can't shoot a powerful stream."

He began avoiding sexual relations with his wife. Rather than confide in her, he told her he "wasn't in the mood" or was "too tired." After several months of rejection, she thought their marriage was in trouble. Finally, he confessed his prostate problems to her and admitted he feared they would also lead to failure in the bedroom.

"She was relieved to know that I hadn't lost interest in her," he said, "and insisted I see a doctor."

The doctor diagnosed BPH and told him that his case required surgery. Jerry left the office feeling that his sex life after surgery would never be the same as it had been before his problems began. He was wrong.

"I was able to get an erection shortly after surgery," he said. "When I was given the all-clear for intercourse again, I was fine. There was no decline in the quality of my erections or the sensations of orgasm. I only wish I'd taken care of the situation sooner."

It may take some time for sexual function to return following surgery. For some men complete recovery takes up to a year. The length of recovery depends in part on how long a man postponed treatment for BPH and on the type of surgery performed. ∎

The Five Steps for Handling Prostate Problems

1. *Get help.* If you're having problems, consult with your doctor. Early diagnosis and treatment will probably eliminate the need for surgery.
2. *Get informed.* Research BPH and prostate cancer. The overwhelming majority of men who have mild to moderate cases never require surgery and don't lose sexual functioning.

3. *Confide in your partner.* Sharing your concerns helps you deal with them and gives her the perspective she needs to understand your behavior.

4. *Don't avoid lovemaking because you fear failure.* If you believe a prostate problem will affect sexuality, it will. Take a positive attitude.

5. *Stay healthy.* Maintaining good general health through diet and exercise can help reduce symptoms of BHP. Talk to a nutritionist about dietary changes you can make. Try saw palmetto berry extract. This natural dietary supplement has a demonstrated effectiveness in relieving the symptoms of BPH.

Quickies

(see "Zipless" Sex)

Recovery Sex

People recovering from a traumatic life event, such as an abortion, or from sexual abuse, rape, or drug and alcohol abuse, often experience sexual difficulties. Recognizing the link between the trauma and the effect it has on sexuality is the first step toward reclaiming pleasure. No matter what has happened, you can recover.

Acknowledge and understand your feelings. If you are angry, learn to channel that anger in productive ways. If you are sad, share your sadness with your partner, friends, a therapist. Sexual healing will begin to take place when you do.

The Five Steps to Recovery Sex

1. *Understand the true effects of the experience on sexuality.* People often think they are okay if they have no physical signs of injury. Psychological and emotional injuries may not be obvious, but they require healing time. When we refuse to give ourselves time, we often shut down sexually.

2. *Expect to feel a lot of anxiety about sex for a while.* After you have faced a problem or opened up to your partner about pain experienced, you will feel more vulnerable for a while. Some of the anxiety you feel will be manifested in sexual worries.

3. *Talk to your partner about what each of you needs and wants sexually.* A man in substance-abuse recovery, for example, might be putting a lot of pressure on himself to prolong intercourse, for example, when his partner would be happy with the lovemaking as long as he took the time to give her an orgasm orally or manually. A woman recovering from rape might initiate intercourse because she thinks he wants and needs it when he would be satisfied with other forms of lovemaking until she is truly ready.

4. *Create new romantic patterns.* Wine and mixed drinks can't be part of the seduction scenario for recovering alcoholics. Replace them with flowers, candles, firelight, and other romantic gestures. Familiar places may remind you of an abusive situation. For a while, at least, avoid those places.

5. *Don't set performance standards for yourself.* A recovering man may experience ejaculation or erection problems. A recovering woman may have difficulty becoming aroused or reaching orgasm. Don't judge yourself a "failure" if you do.

THE SEXUAL AFTERSHOCK OF ABORTION

Though it is typically the woman who has the most severe sense of loss, sadness, anger, or guilt, both men and women can experience emotional distress prior to and after an abortion. Sometimes the distressed partner has difficulty becoming sexual again. This is often more likely to be true of women than of men.

E X A M P L E

Ellen and Jay, both in their late thirties, had been married for 15 years when unexpectedly she became pregnant with their third child. Their two older children were adolescents. Ellen didn't want to quit her job and stay home again with a baby. When she talked about the pregnancy and their options to Jay, she focused almost exclusively on the negative aspects of having another child and the option of abortion. Secretly, he wanted to have the baby, but he felt guilty about that desire and kept those feelings hidden from her.

Ellen had an abortion. Afterward, she was sad for several weeks but determined not to let Jay know how sad. He, too, kept his grief to himself. Within a year, they were having sexual problems. Was there a connection?

Yes, and a therapist helped them see that. When Jay was able to say he'd wanted the baby, Ellen surprised him by telling him her own feelings had been more ambivalent than she'd admitted. Each had been harboring a hidden resentment toward the other for making abortion seem like the only option, a resentment that they had to acknowledge before forgiveness and healing could take place. ▪

Ten Steps to Assist Healing and Restore Sexuality

Here are suggestions for helping a partner (and yourself) to heal. This same approach may be taken when helping a partner deal with loss of sexual feelings due to the trauma of any major loss such as miscarriage, death of a parent, loss of a job.

1. Accept the degree of contact and closeness the person in pain wants. If you are uncertain about how your caring gestures are being received, ask. Say, "Do you want to be held now?"

2. Listen and accept what is said without giving advice or false reassurance.

3. Avoid attempts at empathy that are mechanical or not based on a clear awareness of the other's feelings. If you don't quite understand what she or he is feeling, ask for clarification.

4. Accept the person's feelings without insisting a solution be found.

5. Use your own experience of this (or another) loss as a means of connecting with the sufferer—not as a means of competing for sympathy.

6. When and if appropriate, make timely, sensitive suggestions for rethinking the situation that will lead to positive gain.

7. Let the person in pain set the pace of talking and of working toward resolution.

8. When a lot of emotion is shown, do not attempt to shut off the flow of feelings. Acknowledge the emotion. Identify with the feelings as much as possible. Just being there for the other person is an important way of validating her or his grief.

9. Make good eye contact.

10. Never trivialize the other person's words or feelings. Don't state what he or she *should* be thinking or feeling.

SEXUAL ABUSE

(see also Rape, Vaginismus)

Sexual abuse or rape as a child or adult can cause a variety of sexual problems. Some people who have been sexually abused fear closeness or touching. They may have no interest in sex at all or, they may become indiscriminantly sexual. Abuse statistics vary widely, but most reported victims are women. Women who have been abused may be unable to reach orgasm or to find pleasure in their sexuality. Men who were abused in childhood tend to have problems as adults different from those that women do. (See Paraphilias.)

Sex abuse of children runs the gamut from fondling to rape. On any level it is a violation of the child, whether physical harm is done or not. Sometimes children experience a normal reflex arousal from the fondling. And in some cases, children associate the experience with rewards of candy, toys, or special attention. As adults, they will probably feel guilty for having felt pleasure of any kind.

The severity of the abuse, how often it happened, and at what point in a person's life are the primary factors determining how devastating and lasting the effects will be. Some people, for whatever reasons, seem to be more able than others to recover from sexual trauma. Few will escape such an experience unscathed.

E X A M P L E

❝I *was forced into an incestuous relationship with my adoptive father when I was ten," said Cara. "Once he even asked me to masturbate in front of him. For a long time I felt ruined. I used to let boys and men do whatever they wanted with me. Then I stayed celibate for a long time. When I became sexually active again, I would freeze out during sex. I disappeared into myself and felt nothing."*

Cara's response to childhood abuse, ranging from adult promiscuity to withdrawal, is a typical one. Sometimes abused children grow into highly eroticized teenagers, and the promiscuous behavior is coupled with negligence about the use of condoms and birth control methods. The odds of that teenager resolving the inner conflicts alone are slim. Most people will need a combination of professional help and a loving and understanding partner to establish a healthy adult sexual relationship.

"Two years ago I met a guy who was really interested in me, not just in getting laid," Cara said. "We have managed to work through my trauma together. It was difficult for me tell him everything. I was very uncomfortable even allowing myself to experience being touched or cuddled at first. I could give pleasure but not receive it. It is only recently that I have begun to enjoy making love." ■

$\mathcal{W}$hat to Do if You or Your Partner Has Been Abused

1. See the healing steps under the entry for Abortion.
2. Seek professional help.
3. Know that you are not to blame—and that you are not alone. Many others are struggling with the same problem. If you feel comfortable in a group setting, you might want to join a group of survivors of childhood sexual abuse.

ALCOHOL AND DRUG ABUSE, EFFECT ON SEXUALITY

(see also Medications)

There is a common misconception in our society that alcohol increases desire and improves sexual performance. True, small amounts of beer or wine may relax a person, allow the loosening of minor inhibitions, and increase the desire for lovemaking. Champagne is considered an aphrodisiac by many because of its celebratory properties. In most cases, however, more than a little alcohol will probably dampen desire and hinder performance. Alcohol is a depressant, not a stimulant. A little is good, but a lot is definitely not conducive to a mutually pleasurable sexual experience.

Alcohol consumed in more than small quantities can slow down a woman's response cycle. She will require more time to reach orgasm and feel it less intensely than she otherwise would. Chronic heavy drinking in women can lead to loss of desire and diminished capacity for pleasure as well as wreak havoc with her reproductive system.

When men consume large quantities of alcohol, they require more time and will not become as fully erect. They will likely need more time to ejaculate and may not be able to ejaculate at all. In fact, they may lose interest in making love altogether as the impact of the drinks hits them. The alcohol causes a precipitous drop in the blood levels of testosterone. Up to 80 percent of male chronic heavy drinkers suffer from decreased desire or potency or both. After years of alcohol abuse, men's hormone levels are so disrupted that they may have estrogen levels as high as women's.

Though cocaine, marijuana, and amphetamines have a reputation for being love potions, regular usage of recreational drugs has similar ill effects on sexuality.

- *Amphetamines* create sudden bursts of energy like an adrenalin rush, but leave many users too hyper to have sex.
- *Marijuana* does enhance the sense of touch and gives the impression that time is passing more slowly, which might explain why some people feel it improves sexual functioning. But while some pot smokers swear that their drug of choice enhances orgasm or helps them delay ejaculation, many report no effect at all or find the drug inhibits sexuality. Long-term heavy use disrupts hormonal balances, interferes with fertility in both sexes, and lowers testosterone levels in men.
- In some people, *cocaine* does initially increase the sex drive and loosen inhibitions. The drug stimulates production in the brain of dopamine, a neurotransmitter that acts as a kind of natural aphrodisiac. (Freebasing or smoking the crack form of cocaine further exaggerates the response.) Many people report that after first using cocaine they experienced greater desire, more intense, even multiple orgasms, and, for men, the ability to prolong intercourse. Cocaine may continue to have positive effects on sexual performance for a while, but those effects keep diminishing. Soon the body goes into a state of dopamine deficiency, a natural result of being forced to produce too much of the chemical. Cocaine loses its sex-enhancing properties, and men have trouble getting erections while women can't lubricate or reach orgasm. Sustained use leads to loss of desire.

Barbiturates, heroin, quaaludes, and LSD all dampen ardor in one way or another. They put the user in an altered, even initially euphoric state, in which one is company and two is a crowd.

EXAMPLE

In the early days of his relationship with Kathy, Martin was able to keep his drinking under control. After they were married, she realized he had a "drinking problem," but she thought he would "outgrow" it.

"I rationalized that a lot of men in their twenties drink too much," she said. "And his drinking didn't interfere with his job or his responsibilities around the house. Eventually, it did interfere with our sex life, but I didn't know that was the problem. I thought he wasn't turned on by me anymore."

After five years of marriage, Martin and Kathy were having sex only once or twice a month. Kathy wanted more sex; and she also wanted to get pregnant. Kathy asked her doctor why she hadn't gotten pregnant after two years off the birth control pill and was put through a battery of tests. When there was nothing wrong with her, the doctor ordered tests for Martin. His low sperm count was the red flag that led him into treatment for alcohol abuse.

"I agreed to go into a program the same way an overweight person would agree to spend a month at a spa to lose 20 pounds for a big event," he said. "I didn't think I was an alcoholic, but I wanted to stop drinking long enough to get my sperm count up there and give Kathy the baby she wanted."

Neither Kathy nor Martin recognized that his low libido was also a result of chronic heavy drinking until he entered treatment. Though excessive alcohol consumption is probably the most widespread drug-related cause of sexual problems, few people recognize that as the source of their troubles in bed. Kathy had blamed herself for "not being sexy enough." Martin blamed stress, fatigue, anxiety—anything but alcohol. With therapeutic help, they worked through the problems alcohol had created in Martin's life and in their life together. Now they have a satisfying sexual relationship and look forward to the birth of their first child in several months.

"The most scary thing," Martin said, "was having sex sober for the first time. I'd always relied on alcohol to take away my inhibitions."

If you or your partner are confronting the same problem, be reassured that you can have great, sober sex. ■

RAPE

Rape's long-lasting effect on sexuality

Prevalence of rape estimates (in the United States) range from 5 percent to over 20 percent of adult women. Figures vary so dramatically because there is disagreement on approximately how many rapes likely go unreported. We do know that in the United States reported rapes are 35.7 per 100,000 women versus 5.4 per 100,000 women in Europe—a startling contrast.

Survivors of rape go through a variety of emotions and stages of healing that may last for years. Initially, the woman may evidence some degree of denial or dissociation. She may talk about the rape almost as if it had happened to someone else. Denial may give way to shame and guilt and then to rage, anger, or sadness and finally, acceptance, possibly forgiveness. During this process she may have any of a number of symptoms of post-traumatic stress disorder, including but not limited to sleep disturbance, nightmares, flashbacks, anxiety, fear, excessive feelings of guilt and shame, and sexual difficulties.

EXAMPLE

Newlyweds Ellen and Keith decided they needed professional help because she had little desire for sex. During the taking of her history, she told the therapist that she'd been raped two years ago, just before meeting Keith.

"That experience is over for me," she said. When pressed, she said she'd told Keith about it early in their relationship. "He felt sad for me, but neither he nor I saw the need to talk about it very much."

In other words, he'd been just as happy to avoid the issue as she was. They were both angry when their therapist gently prodded them to talk about the rape and the traumatic aftermath in greater detail. Eventually, they took his advice. The resulting discussions were painful and caused a lot of tears on both their parts. For the first time Ellen acknowledged feeling "dirty and shamed." Keith's compassionate response went a long way toward helping her begin the healing that hadn't taken place because she'd hidden the wound.

After several months, Ellen gradually became sexual again. If they'd never had that talk, she might have remained frozen in an emotional and sexual impasse. ■

The Five Steps to Helping Yourself (or Your Partner) Become Fully Sexual Again

1. *Seek intervention.* Every survivor should have some kind of post-rape therapy. Hospitals, physicians, and crisis centers can help put you in touch with a therapist and/or a survivors' group.

2. *Understand that rape is a crime of violence.* It is not a response to sexual provocation. The survivor is blameless.

3. *Recognize that spouses, lovers, and sometimes other family members also may need help to handle their own emotional turmoil.*

4. *Follow the help suggestions under "Abortion, the sexual aftershock" of on page 223.*

5. *Be patient.* There should be no sexual contact that makes the woman uncomfortable. Becoming fully sexual again may take some time.

Romance

(see also Marriage)

Romance is an important and often misunderstood subject. Sometimes when people talk about romance, they really mean sexual passion. And some people confuse romance with the romantic love phase of a new relationship. When they say, "The romance has gone out of our relationship," they mean, "The euphoria we felt while falling in love has subsided." Passion does ebb and flow. Euphoria most assuredly subsides, typically within three to six months. Romance can and should be a lifelong expression of love between two people.

Sometimes in a misguided attempt at finding lasting romance people pursue one lover after another, discarding the relationship when the newness has worn off. Their unrealistic expectations lead to nothing but grief for them and their partners. We idealize that behavior when we describe such people as "incurable romantics." They seek the euphoric rush, not true romance.

Though they may have trouble defining the term, most people know when romance is missing from their lives. They have stopped feeling loved and desired by their partners. Thoughtful gestures and words of love require some effort. When the effort is no longer being put forth, people ask: Am I still loved? Romance is probably more important to women than it is to men, but men, too, need and want romance in their lives.

*C*all your partner at the office at about 10:30. "Sweetheart," you'll say, "check your briefcase—I left something in there for you." Inside, he will find a sealed envelope on which is written, "Guess what's for lunch?" Inside is a pair of edible panties.

The exciting thing about this time together is that it's got to be quick, so you may want to suggest what you'd like to do with him on the back of the envelope. "All I want for lunch is you," paints an explicit picture, as does, "you make my mouth water."

When he walks through the door, you aren't there. Instead, he'll hear the sounds of music coming from somewhere else in the house. You've taped a piece of paper to the banister. A red arrow piercing a heart points in the right direction.

You are waiting behind a door (not necessarily the bedroom door) with only your underwear on and a bunch of grapes in your hand. You have put on a favorite CD, and the shade on the skylight is raised, letting sunlight stream over your body.

Undress him, and don't let him lift a finger to help. Punctuate your movements with little endearments—a butterfly kiss in the hollow of his neck as you rip off his tie and then his shirt; a soft stroke on the inside of his thigh as you undo his belt buckle, pop the button or clasp, and pull down his zipper. Cup his penis and testicles with both your hands and tell him how warm he is and how hot you are.

Let the clothes fall away and quickly drape them over a chair (remember, you have to get back to the office after this).

Start standing, holding one another and exploring the territories that are usually hidden, in the dark. See where the sun hits you and direct his kisses to those places—under your arm, behind your knee, at the nape of your neck. Wrap one leg around him so that he can easily reach under the elastic of your pants.

Now snake out of your underwear. You want to expose yourself completely to your lover, let him see all of you. Let the sun caress the curve of your breast, the roundness of your belly. Put his hands just where you want them as you run the tip of your tongue around his lips. Take a grape into your mouth and gently, as you kiss him, transfer it to his. You can drape a few grapes over your ear so that he can nibble them off; you can put a cluster over his penis and suck on each one until you reach the flesh.

When neither of you can stay on your feet because of your excitement, drop to your knees and put your arm around his neck. If he is completely erect, you can move forward so that you straddle him and move slowly back and forth, gripping him with your thighs.

You know he has a committee meeting at two, and you have a project to finish by the end of the workday. So this is the time. You take the lead, pushing him onto his back to that you can be on top. Together, you can polish off that lunch right away. ∎

EXAMPLE

"My wife is unhappy with me because I'm not romantic enough," said Carl. "I love her. We have a good life together, good sex, good communication. I send flowers on our anniversary, Valentine's Day, and her birthday. I'm not sure what it is she thinks is missing."

His wife Suellen thought romance *was* missing.

"He sends me a dozen roses three times a year and thinks that's romance," she complained. "I don't even like roses. My favorite flowers are gardenias, but he's never noticed."

Suellen craved a special kind of attention she wasn't getting from Carl: close attention to her likes and dislikes. After ten years of marriage, she couldn't understand why he still didn't know she liked gardenias, not roses. That was the first example she gave him when they sat down to their "summit on romance."

"I got the message that she would rather have a gardenia or a bunch of flowers I bought in the market on impulse than two dozen roses arranged in a crystal vase," he said. "Once I understood that, I began listening to her more closely and watching what she bought for herself to get clues about her."

They agreed to stop and ask themselves, "Does this spell love to my partner?" before buying gifts or doing favors, even showing affection. He finally told her that he hated it when she "patted" him on the back while they hugged because it made him feel like a little boy with his mother. Suellen learned that, for Carl, a rub on the back was more romantic than a pat. ■

If you want your partner to be more romantic, first examine the ways in which you are romantic. Are you giving him or her what is wanted or what you want to give? And don't withhold affection as a way of punishing the unromantic partner. When your partner does perform romantic gestures, reinforce the behavior with a smile, a kiss, a warm thank you.

Say, "I love you," often.

$\mathcal{S}$ix Ways to Keep (or Put Back) the Romance in Your Relationship

1. *Empathize.* True romantics are able to put themselves in their partner's place. They can see and feel the world as he or she does. Empathy makes it possible for them to personalize the words and gestures of love, to give what the partner desires, not what the giver would like to give.

2. *Be adventursome.* In the euphoric stage of love, the brain produces a potent love hormone, phenylethylamine (PEA), that creates a natural high. Excitement, adventure, and risk also cause the body to produce PEA. If you want to duplicate the feeling of falling in love, go white-water rafting together. Climb a mountain. Travel to foreign countries. Explore New York City via subway.

3. *Be sexually adventurous, too.* The state of advanced sexual boredom is not conducive to romance. Try something new. See the many suggestions in this book for adding variety to your lovemaking.

4. *Show physical affection.* Kisses and caresses that are not meant to be preludes to lovemaking are romantic gestures. Touch in the way your partner likes to be touched.

5. *Do something romantic every day.* Say, "I love you." Change the cat litter even if it isn't your turn. Go a few blocks out of your way to pick up his cleaning or her favorite brand of frozen yogurt. Romance doesn't have to cost money.

6. *Flirt with each other.* Flirting is both playful and sexy (see Flirting). It makes us feel desired. When is the last time you flirted with your partner?

Safe Sex

(see also Condoms, Masturbation, Noncoital Sex, Oral Sex, Sexually Transmitted Diseases)

"Safe sex" generally describes no- or low-risk sexual activity. That can mean sexual expression without the exchange of any bodily fluids, including saliva, in activities such as mutual masturbation, erotic massage, or telephone sex. Such extreme caution is warranted when a partner is known to be infected with HIV or falls into a high-risk-for-HIV category. Most often "safe sex" is really *safer* sex: partners who do not fit into high-risk profiles using condoms and spermicide during intercourse. While that degree of safety will not provide 100 percent protection, it does dramatically decrease risk. Driving a car or walking across a street are not 100 percent safe activities either.

Everyone who has sex outside a monogamous relationship should practice *safer* sex.

235

✑ex Activities in Ascending Order of Risk

1. *Kissing*. There is no evidence that AIDS is spread by kissing unless both partners have open sores in their mouths or bleeding gums. Saliva does not carry the virus. No risk.

2. *Mutual masturbation*. No risk, as long as the male does not ejaculate on his partner.

3. *Erotic massage*. No risk in touching and stroking.

4. *Oral sex.* Transmission could take place if blood or fluids come in contact with cuts in the mouth. To be completely safe, a woman should put a condom on a man before she performs fellatio. Minimal risk.

5. *Vaginal intercourse*. The virus can be transmitted this way. Check your partner's genitals for obvious signs of ill health or injury—and use condoms. Risk activity.

6. *Anal intercourse.* Infected semen can easily enter the bloodstream through the membranes of the rectum and through tears that may occur during intercourse. If you do have anal intercourse—which I don't recommend with casual partners—use specially designed anal condoms and a lot of water-soluble lubricant. High risk.

Seasonal Sexual Slump

The old adage, "In spring a young man's fancy turns to thoughts of love," may have a biological basis. Sexual desire does seem to increase in the spring and summer for many people. Their libidos may fall with the temperatures, making winter truly the season of discontent for their partners who are not similarly affected.

Researchers have known for some time that the body may produce greater quantities of testosterone during warmer months. A sex hormone present in both women and men though in greater amounts in men, testosterone is the hormone of libido, affecting levels of desire in both sexes. If the weather affects testosterone, why would it not libido?

In the past decade some researchers have suggested that weather's impact on libido may be more complicated than the simple temperature/testosterone link. Sunlight, they believe, may affect libido as it does mood in the common syndrome, seasonal affective disorder, or SAD. Sufferers from this disorder feel continually tired, irritable, and sad during the winter months. Not surprisingly, they don't report having much interest in sex either. Sexual desire is one of the first functions to be short-circuited by illness of any kind.

If your libido dips precipitously in the fall, you may be in a seasonal sexual slump.

EXAMPLE

"I suffered several years of the winter blues before I began to look closely at what was happening," Donna said. "Each winter I would lose my desire for sex and feel generally unmotivated and lethargic. At first I thought I simply missed the outdoor fun and lightheartedness of summer. I was in mourning for better weather. My husband felt rejected. We argued about having sex a lot.

"Then I noticed how much better I felt if I just took a vacation in a warm climate during the winter. I investigated the subject and discovered SAD. I realized I was one of those people who suffered from it."

Donna consulted a doctor familiar with the syndrome who prescribed light therapy. In this treatment, patients are typically exposed to lamps of approximately 2,500 lumen, the same amount of light you'd get sitting in the window on a sunny spring day. The light is placed at eye level about three feet away from the patient. Though most doctors prescribe a daily regimen throughout the winter months, the timing and the dosage of the light vary. Some doctors advise two hours of light in the mornings, for example, while others recommend two to four hours of light at midday. This does seem like a lot of time under a light, but patients can read, write, eat, talk on the phone, work at a computer, and do anything else they would do sitting in the sun. And some people who are able to sleep under the light set timers to give them therapy during their pre-waking hours.

"When I started light treatment, it was like a miracle," Donna said. "I was back to my old self. I had a healthy libido again. I bought my own treatment lamp and use it every morning to take a light bath during the winter."

Donna's pattern of behavior was typical of SAD sufferers, but not everyone who loses interest in sex during the winter has the syndrome. There may be other seasonal factors contributing to depression and loss of libido. Some peo-

ple may be out of work during the cold months. Others may have extra work or family responsibilities at that time. ■

If you are diagnosed as a SAD sufferer, the light treatment is certainly worth trying. There are no side effects; and the treatment will probably work within a few days. For more information on research programs, companies making lamps, and private practitioners who treat SAD nationwide—call The Light Therapy Information Service in New York City at 212-960-5714.

Secrets, sexual

Almost everyone has at least one sexual secret, a piece of relevant information withheld from partners. Most sexual secrets fall into one of three categories: partner histories, arousal preferences, and fantasies. Sometimes the secret is an affair, which is a category unto itself. (See Extramarital Affairs.)

Why do people keep secrets from each other? Most fear their partners would be disturbed or turned off by the undisclosed information. A man who fantasizes making love to two women—a very common male fantasy—might think his wife would be jealous, threatened, or repulsed. Another man who is very aroused by having his nipples stimulated may not tell his partner what he wants because he thinks his preference is unmanly. A woman might not tell her husband she masturbates because she fears he would feel emasculated or consider her oversexed if he knew. Even faking an orgasm is a form of a secret, the secret being the person did not have the response they feigned to have.

Sometimes these fears grow out of negative sex attitudes learned in childhood. Shame and furtiveness often accompany sexual experimentation in adolescence. As adults in intimate relationships, some of us continue to behave as though our sexual thoughts and feelings were shameful.

People may withhold sexual information out of fear of rejection, too. They may be anxious about their fantasies or desires and project that anxiety on the partner who, they fear, couldn't possibly love them if the truth were known. Or they may consider the partner less adventuresome than they are and keep their secrets to protect the other's sensibilities. Many people are reluctant to share their fantasies for these reasons.

Keeping quiet about a sexual past is another matter. Former lovers, a homosexual experience, use of prostitutes, or participation in one night stands or group sex may or may not be relevant to the present relationship, depending on level of health risk and whether the behavior is recurring or not. Some people also withhold a history of rape or sexual abuse, partly because discussing the episode would be painful.

Should you share sexual secrets with your partner? There are good reasons for doing so—and a few bad ones. Telling your partner about your fantasies and desires can promote better understanding of your sexual needs and open the door to similar confessions from him or her. Mutual sharing can enhance the relationship by opening the channels of communication, help heal past hurts, and possibly expand your lovemaking to include those hidden desires. Most people can handle sexual secrets better than their partners think they can. On the other hand, confessing in anger that you had a brief liaison with his or her best friend before the wedding only causes pain. Revenge is not a good motive for sharing a sexual secret.

What Men and Women Say About Sexual Secrets

From a 38-year-old man: "My wife and I were separated for six months. During that time I had brief liaisons with a dozen women. When I got back with my wife, I didn't tell her about the other women until we had our first big fight. She accused me of being selfish in bed and I retorted, 'Selfish! I had a dozen women during the months we were apart. None of those women had any complaints. Selfish, my ass. You're never satisfied, that's your problem!' We were in counseling for months after that."

A 33-year-old woman says: "John and I were together for three years before I considered telling him something I had never told anyone. I told him because I wanted him to understand me better. He frequently asked me to give him oral sex and I resisted. John thought I didn't love him enough. There was another reason. When I was a child, my mother left me with a male babysitter. One day this guy talked me into oral sex. I did it because I was scared and I wanted him to like me. I gagged and felt terrible afterward. He never made me do it again, but the experience scarred me. When I told John, he was understanding. The tension between us evaporated. Eventually, I was comfortable with performing oral sex on him."

A 50-year-old man says: "I cheated on my wife in our early years together, but I have never told her. We are approaching our twenty-fifth anniversary together. She would only be hurt by that information. It might ease my conscience, but at what cost to her? I keep my silence."

And a 39-year-old woman says: "I have never told the men in my life about my fantasies. They are often wild and sometimes violent. I fantasize being whipped and whipping, having sex with more than one man and with a woman. My fantasies are like something that would be censored on cable. I am not exactly guilty about them, but I'm not proud. And if I told a man, he might get the wrong idea about what I am really like in bed. Not like that!"

The Five Keys to Sharing Sexual Secrets

1. *Think before you share.* Examine your motives for sharing a sexual secret. Are they good ones?

2. *Give yourself a break.* Your fantasies and desires don't make you a terrible person. Stop being your own worst sexual critic.

3. *Initiate the discussion in a nonthreatening way.* Use "I" statements and express your feelings. Your partner may be threatened by disclosures that make him or her feel inadequate.

4. *Help your partner share in return.* If you have a hidden desire or secret fantasy, isn't it reasonable to assume your partner does too? Don't insist on a quid pro quo swap of secrets, but do encourage an exchange of wish lists.

5. *Give it more than one try.* Sharing may be awkward for you or your partner or both. Don't let discomfort discourage you from opening up again.

Sensuality

(see also Aural Arousal, the Kiss)

Good lovers are sensual people who revel in all five senses: taste, smell, sight, touch, and sound. Lovemaking is more than technique and genital connection. Many people confine themselves to that narrow definition in part by limiting their sensory input to familiar touch, sight, and some sounds. Awaken your senses and your sexuality will expand.

In lovemaking, the body's sense of *taste* serves a dual function, helping us define what we are touching as well as tasting. You feel your partner's genitals with your tongue when you lick them. Kissing is a way of exploring the taste and feel of another's lips, tongue, and inner mouth.

The sense of smell is an integral part of sexuality for the obvious reason: semen and vaginal secretions have a scent. Many women and men use fragrance as a seductive tool. Scented candles, perfume, flowers, even the aroma of special foods being prepared help set the mood for lovemaking. In the United States, bathing or showering is often part of the preparation for sex, but in other countries the body's natural scents are considered more erotic than clean skin. Whether you enjoy body odors or prefer the scent of perfumed soap is a matter of individual taste though, in general, women are more likely to opt for the bottled fragrance than men are. While further research needs to be done, evidence also exists that everyone has a sixth sense, a tiny organ in the nasal cavity that responds to pheromones, the chemicals that play a role in human emotions such as love.

Sight, touch, and *sound* seem more obviously connected to sex than taste and smell. For that reason, these senses may become dulled. The feel of a lover's skin and the sound of his or her voice in bed may seem too familiar to be exciting anymore. But the senses can be revived.

How Men and Women Describe Their Sensuality

From a 39-year-old man: "I received a sensual jolt last year when my lover asked me if I wanted to play a game called 'heat and ice.' After holding ice cubes in her mouth, she performed fellatio on me. When her mouth warmed up, she filled it with hot tea to make it even warmer and went back to fellatio. Later, during intercourse when I was ready to come, she grabbed a handful of ice from the bowl beside the bed and slapped it against my scrotum. For weeks afterward, my skin was more sensitive during lovemaking."

A 36-year-old woman says: "My husband and I explore our sensuality in many ways. We lick honey off each other's nipples, fondle each other's genitals through silk, and make love to our favorite piano concertos. Sometimes we make love blindfolded to increase our sensual perceptions."

And from a 27-year-old woman: "I knew I had found the man I was going to marry the first time we kissed and he held me in his arms. I buried my face in his neck and took a deep breath. I loved the way he smelled. I knew I was home."

Five Exercises for Awakening Sensuality

1. *The sensory surprise.* Take turns planning a lovemaking session with emphasis on sensory delights. If he is in charge of the planning and she loves flowers, he might spray the room with rosewater and put rose petals on the bed. Add some detail that will ignite each one of the five senses.

2. *Touch focusing.* Close out everything else and concentrate solely on what you are touching. Feel your lover's skin under your hands as you stroke his or her body. Note how the texture of the skin changes from one place to another, how varying the pressure makes touch a different experience.

3. *Touch expanding.* Introduce some unusual materials into your lovemaking—fur, silk, feathers, velvet, leather, warm water, ice.

4. *Sound play.* Put some excitement into the pillow talk. Have phone sex. Bring music into the bedroom.

5. *Awareness expansion.* Every day for at least ten minutes pay attention to your surroundings in a new way. On a familiar walk, look at the trees. What do you notice about the trees that you didn't see before?

Sex Education

(see also Masturbation, Teenage Sex)

Sex education is one of the most critical tasks of parenthood, too important to be totally left to the schools and churches. What does a parent have to do to educate offspring? Provide children with good sex information, instill positive attitudes about sexuality, and teach them how to behave in a sexually responsible way.

Some parents do nothing at all about sex education. The subject, sex, is never mentioned in their homes; and the unspoken hope is that their children won't "discover" sex until they're safely out of those homes, living adult lives. Some parents preach against sex, equating pleasure with sin, and their hope is that their children won't "discover" sex until they are married and want to reproduce. And some parents focus obsessively on the negative aspects of sex, warning against abusive people, STDs, unplanned pregnancies, promiscuous lifestyles; and their fervently expressed hope is that their children will not be hurt by sex.

Some people fear that talking about sex will make them want to become sexual. They hope that ignorance will keep their children from finding their own genitals or acting upon the urges they develop in adolescence when their hormones kick in. Nothing could be further from the truth. The human race was multiplying long before humans had the words for sex education.

Whatever you do or don't do, your children will explore their own sexuality. Good sex information will help them understand, appreciate, and respect that sexuality. If they know the pros and cons of becoming sexually active and how to protect themselves when they choose to do so, they will make better sexual choices for themselves and their partners. In other countries, particularly the Netherlands, Sweden, and Finland, where sex education is part of general education, teenagers have sex at an average later age than U.S. teens do and have dramatically lower incidences of pregnancy and STD infection than do our teens. The United States leads the industrialized nations in teen pregnancies—not a distinction to make us proud.

Sex education is a lifelong process. At any age, we can learn more about making love. If you think you learned everything you needed to know about sex in high school, think again.

The Top Ten Questions Parents of Children and Teens Have About Sex

1. *How do I talk to my children about sex?*

Answer their questions honestly and without embarrassment, but give them only the information they need at the time. A three year old who wants to know where babies come from doesn't need and won't understand all the details of reproduction. She'll be satisfied with being told babies grow in a special place inside her mother's body. (If you do give too much information, however, don't worry about it. She won't remember it anyway.) A thirteen year old knows where babies grow and probably how they got there, but she might have some erroneous information and want to know exactly what sexual activity leads to pregnancy or how to prevent that from happening. Don't treat children's questions about sexuality any differently from the way you would questions about other areas of life.

2. *What do we say to a child who has caught us in the act of making love?*

Don't overreact. Pull on a robe and take the child back to bed. Explain that you and your partner were not fighting or hurting each other, a common childhood misinterpretation of intercourse. You might want to say that you were playing vigorously or showing your love for each other in the way adults sometimes do. Be affectionate and reassuring.

3. *At what age should we plan to have The Big Talk with our kids?*

Forget about "The Big Talk." Children learn about sex over time and through the answers to individual questions. Planning to sit down with them and tell them all they need to know in one session is unrealistic.

4. *How do I handle questions asked at inappropriate times?*

If a child asks a question about sex in a public place or even when you're too busy to provide a thoughtful answer, you can simply say, "We'll talk about that later."

5. *What words should we use for genitals?*

The right words. Penis and vagina are not dirty words.

6. *How do I convince my teenagers not to have sex yet?*

You may not be able to convince your teenagers to wait as long as you would like, but research suggests that adolescents who talk to their parents about sexuality are less active than those who don't. Give them good information, including facts about birth control and STD prevention. Teach them to value their own sexuality and that of others. Tell them you hope they will wait to become sexually active until they are old enough to handle all the feelings that will engender. Let them know they can always talk to you about sexuality issues. Then you have to trust that they will behave in a sexually responsible way at whatever age they become active.

7. *How do I know if a sex education class is a good one?*

Public schools are required to allow parents to review sex education materials. If you have concerns, make an appointment to talk to the teacher about the curriculum. A good teacher should be able to talk openly about the subject.

8. *I've caught my teenage son with pornographic magazines and videos. What should I do?*

Don't overreact. This is not a problem unless the materials are violent and degrading or he is spending an inordinate amount of time on them. You can tell him you find the material offensive. If you punish him for looking at them or overdramatize your response, you risk making the magazines and videos more alluring to him.

9. *My six-year-old daughter and a neighbor boy were playing "doctor" and examining each other's private parts. What should I do?*

This is not unusual childhood behavior. Calmly tell them that "private parts" are just that—private—and they shouldn't let other people touch them in those places. Suggest another game.

10. *How do we explain homosexuality to our kids?*

Many, if not most, families have a gay or lesbian relative, friend, or neighbor, and gays and lesbians live more openly now than they did in the past. Children will probably ask about relationships of people they know. Tell them some men love other men and some women love other women.

Sex Therapy

Sex therapy is a relatively new practice. In 1970 pioneering sex researchers Dr. William Masters and Virginia Johnson revolutionized the treatment of sexual problems, an area that had been ignored by the medical profession and treated with little success by many psychotherapists. Now sex therapy enables people to solve once nearly insoluble problems such as impotence and the inability to have an orgasm in a matter of weeks or months through a combination of physical and psychological processes: talking about issues and problems and "homework," erotic exercises performed by the couple at home. Many of the prescriptions for dysfunctions such as premature ejaculation are so easily conveyed that couples can "cure" themselves with the aid of books such as this one.

The aim of sex therapy is twofold: to help couples resolve the psychological and emotional difficulties that stand in the way of their having a satisfying relationship and to help them improve the physical quality of their lovemaking through the use of various exercises and techniques. For therapy to be successful, couples must talk honestly to each other and the therapist. Open discussions of sexuality are the catalyst for improving relationships by increasing pleasure.

Why see a sex therapist? If you haven't been able to solve the problem on your own, professional intervention is a good idea. Some couples seek help even after they have corrected a minor problem because they want to increase their sexual pleasure and deepen their relationship.

Ask your doctor or other trusted source such as clergyperson for a referral. Or find help through a medical center or a teaching hospital that has a sex therapy clinic on premises. A good sex therapist will first take a thorough medical and sexual history and, in some cases, recommend a medical examination before treatment begins. Early in treatment, you should identify goals and establish a realistic time frame for the achievement of those goals. Unlike psychoanalysis, which is open-ended and can last for years, sex therapy usually works within a time frame.

Many therapists treat couples only, though some will work with individuals. Typically, for uncomplicated issues, couples see the therapist once or maybe twice a week, with an average number of 15 to 20 sessions. The therapist educates the couple about sexuality, dispelling some of the myths and misinformation they may have, gives them permission to explore and enjoy their sexuality, helps them establish effective communication and resolve emotional conflicts, and sends them home with prescriptive exercises. They report back about their experiences with those exercises on the following visit. Sex therapy *never* involves sexual interaction with the therapist. Nor should he or she ever suggest observing sex acts in the office.

To get the most out of sex therapy, be prepared to talk as openly as possible with your therapist. As is the case with any therapist or doctor, you need to feel comfortable with this person and have a reasonable degree of trust in him or her. If you don't, seek help somewhere else.

EXAMPLE

"I had to drag Len into therapy," Bonnie said. "First he said there was nothing wrong. Then he said he couldn't talk about our private issues, especially sexual ones, with a stranger. He finally consented to go with me because we had reached a stalemate."

In their early thirties and married seven years, Bonnie and Len were rarely making love. They had blamed their lack of desire on overwork, stress, their travel schedules. Bonnie was the first to recognize deeper problems.

"When we did have sex, it wasn't satisfying," she said. "It hadn't been for a long time."

In therapy, they explored the nonsexual issues that had been wreaking havoc with their sex life. He resented her career success, which had outpaced his. She resented his pushing her to get pregnant when she wasn't ready to do so. He accused her of never being in the mood for sex, while she said he never tried to please her sexually.

At the end of treatment, they had reestablished good communication. Though all their differences weren't resolved, they were talking about them outside the bedroom, and their lovemaking had improved dramatically. ■

ℱive Warning Signs Indicating Therapy Is Needed

1. *Frequent arguments about sex.* Do you often argue about frequency or the kinds of lovemaking each prefers? Are you unable to resolve the conflict to each partner's satisfaction?
2. *Avoidance of sex.* Do you rarely make love? Or, have you stopped making love altogether?
3. *Strong feelings of sexual frustration and disappointment.* Is she rarely or never orgasmic and often frustrated? Is he often frustrated and disappointed at his inability to get or sustain an erection?
4. *Inability to talk about sexual problems or desires to each other.* Are you unable to tell your partner what you want and need sexually? Are you faking orgasm rather than expressing your needs?
5. *Extramarital affairs.* Is one or both partners seeking sexual satisfaction outside the marriage?

If you feel the need for therapy, but your partner balks:

■ *Explain, but don't accuse.* Tell him or her why you want to get help without saying, "It's all your fault." Use "I" statements. "I want to make our sex life better."

■ *Ask for his or her help in solving the problems.* Your partner still doesn't want to go to therapy? What plan does she/he have for resolving the difficulty? Help your partner see that the plan might be more easily implemented with professional help.

■ *Don't give up with one try*. Bring up the subject again another time. Some people need time to adjust to the idea of seeking help before they can agree to do it.

■ *Go alone.* If your partner won't go with you, go solo.

Sex Toys

Sex toys include vibrators, dildoes, feathers, various forms of restraints, ben wa balls (inserted into the vagina) cock rings, even whips, paddles, costumes, and nipple clamps, the accoutrements of S/M. (See Kinky Sex.) Any object used to arouse a partner and/or prolong and intensify lovemaking could be considered a sex toy. The use of such items has increased in recent years, partly because they are more generally available both in shops and through catalogs. Many people have seen the toys in X-rated videos and been inspired to try them. (Two excellent catalog sources for all kinds of toys and accoutrements are Good Vibrations, 1210 Valencia Street, San Francisco, CA 94110 and Eve's Garden, 119 W. 57th Street, New York, NY 10019.)

The most commonly used sex toy is the vibrator. There are several types and the basic varieties, marketed as "personal massagers," can be purchased in drug, department, and variety stores, typically next to the blow dryers and curling irons. Electric vibrators were first manufactured in this country in the early 1900s and prescribed for some women by their doctors as a treatment for "female hysteria." Currently, some sex therapists recommend their use as a learning aide for women who have difficulty reaching orgasm or who have never reached orgasm at all.

There is some controversy among therapists about "prescribing" vibrator use because there are more sophisticated ways of treating the problem. A woman can, for example, explore her own sexual past to find sources of arousal and replicate those situations with her partner. On the other hand, some women, particularly those who have never had an orgasm, can learn how to be orgasmic fairly quickly with the vibrator and move on to being orgasmic during manual masturbation and finally with a partner. For women who are receptive, I often suggest the vibrator as a starting place. Once the woman has the orgasmic experience it is easier to duplicate with other forms of arousal.

Vibrators are often used, especially by women, for solitary pleasure during masturbation, but an increasing number of couples are incorporating them into loveplay. They can take the performance pressure off a man while adding variety to lovemaking. Some men also enjoy vibrator stimulation of their genitals.

What People Say About Sex Toys

From a 36-year-old woman: "The vibrator is the easiest way for me to have an orgasm. I love it when my husband does it to me because his technique is better than mine. We sit on the floor or on the bed, my back to him, with him snug up against me. Lots of skin contact! He reaches around with one arm and uses the vibrator on my clitoris while holding and stroking me with the other hand."

A 40-year-old man says: "When I was younger, I was threatened by the idea that a partner of mine would use a vibrator. Now I enjoy using one with her occasionally. I find it exciting to have the underside of my penis and the ridge around the head stimulated. Direct pressure is too much. My partner uses the hand-held vibrator and takes my penis in her hand."

And a 31-year-old man says: "My fiancee and I got a box of sex toys as a shower gift from friends. At first we laughed at the stuff. Then we decided to try it. We put honey dust on each other and licked it off, fastened each other to the bed with Velcro restraints, and used every attachment for the vibrator. Toys are fun!"

ive Tips for Enhancing a Couple's Vibrator Use

1. *Maintain emotional closeness*. Using a vibrator doesn't have to turn sex into a mechanical experience. Look into each other's eyes. Caress, fondle, kiss.

2. *Experiment with different sizes, shapes, and attachments*. Why be a one-vibrator couple? Each attachment creates a different sensation.

3. *Use lubrication*. Vibrators can cause friction.

4. *Start by massaging your partner's body with the vibrator*. Use it on the back, neck, arms. legs. Move slowly to the genitals, just as you would if you were using your hands or mouth.

5. *Combine penetration and the vibrator*. Hold the vibrator on her clitoris while slowly thrusting into her vagina with your penis.

Sexually Transmitted Diseases and sexuality

(see also Condoms, Safe Sex)

Approximately 12 million Americans will contract a sexually transmitted disease, or STD, this year. With the exception of AIDS, these diseases, transmitted through sexual contact, are curable, most of them easily treated by antibiotics. When left untreated, some of them can lead to serious complications such as infertility. Many STDs are largely asymptomatic, making prevention and regular testing that much more important. For specific diseases with symptoms and treatments, ask your doctor to recommend a book.

Sexually active adults who are not in monogamous relationships should practice safe sex, using condoms and nonoxonyl 9 during intercourse. In addition, they should discuss with their doctor periodic testing for STDs. When two people decide to make a commitment to each other, they should be tested for STDs before they discard the condoms.

Many older adults mistakenly believe that only the young get STDs. While the majority of cases are among those under 25, fully one third represent people over that age. If you've reentered the dating scene after a divorce, you can't afford not to use condoms.

STDs and the fear of them affect sexuality. Some people are reluctant to be sexually active again after contracting an STD. Others use the fear of "catching something" as a reason for staying out of sexual relationships. It's foolish to ignore the risks inherent in sex outside a monogamous relationship, but don't let fear dictate your sexual and emotional choices.

The Top Five Questions People Have About STDs

1. *How can I tell if someone has an STD?*

You probably can't. While some STDs have visible symptoms, many others don't. Chlamydia, for example, the most prevalent STD, is largely asymptomatic in men and women. And you certainly can't tell by looking at someone if they are infected. STDs affect people from all socioeconomic groups.

2. *How can I get a partner to share sexual histories?*

You should talk with a new partner about your sexual histories—past partners and experiences relevant to sexual health, as well as attitudes about sexuality—before you become sexually involved. That doesn't mean getting names of past partners. Begin by expressing your discomfort with the subject to put the other person at ease. Share your own information. Don't be critical or judgmental when it's your turn to listen. But don't throw caution to the wind either.

3. *How can I tell a new partner I have herpes?*

Don't wait until you have begun lovemaking to bring the subject up if you have herpes or another condition such as genital warts that hasn't been completely cleared up with treatment. Let your partner know early in the relationship. Explain the kinds of sex you can safely have without risking infecting another person. Most people will appreciate your honesty and caring.

4. *How can I get over the shame I feel about having had an STD?*

Having an STD is no more shameful than having any other disease. Fear and ignorance cause us to label STDs "dirty" diseases. Promise yourself you will practice safe sex in the future and put this behind you. If your feelings of shame persist, you may need to talk to a professional.

5. *My new husband swears he hasn't cheated on me, but I was just diagnosed with an STD. How can that be?*

This situation is more common than you realize. Either one of you may have contracted an STD from a previous partner before you met each other. Some STDs are asymptomatic and are missed in routine medical exams. The infection may run its course or be cleared up by antibiotics prescribed for another condition. Often the disease is not detected until a couple try to conceive and discover that an undiagnosed STD has scarred her fallopian tubes or lowered his sperm count. Testing is the only way to be sure you don't have a disease.

AIDS

Acquired immunodeficiency syndrome (AIDS) is caused by the human immunodeficiency virus (HIV). Once a person has been exposed to the virus, she/he tests positive for HIV and can transmit the disease even if no symptoms are present. Approximately 50 percent of HIV-infected people will develop AIDS within five years. Early symptoms can include fatigue, weight loss, diarrhea, night sweats, and infections of the mouth and mucous membranes. Drug treatment can help improve and prolong life for HIV-infected people, but there is no known cure.

You cannot catch the AIDS virus as easily as you catch a common cold from casual contact with others. The disease is transmitted by semen-to-blood or blood-to-blood transmission, with the most common means being shared needles in drug use, anal intercourse, and vaginal intercourse when STDs or other factors have caused tears or lesions in the vaginal wall and/or similar conditions in the skin of the penis. A minute break in the skin can provide the entryway for the virus. Infected mothers also pass the virus along to their babies during pregnancy or delivery. (The risk of contracting HIV from a blood transfusion, which happened early in the epidemic in the United States, has been greatly reduced by blood screening.) In this country, early outbreaks of AIDS occurred in the gay community primarily among men who'd had many sexual partners. In Africa, the majority of people first infected with the disease were heterosexuals. No one should consider themselves immune.

How can you tell if someone is HIV-infected? *Not by looking.* A person with the virus can appear to be healthy until she/he develops the cancers and infections associated with full-blown AIDS. *And often not by asking either.* "Exchange sexual histories" is advice often given to singles these days. People do lie about their sexual history, particularly if they feel ashamed of a bisexual or a promiscuous lifestyle. They may also lie about past drug use. Some men and women are HIV positive without knowing they are because they haven't been tested or were tested too soon after they contracted the virus. To be sure you are negative, you need to be tested several times over a period of months after a sexual encounter with an infected person.

It is not possible to know for sure if a potential new sex partner has an HIV infection. Therefore you must protect yourself by practicing safe sex until you and your partner have agreed to be monogamous and have been tested for HIV as well as other STDs. This does not have to take the joy out of sex. There are many ways of giving and receiving pleasure that do not put people at risk.

It is my belief that some people, particularly right-wing commentators, have gleefully seized upon the AIDS epidemic as an excuse for endorsing sexual repression. Everyone, particularly the nation's youth, needs access to good sex information and contraceptives. Scaring people only guarantees they will take more sexual risks because they don't know what is safe and what isn't or how to protect themselves. The human sex drive is too strong to be suppressed.

For ways of making love to an infected partner, see Aural Arousal, Masturbation, Massage, Noncoital Sex, Oral Sex, Romance.

Smoking, effect on sexuality

(see also Health and Sexuality, Illness or Disability, Medications)

If you or your partner need one more reason to quit smoking, here it is: Smoking may contribute to impotence. Smoking constricts blood flow through the body's arteries, and erections depend on good blood flow to the penis. To a lesser degree, women's sexual functioning is affected by smoking. Women have greater sensation when their genitals are fully engorged, and again, smoking constricts the blood flow, reducing blood circulation to the genitals. In some women, this may make clitoral stimulation and orgasm difficult.

For both men and women who smoke, the biggest gift—for long-term better sex—they can give themselves and their partners is smoke cessation.

Taoist and Tantric Sex or Eastern Sexual Techniques

(see also Ejaculation [premature, techniques for delaying], Kegels)

Two sex-advice books written two thousand years ago have had a lasting impact on the world. The basis of the Eastern sexual philosophies, the *Tao* of China and *The Kama Sutra* of India, are as graphic as today's sex manuals—and more erotic. The positions and techniques they described helped couples prolong and intensify lovemaking and achieve a closer, more spiritual union at the same time. Renewed interest in that approach to sexuality has been steadily increasing in this country over the past several years.

Taoist teachings stressed male ejaculatory control. The man's aim was to please the woman and give her as many orgasms as possible while holding back his own. Ideally, he would not have an orgasm every time he made love and, if he did have an orgasm, would not ejaculate. Reputedly, Taoist masters ejaculated only a few times a year. The Tantric approach also encourages prolonged lovemaking but with less emphasis on the man's holding back his own orgasm. Strong PC muscles are necessary for Eastern lovemaking. For true devotees, sex is a way of life, not a part of life.

Many books interpret Eastern sexual philosophies for modern lovers. Frankly, most of them are not very accessible to the average couple who may not be interested in the spiritual theories and probably do not have the time to devote hours to lovemaking every time. I do recommend *The Art of Sexual Ecstasy* by Margo Anand for those wishing to read further. In addition, many workshops and seminars across the country, particularly in California, teach the ways of Eastern sex.

There are techniques a couple can learn to prolong and intensify their lovemaking while still leading full and active lives outside the bedroom. Pleasure-oriented rather than goal-oriented, this kind of lovemaking has one simple underlying principle: Using a low level of stimulation, keep arousal at low levels, especially for the man, for as long as possible. Arousal builds very slowly toward a strong climax. Men over 40 can do this more easily than younger men can. And the aging of the baby-boom population may go a long way toward explaining the new popularity of an ancient way of making love.

What Men and Women Say About Taoist and Tantric Sex

From a 35-year-old man: "My wife dragged me to a weekend workshop on Tantra. The instructors were too full of themselves, and I resisted the pitch. But I admit we got some things out of it. The breathing and the Tantra kiss. Excellent!"

A 40-year-old woman says: "My husband and I needed something to add excitement to our sex life, and this was it. We learned a few new positions and, more important, began spending more time on sex."

And from a 28-year-old woman: "I am involved with a man 20 years my senior. Tantra was his idea. I think it's great for women. It's all about pleasing us. What could be better?"

The Four Eastern Sex Techniques Any Couple Can Use

1. *Deep breathing.* Learn how to breathe deeply and slowly, letting the air fill your chest cavity and expanding it, before slowly exhaling. Use the slow breathing to slow the arousal process. Try these exercises to use breathing as a way of getting closer to your partner: (1) Lie

together spoon fashion. Imagine you have a nose on your chest and are breathing your partner into your body as you take deep breaths. (2) Again, nestled as spoons, close your eyes and breathe together for five minutes. Inhale, hold your breath, exhale.

2. *The eye lock.* Don't close your eyes while making love. Look into each other's eyes. You'll be surprised at how this intensifies the pleasure of lovemaking.

3. *The Tantric kiss.* Stop lovemaking before either reaches orgasm. She sits on his lap, his penis inside her, their legs wrapped around each other. Remain as still as possible. Press foreheads together. With eyes open, put your mouths together and exchange breaths. As he inhales, she exhales, and vice versa. If you can do this for even a few minutes before becoming so aroused you have to kiss passionately and move toward orgasm, you will both experience stronger climaxes.

4. *The set of nines.* During intercourse, he takes seven shallow strokes, allowing only the head of the penis to penetrate the vagina, then takes two deep thrusts. Now six shallow and three deep, and so forth until he is taking nine deep strokes. Very exciting for both partners— and helps a man delay orgasm.

Teenage Sex

(see also Sex Education)

Whether their parents are aware of it or not, sexual activity is commonplace among American teenagers. Today, one third of adolescents have had sex by age 15. Our society frowns on teen sex. Many national leaders preach "just say no," favoring that approach over educating teens on sexuality and birth control. Yet we have the highest rate of teen pregnancies of the industrialized nations, and every year 2.5 million teens are infected with an STD. The combination of denying reality while delivering a message of piety isn't working.

I don't advocate sexual activity among teens, but I do encourage parents, educators, and religious and political leaders to acknowledge that activity and realistically assess the problems it creates for our nation's youth. How else can we solve them?

Teenagers are biologically ready for sex. Stern adult warnings and admonitions are feeble weapons against burgeoning sexuality. That doesn't mean teens can't stop themselves from having intercourse—

or that they shouldn't stop. Few teens, especially younger ones, are emotionally and psychologically prepared for intercourse, though their bodies may be ready.

Adolescent sexuality is a strong force that must be respected—and reckoned with—as is adult sexuality. Educate your teens about birth control and disease prevention. Create an environment in which they can comfortably talk about sexual issues and concerns. Denying their sexuality won't keep them chaste and safe from harm. In fact, it may have the opposite effect.

There are ways of enjoying sexual stimulation and obtaining release outside of intercourse. Masturbation, noncoital sex such as outercourse, and fantasy can fulfill needs safely. Teenagers who don't rush headlong into intercourse but choose these sexual activities instead learn more about their bodies and what gives them pleasure as well as protect themselves from the emotional and physical risks they aren't ready to handle.

EXAMPLE

"My parents would be angry if they knew how close I am to actually doing it," said Robin, who just turned 15. "Having sex feels right to me now. I think I am ready."

Several of Robin's friends have already become sexually active. They talk about their boyfriends and their sexual exploits, whetting her appetite for experience. In the competitive world of teens, she feels they are outpacing her.

"I have had an orgasm from masturbating," she said. "I wonder what it will feel like to have intercourse. I masturbate about once a week, but that's not the same thing."

Her parents have warned her about the dangers of sex. They've lectured her about AIDS and unwanted pregnancy. But she doesn't think that will happen to her.

"Especially the AIDS," she said. "I don't know that kind of people. I'm more worried about how my boyfriend will act if I ask him to use a condom. Will he get mad? Will it make sex less fun for him? I know a girl whose boyfriend dumped her over the condom issue. He said they ruined sex for him."

Robin is on the verge of making one of the biggest decisions of her life. What she does now could change her future. If you know a teenager like Robin, give him or her this list. ■

The Five Crucial Teen Sex Guidelines

1. *Joyously acknowledge your sexuality.* The sexual awakening is an exciting period of life. Don't deny your feelings. And don't let negative sex messages, whatever the source, make you feel bad about your developing sexual interest.

2. *Explore your body yourself.* Masturbation is a normal, safe, and readily available sexual outlet. What you learn about your body during self-pleasuring will help you become a better lover.

3. *Set your own ground rules for sexual experimentation.* Don't be influenced by peers or media images. If you want to stop at kissing, caressing, outercourse—bringing a partner to orgasm without intercourse—then stop. The majority of women do not reach orgasm during intercourse only anyway. And the most intense orgasms are achieved through masturbation. Your friends are probably exaggerating the pleasures of their experiences.

4. *Indulge in fantasy.* But know the difference between fantasy and fact. Many young people, especially girls, convince themselves they are in love because they are aroused. Love can be a dangerous fantasy if it leads you to have intercourse before you are emotionally ready and/or to commit to a "relationship" with someone who is best enjoyed as a crush.

5. *Accept the consequences of sexual involvement.* Sex is a natural and beautiful part of life, but sexual relationships have consequences, both physical and emotional. Be prepared for intercourse. Use condoms. And be prepared to handle the change in a relationship that intercourse will bring.

Trust

Erotic love is a combination of elements, including desire and acceptance, openness and vulnerability. But the elements of love float loosely in disarray if not bound by *trust,* the invisible connective thread. Some people find it unusually hard to trust, while others too easily place their trust in the wrong people. Some betray the trust of their partners by having extramarital affairs or behaving in other hurtful ways. If a relationship damaged betrayal is to be repaired, the partners must learn to trust, and be trustworthy, all over again.

Whenever couples list their areas of conflict, they are talking about the issue of trust though they may not use the word. The issue is sex? One of them has an affair, breaking the marriage vow. Money? One continually overspends, violating a budget, the monetary agreement they've made as a couple. Children? One goes behind the other's back in granting concessions and winning favored-parent status. In-laws? One partner betrays another by putting loyalty to his or her family ahead of loyalty to the marriage.

Even the seemingly smaller daily matters that reduce couples to bickering have their basis in trust. Intimate confidences are betrayed and promises broken. He "never" does what he says he will do. She tells her friends about his sexual problems. This buildup of "minor annoyances" make people so angry because they sense they can't trust their partners anymore.

Trust is not an optional component in love relationships. It is bedrock. Can you have good sex without trust? Maybe, but not on a consistent basis.

Do you trust your partner? Can your partner trust you? Sometimes the answers to those questions aren't obvious. Trust issues aren't always immediately evident.

It's vital to recognize the early signs of trouble, the trust distress signals. Many of the couples I've counseled asked me how they could do that. To help them, I developed the Trust Scale, an inventory that indicates how much you trust your partner. The 15 points reflect the concerns and fears of most couples. I've used the scale successfully over the past several years with well over a hundred couples.

Trust Scale

Read each of the following statements and decide how true it is of your relationship and your feelings about your partner. Circle the number that most closely corresponds to your view. Unless there has been a dramatic betrayal recently—in which case the inventory is superfluous—do not lend too much weight to a particular incident, positive or negative. Instead, consider overall behavior over a prolonged period of time.

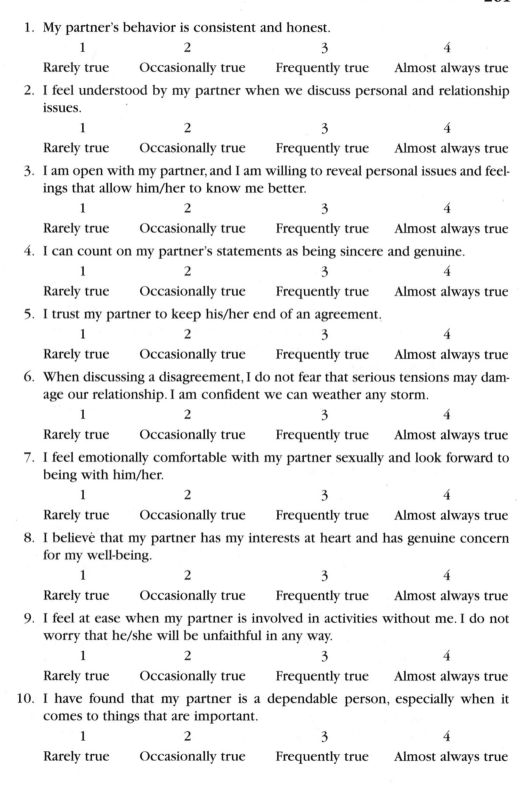

1. My partner's behavior is consistent and honest.

1	2	3	4
Rarely true	Occasionally true	Frequently true	Almost always true

2. I feel understood by my partner when we discuss personal and relationship issues.

1	2	3	4
Rarely true	Occasionally true	Frequently true	Almost always true

3. I am open with my partner, and I am willing to reveal personal issues and feelings that allow him/her to know me better.

1	2	3	4
Rarely true	Occasionally true	Frequently true	Almost always true

4. I can count on my partner's statements as being sincere and genuine.

1	2	3	4
Rarely true	Occasionally true	Frequently true	Almost always true

5. I trust my partner to keep his/her end of an agreement.

1	2	3	4
Rarely true	Occasionally true	Frequently true	Almost always true

6. When discussing a disagreement, I do not fear that serious tensions may damage our relationship. I am confident we can weather any storm.

1	2	3	4
Rarely true	Occasionally true	Frequently true	Almost always true

7. I feel emotionally comfortable with my partner sexually and look forward to being with him/her.

1	2	3	4
Rarely true	Occasionally true	Frequently true	Almost always true

8. I believe that my partner has my interests at heart and has genuine concern for my well-being.

1	2	3	4
Rarely true	Occasionally true	Frequently true	Almost always true

9. I feel at ease when my partner is involved in activities without me. I do not worry that he/she will be unfaithful in any way.

1	2	3	4
Rarely true	Occasionally true	Frequently true	Almost always true

10. I have found that my partner is a dependable person, especially when it comes to things that are important.

1	2	3	4
Rarely true	Occasionally true	Frequently true	Almost always true

11. My partner handles money matters between us in an open and fair manner.

1	2	3	4
Rarely true	Occasionally true	Frequently true	Almost always true

12. I am confident that during discussions of conflict my partner will not get out of control. He/she doesn't make me feel afraid.

1	2	3	4
Rarely true	Occasionally true	Frequently true	Almost always true

13. My partner treats me as an equal. He/she behaves toward me in a manner that conveys respect.

1	2	3	4
Rarely true	Occasionally true	Frequently true	Almost always true

14. Following a fight, my partner will make up promptly and sincerely rather than carrying a prolonged grudge.

1	2	3	4
Rarely true	Occasionally true	Frequently true	Almost always true

15. Though the future is never certain, I am comfortable with the emotional investment I have made in our relationship because I am confident about what lies ahead for us.

1	2	3	4
Rarely true	Occasionally true	Frequently true	Almost always true

What Your Answers Mean

1. Consistency and honesty

If you feel like a private investigator, you have a problem. When you trust your partner, you don't question every small action. You view his or her behavior as reasonably predictable. Too many questions and puzzled responses to actions indicate a lack of consistency and honesty.

2. Feeling understood

If you don't feel understood by your sex partner, who should know you well, your feelings of love and ardor will soon be dampened by resentment.

3. Being emotionally open

When we feel understood, we are encouraged to expose more of ourselves. The cornerstone of intimacy is the willingness to be self-disclosing while being empathetic to your partner's disclosures. Do you find yourself holding back? Is conversation between the two of you diminishing to necessary exchanges of information? Have long periods of silence become commonplace rather than occasional?

Your lack of intimacy may be caused by a growing sense of distrust.

4. *Being sincere and genuine*

Insincerity causes others to be guarded. It creates relationships lacking in trust and passion.

5. *Keeping an agreement*

Agreements that have been made without coercion are important trust builders. The disappointments, small and large, that occur as a result of a failure to keep the agreement erode trust.

6. *Confidence in resolving disagreements*

We want to trust our partners to work through whatever feelings come up until both feel cleared and settled about those feelings. That's part of commitment. The fear of disagreement or confrontation often inhibits couples from raising important issues. If these important issues are not resolved, they will stand as bricks in a wall blocking intimacy.

7. *Feeling desirous and emotionally comfortable with sex*

Sometimes when trust has been damaged, your body tells you before your head does. Although sex is only one link in the chain of relating intimately, this physical expression of love is, to most of us, invested with a great deal of importance. Of the many forms of intimacy, sex is probably the most sensitive and provocative. The changes in a couple's emotional bond are acted out most vividly in the bedroom. When distrust exists between them, they may have less desire for sexual relations or they may behave with less freedom when they do make love.

8. *Having your well-being and interests at heart*

A basic element of trust is the belief that your partner is on your side—for you, rather than against you. Your partner may disagree with you, but he/she should respect your vulnerabilities. True, some people are overly sensitive to criticism, even stated tactfully and in private. In most cases, however, a person who feels consistently ill-used and let down—or put down—has good reason for feeling that way.

9. *Trusting your partner when you're apart*

When your partner pursues an independent activity, do you feel abandoned or neglected? Perhaps you interpret her/his need for time alone as a sign of rejection. You imagine your partner is saying: I don't like you and I want to be independent of you. In fact, everyone needs to have interests outside a relationship.

Maybe you feel this way because you don't believe you are important enough to your partner. Or, you may be worried that he will find someone else more appealing. Trust is the real issue here. Has your partner done something to create distrust?

10. *Dependability*

People choose their partners for many reasons: sexual attraction, shared values and beliefs, among others. They should be looking for the person they can trust, the one who makes them feel safe. Imagine you are climbing a mountain. Do you want this person tied to you by a rope? Can you trust him or her with your life?

You trust your partner because you can depend on him/her when it counts. That trust develops over time. He always calls when he says he will. She takes care of the bills each month as she said she would when the family responsibilities were divided. More important, you know you can depend on your partner in situations when you would feel hurt or rejected if he let you down. He offers support when you're stressed from work. She was at your side when you were hospitalized and took care of you during convalescence.

11. *Handling money fairly and openly*

Money, like sex, is one of those issues fraught with many expectations. Money can give or take away power, self-esteem, reassurance, and emotional fulfillment. Like sex, money often fails to deliver on the promises we have assumed.

Conflicts about money are symbolic of underlying trust problems. The conflict can take many forms, including withholding money, lying about income or expenditures, spending too much and stressing the household budget, or being more frugal and controlling than is warranted. In a trusting, collaborative partnership, money conflicts are settled without undue hard feelings.

If money issues aren't resolved, they promote secretiveness and sap the partners' emotional energy.

12. *Feeling safe during disagreements*

Relationships provide fertile ground in which the germs of conflict can flourish, like the petri dishes in your high school biology class. Conflict, whether deep-seated or superficial, is inevitable. To completely avoid or deny disagreement is a sure way to deaden a relationship. In contrast, the emotionally charged atmosphere created by repeated conflict discourages resolution. Sometimes the conflict can be frightening.

Intimidated by a partner's explosive reactions, one may likely withhold feelings—the beginning of falling out of love.

13. *Feeling respected*

It can be difficult to feel intimately connected with someone who sees the world very differently from the way you do. But a strong intimate bond can be forged between two such people if each respects the other's viewpoints, values, and feelings. If your feelings, thoughts, and behaviors are rejected, not occasionally, but regularly, you will feel alienated. As a result, you may become preoccupied with protecting your sense of worth, rather than building a stronger love.

We need to know that our partner's respect for us does not hinge on our conformity to his or her beliefs. Respect, in the face of differences, leads us to trust that we will be accepted and loved.

14. *Letting go of anger*

Each time one partner withdraws emotionally, the other may find his/her feelings of love becoming less strong. Eventually those feelings dry up and the couple separates. Don't let anger linger. Think of retained anger as a toxic substance capable of destroying your love.

15. *Confidence in the future*

We can't predict the future or promise that a love will grow and not die. But most of us need a modicum of stability and hopefulness about the future in a love relationship. For some, hope frees them to be sexually responsive.

Possible scores range from 50 to 60. Scores above 40 are high, while those below 25 should be considered low. In general, the higher your score, the more trust you feel in your partner. Discussing each item of the Trust Scale with your partner is important, but you don't need to make him or her sit down and take the quiz. Rather, you can use the subjects of the questions as talking points if that is more comfortable for both of you. Some people may feel coerced or restrained by a question-and-answer format while others respond to it enthusiastically.

Vaginismus

(see also Painful Intercourse)

Vaginismus is a sexual disorder that can make intercourse difficult or impossible. Involuntary spastic contractions of the vaginal entrance constrict it so that penetration cannot occur. Some women who have this condition cannot even insert a tampon or their own finger into their vaginas. Obviously any attempts at intercourse are painful for both the woman and her partner.

This can be a temporary condition, associated with an abscess or severe inflammation of the vagina. If chronic, vaginismus may be the result of physical disease, but is more likely caused by psychological factors. Those factors include shame and/or guilt about sexuality, a traumatic sexual assault (see Recovery Sex), or a pathological fear of penetration.

Though vaginismus is, to say the least, a difficult experience for a couple, it is 100 percent reversible. Some women can cure the problem at home themselves. Others respond relatively quickly to therapy.

EXAMPLE

❝I was ashamed to tell my doctor my marriage had never been consummated," said Helen, age 26.

Married three years, Helen and her husband, Phil, regularly stimulated each other to orgasm. But every time they attempted penetration, Helen's vagina tightened involuntarily, making it impossible for Phil to enter and causing her and sometimes him extreme pain. These experiences ended in tears on her part and confusion and hurt feelings for both of them. After a year of sporadic attempts at intercourse, they became so discouraged they stopped trying.

"We were frustrated by the situation, but we didn't seek help to ease our frustration," Helen reported. "We wanted to start a family. I swallowed my embarrassment and told my gynecologist what was happening."

An exam indicated no physical reason for her condition, which the doctor told her was vaginismus. He sent them to a therapist. After 12 sessions with the therapist—centering around simple home exercises and exploration of her fears—the problem was corrected. Their sexual relationship improved dramatically. Helen is now pregnant with their first child. ■

> If you suffer from vaginismus, seeing a therapist is a good idea, even if you are able to cure the problem with the following exercises. Understanding the underlying psychological issues will help you become more fully sexual.

The Eight Steps for Curing Vaginismus

1. *Relax.* Lie down in bed. Lock the door and turn off the phone so you won't be disturbed. Breath deeply, in and out. Keep your mouth open while you slowly exhale. Some women find that having this experience in the bathtub is even more comfortable in the beginning.

2. *Insert one lubricated finger into your vagina.* Keep breathing deeply. Say to yourself, "This is my finger. No one is hurting me."

3. *Explore your vagina.* Move your finger around inside your vagina.

4. *Voluntarily tighten the vaginal muscles around your finger.* Imagine you are trying to stop a flow of urine. Tighten the muscle. Then relax. Now repeat.

5. *Repeat steps 3 and 4 for five minutes twice a day.* After a couple of weeks or when you feel comfortable with the preceding step, insert two fingers in your vagina.

6. *Now, add your partner.* When you are comfortable with having your two fingers in your vagina, have your partner place one lubricated finger in your vagina. Continue to breath slowly with your mouth open as you have done before. When you are ready, have him use two fingers. Guide his movements. You should be the active partner and he the passive one.

7. *Incorporate the exercise into sex play.* Again when you are ready, have him arouse you by stroking, caressing, kissing. Straddle him and place his erect penis partially into your vagina. Contract and relax your muscles around his soft penis while he strokes your clitoris. Continue with the breathing and insert his penis into your vagina as you feel ready. Discontinue if you feel pain.

8. *Give yourself time.* Response varies widely from woman to woman. Take as much time as you need.

Wet Dreams

(see Ejaculation, Erection, Orgasm)

Zipless Sex or Quickies

"Quickies" are brief episodes of lovemaking centered around intercourse. Thanks in part to the phrase "wham, bam, thank you ma'am" used to describe a man's rushed and selfish lovemaking style, quickies have gotten a bad name. There is room for an occasional quickie in a sexual relationship. The urgency and excitement inherent in the brief encounter can make it a stimulating and pleasurable experience for both partners.

In the best of all possible quickies, a man and a woman look at each other and ignite. They come together with both partners at the boiling point. In the real world, a quickie may be her accommodation to his needs, a loving gesture on the part of a generous spouse who knows that next time he will lavishly worship her clitoris in return for this moment's favor. There's nothing wrong with that.

Few couples have the time for languorous lovemaking sessions every time one or both of them desires gratification. Jobs, children, and other responsibilities get in the way. Too often they don't make love because they don't have time to make it a complete sensual and sexual experience. "Seize the moment!" is a motto few couples apply to their sex lives, and that's too bad.

A few minutes of passion can act as a jolt of sexual caffeine into the bloodstream of your relationship.

What Men and Women Say About Quickies

From a 29-year-old woman married to a 25-year-old man: "We have morning quickies once or twice a week. There's no time, we're late for work, but I see that glazed look in his eye and I think, what's five more minutes? I don't have an orgasm, but I enjoy the experience. I like feeling him inside me and knowing I've pleased him. It gives me an erotic charge."

A 40-year-old woman says: "Fast and frenzied sex is exhilarating whether you come or you don't. I love the occasional quickie. We always have great sex for days afterward."

Her husband adds: "In my first marriage, sex was always a great big deal. Sometimes I didn't initiate lovemaking because I wasn't up to the challenge. In this marriage, I feel much freer. She is up for a quickie now and then, and she's ready to unplug the phone for the night too."

A 36-year-old man says: "Any man who says he never wants a quickie is lying. Sometimes you want to grab her and do it. A woman who can get into that is a woman to treasure."

And from a 31-year-old woman: "Quickies are fun. On the one hand, they are transitory, over in minutes. On the other hand, they last a long time, the good feelings they generate radiating throughout your life together. Some of our best memories are quickies, like the time we did it standing up in the dressing room on the Metroliner between D.C. and New York."

The Five Golden Rules of Quickies

1. *They should be a "sometimes" thing.* If this is the only way you make love, he really is one of those "wham bam" guys.

2. *Foreplay doesn't have to be done at the scene.* Who says a quickie can't be arranged? Maybe she's awake before he is. In the shower, she masturbates but not to orgasm. Then she wakes him.

3. *She doesn't have to have an orgasm.* He needs to believe her when she says she doesn't need an orgasm every time. Many women won't

have an orgasm in the space of a quickie. That doesn't mean they didn't enjoy the experience.

4. *Be open to erotic opportunity.* No time for lovemaking until the weekend? Slip into the bathroom together for those few minutes the children are engrossed in *Sesame Street.* You're probably overlooking opportunities because you tune out sexual thoughts unless the time and place are "right."

5. *If there's time and energy for something more, let it happen.* Maybe you meant it to be a quickie so you could both get back to the piles of work you brought home from the office. Sometimes plans, duties, schedules, and responsibilities have to be put aside.

I ndex